THE FORTUNE BUILDERS

EDWIN DARBY

THE FORTUNE BUILDERS

DOUBLEDAY & COMPANY, INC.
GARDEN CITY, NEW YORK
1986

For G.K. and Susan

Library of Congress Cataloging-in-Publication Data

Darby, Edwin.
  The fortune builders.

  Includes index.
  1. Capitalists and financiers—Illinois—Chicago—
Biography. 2. Wealth—Illinois—Chicago—History.
I. Title.
HG184.C4D37 1986   332'.092'2 [B]   86-6284
ISBN 0-385-12369-8

CONTENTS

CONTENTS

FOREWORD

Virgil Vogel, for years a professor of history with the City College of Chicago and a dedicated scholar in Indian lore, says he has thirty-nine spellings of Chicago in his files and fourteen supposedly correct explanations of how Chicago got its name. That is as it should be. More so than most crossroads, Chicago has always been a city of paradox and contradiction. In fact, it got its name before it was anything resembling a city or even a village. The first extant and recorded use of the name along with an explanation of the meaning is found, Vogel says, in the journal of a Frenchman, Joutel, a member of a La Salle expedition in 1687. "We arrived at a place called Chicagou," Joutel wrote, "which, according to what we were told, has been so called on account of the quantity of garlic growing in this district, in the woods." Wild onions growing in the swampy lands in the district sounds more logical than garlic and that's the way the story goes most often today. It is more easily accepted in that it is possible the Indian word meant not only onion, as in strong smell, but also anything big, or great.

In the United States there are two great and big world-class cities. Chicago is the other one.

If you want it, you don't have to send for it. It can be had just around the corner whether it happens to be grand opera of a quality to rival La Scala, professional sports of Super Bowl or World Series class, foods prepared by chefs from every corner of the world, France to Lithuania, China to Ethiopia, or the most mundane of goods and services. If it is a service or a product, it is easily available and very possibly the product was manufactured nearby. The city lists some 13,000 firms that are officially classified as manufacturing companies.

This book has been an extraordinarily long time in the composition. One reason is that Chicago is such a vital and volatile city. Frequently someone or other makes an effort at putting together a phrase to characterize Chicago. Most often action, praiseworthy or not, is implied as in "City on the Move" or "City on the Make."

If French explorers "discovered" Chicago—that is, its great crossroads location—it was built by New Englanders as well as Virginia Anglos. The Irish flooded in to do the construction work on the early canals linking the Great Lakes to the Mississippi waterway system, and the city retains distinct neighborhoods today of every ethnic grouping known to the globe. By the end of World War I blacks made up a sizable portion of the city's population and the trend has continued upward ever since, with the flight of blacks from the South and the flight of whites to the suburbs. The black population doubled in the twenty years before 1970, and in 1980 the city elected its first black mayor, Harold Washington. But by then Spanish-speaking people, predominantly Mexican and Puerto Rican, outnumbered blacks.

An accepted cliché in Chicago has it that if you can't make it in Chicago you can't make it anywhere, meaning that opportunity abounds in the city. Power, clout, money all change rapidly, too rapidly for a biographer of the city to track.

Marshall Field V is the only representative of old Chicago money on the 1985 list compiled by *Forbes* magazine of the country's 400 richest persons. John Herald Johnson, at age

66 that year, was the only Chicago black to make the list, based on individuals with a net worth of at least $150 million. Johnson, who took $500 borrowed from his mother and built it into a magazine *(Ebony)* and communications empire, was accorded a fortune of $160 million by *Forbes.*

Searching the country, *Forbes* found fourteen billionaires but no one of that vast wealth in Chicago. However, three Chicago families are in that exalted category. After assorted members of the Searle family, led by Daniel, decided to walk away from G. D. Searle, the pharmaceutical company, they could bring a billion dollars to the table without inviting several cousins to the party. The Pritzkers, in spite of what the Braniff tailspin may have done to the family exchequer, would weigh in with at least a billion and a half. And even with the troubles of General Dynamics, the Crown family, or the Colonel and his son Lester alone, could easily lay hands on a billion if ordered to add everything up.

The problem, of course, for anyone taking a look at the wealth of Chicago is finding room for more than a sampling. More than a little should be said about a striking young Chicago woman, Abra Rockefeller Prentice Anderson, wealthy enough to solve the problem of enlarging her penthouse apartment on the Gold Coast by having a helicopter drop off such materials as steel beams. The Rockefeller in Abra's name connotes old money.

But Chicago teems with new money and people who will be movers and shakers in the city for years to come. Neil Bluhm and his partner Judd Malkin no doubt can account for the $300 million *Forbes* says each has made in real estate development and syndication.

The *Forbes* list itself is wanting. Ira Kaufman, principal of a thriving investment banking and brokerage house and also of the Exchange National Bank and wealthy enough to keep a yacht on Lake Michigan and a second yacht, this one 115 feet long, in Florida waters, is not mentioned by *Forbes.* William F. Farley, age 42 in 1985, is credited with a self-made $250 million. His net worth may easily be twice that.

Among other things, he and several friendly banks own Northwest Industries. A few years back and before Farley bought all of the company's shares, the stock market put a value of $1.6 billion on Northwest.

Something else: to paraphrase a classic remark, there are dozens of millionaire Chicagoans who are just as wealthy for practical purposes as those *Forbes* credits with $150 million and more. Who counts after 10, or 20, or 50 million? For example, young William Lane owns a chain of prospering neighborhood banks, is a major stockholder in the General Binding Corp., and fell heir to a real estate empire that includes a ranch of 300,000 acres in New Mexico and an 11,000-acre farm in the Virginia horse country.

To know the people of Chicago is to know that the city will go as far as any toward solving the problems of urban living in the 20th and 21st centuries. It remains a city of solid builders and brilliant innovators.

There is more than a little truth in the observation that New England won't touch it unless it is just the way it was when Grandfather was around, that the West Coast likes it only if it is 100 percent new, and that Chicago and the Midwest think well of it if it embodies an innovative improvement on the tried and true.

For more than a quarter century I have been watching this exciting city and reporting on the innovative improvements generated by a vigorous commercial, industrial and financial community. For all that time I have written a column for the Chicago *Sun-Times*. Focused on the working world, the column appears five times a week at least forty-eight weeks a year. At a minimum 800 words, that works out to something like 5 million words.

Chicago, a vital and finally representative part of this nation, has always kept me interested.

Chicago has a beautiful sound because Chicago means money.
　　　　　—attributed to actress Ruth Gordon

I

ARMOUR

There was nothing strange about Carbon Petroleum Dubbs. Not really. It could be said that others were responsible for his name and he did without a doubt have good reason to wear roller skates at home.

Or in one of his homes. He built the first house in Wilmette, one of the wealthy suburbs that line the shore of Lake Michigan north of Chicago. It cost $250,000 and was designed by Dubbs for ease of living as he saw it. In the form of an L, it had twenty rooms, but it was only one room wide. The Paget, Bermuda, house was the problem. Dubbs bought the Bermuda house and was only responsible for extensive remodeling and additions. A coral-stone villa, it was huge with terraces and garden walks and guest houses sprawling all over a hilltop. Why wouldn't someone touched with imagination—and Dubbs was an inventor of some genius—immediately think of roller skates as the best way to get from here to there? Tall, well built, athletically inclined, and a demon sailor on water, Carbon Petroleum didn't need to worry about his glasses falling from his strong, square-jawed face and shrewd blue eyes as he streaked about the house; at bottom he was a conservative man and his glasses were always secured by a ribbon.

Not too many Americans have ever heard of Carbon Petroleum Dubbs, but his name rightly should be familiar to all inhabitants of the United States, the nation created by, for, and of the automobile. By helping to make gasoline and oil plentiful and cheap, he and his father—and J. Ogden Armour—played a considerable part in the development of the automobile age and the vast changes that eventually made the nation's comfort and prosperity dependent on the dictates of Arab sheiks.

As far back as anyone knows, the men in the Dubbs family were apothecaries and chemists. Jesse A. Dubbs, Carbon's father, was a fortunate member of the line in that he found himself in the late 1800s a resident of Franklin, Pennsylvania. Franklin is in that part of the country where Indians once skimmed an oily substance from streams and swamps and made use of it as a cure-all for the ailments of natural man. And Franklin is in that part of the country where curious and energetic white men first learned that the same substance could be extracted in seemingly unlimited supply from the ground by sinking wells. A simple distillation process would provide a product that would beach the New England whaling fleet in time to save some species of ocean mammals from extinction. Edwin Drake sank his first well in Titusville, Pennsylvania, in 1859 and soon kerosene was lighting the nation's (whale oil) lamps.

While John D. Rockefeller, from his base across the Pennsylvania border in Ohio, was working day and night putting together a corporate combination to control the sources, the refining, and the transportation of petroleum, Jesse Dubbs was taking a chemist's interest in the process of distilling useful products from Pennsylvania crude oil. Rather obviously from the years he put into his research, the senior Dubbs was no light-bulb-Eureka inventor. But just as obviously, he was a determined man and so single-minded that he named his son Carbon after that essential element of Pennsylvania coal and petroleum.

The son always insisted that his middle name was a bit of fun and not really legitimate although he did use it all his adult life. "I put the initial 'P' in just to make the name euphonious," Carbon always told anyone who asked. "Then people started calling me Petroleum for fun, and I've been called Carbon Petroleum ever since."

In any event, it was not until 1914 that Jesse Dubbs thought he had worked out something of real value. On January 5, 1915, he was granted his first patent for "Treating Oil," as the patent was titled. Still, that was only a piece of paper, and neither the oil companies nor investors beat a path to the Dubbs door. However, Dubbs did find his own way to the door of Jonathan Ogden Armour. He was well and even lavishly received.

The second son and heir of Philip D. Armour was lectured from childhood in all the hard-work and penny-saving virtues, but perhaps J. Ogden was more impressed with some of the spectacular things his father had done in his lifetime than he was with what P.D. said. Or perhaps J. Ogden inherited a touch more of the Irish romantic from the family than he did of the frugal Scot. He was always a sucker for a long shot.

"You can not be too careful of yourself in husbanding your money," P.D. once wrote to his sons, then grown men. "Don't try to get rich too fast and never feel rich."

J. Ogden not only felt rich; he also believed that he could get a lot richer in a hurry by scattering some of his money around in likely places instead of husbanding it. One promising place, in Armour's eyes, was a California valley with a glittering name, Sutter's Basin, as in Sutter's Mill, where gold was first discovered in 1848. Even if John Sutter of Sutter's Mill had not piled up millions for himself in gold, John Sutter of Sutter's Basin and J. Ogden Armour thought they could extract millions from the land. John Sutter, with the same single-minded purpose exhibited by Jesse Dubbs, had spent the greater part of his life trying to make use of irrigation techniques to turn parched acres into a Garden of Eden. J. Ogden put his trust and considerable money into Sutter's dream. Perhaps a half century too soon.

In 1913, Armour, a wintertime visitor to California, organized the Sutter Basin Co. It was no penny-ante venture. The company owned 54,000 acres, the capital stock was valued at $6 million, and Armour not only was the big investor but also signed and personally guaranteed $7,500,000 in bonds sold to others. Before Sutter Basin dried up and blew away, J. Ogden poured upwards of $17 million into it.

Freudians might pause and take a longer look at J. Ogden's stubborn gamble on wringing riches out of a California irrigation project. Presumably he knew that his brilliantly successful father had made his first stake on the way to millions by constructing ditches and selling sluicing water to the California gold miners of the 49er era.

To J. Ogden, Jesse Dubbs's plans sounded just as promising as Sutter's. Dubbs was a man who had patents on the very best process for refining petroleum, and by 1916 even a man who made his living in cattle and hogs could see that the age of the gasoline-powered internal-combustion engine had arrived.

Armour put $2 million into Dubbs's company, grandly named Universal Oil Processes, Inc. (later Products, Inc.), and set Dubbs up in a secret laboratory on a two-acre site near Independence, Kansas. It is the younger Dubbs, Carbon Petroleum, who is given the credit for perfecting the process. In July 1919, what is conceded to be the world's first petroleum thermal continuous-cracking process went on stream at the Independence laboratory.

The petroleum industry had been getting along quite nicely until then without either of the Dubbses and had, of course, supplied the suddenly big demand for gasoline and oil occasioned by the military's need for land, sea, and air transport in World War I. So it was three long years later before the first commercial Dubbs-process unit was in operation—at the Wood River, Illinois, refinery of Roxana Petroleum Corp. (Dubbs, like Howard Hughes's father with the Hughes patented oil-well drilling bit, chose to license his process instead of selling it, in the hopes of keeping royalty payments gushing in for years.)

Dubbs very definitely had something of great value to the burgeoning oil industry. The word "continuous" is one key. The refining processes in general use at the time had to be shut down periodically while clogging deposits of coke were cleaned out, a costly and time-consuming operation. The Dubbs system had "clean circulation." Of greater importance, Dubbs guaranteed a higher percentage of gasoline of specified quality from the breakdown of crude oil. Simple crude-oil distillation processes yielded only about 26 percent gasoline—four barrels of crude to get one barrel of gasoline. There was also a yield of oil and kerosene, but Edison had pretty well taken care of the kerosene market by the 1920s, and more than half of a day's production of a conventional refinery could be sold only as fuel oil at bargain-basement prices or reduced to even less profitable asphalt.

Standard Oil of California was the second company to go for the Dubbs thermal cracking system and it was Dubbs who really made the growth of California's "black gold" industry possible. It seems that California crude is heavy—a high specific gravity—and the stuff was very difficult to refine until the Dubbs thermal cracking process solved the problem.

In 1923, Universal Oil Products was bubbling along. Carbon Petroleum and J.O. were happy to report that sixty-five thermal cracking units were installed that year. But this was not the big time; the sixty-five units had a total capacity of only 42,000 barrels a day. Universal was not so universal as it hoped. There were a number of competing systems, and engineers argued vehemently and jealously about their merits. (In the nature of things and of corporations, outsiders are resented and rebuffed. The virulent form of the disease is known in corporate research circles today by the initials NIH, for Not Invented Here—and we don't want any part of it.) Naturally, and even deliberately, the growing giants of the still-infant industry sought to develop their own refining processes, skirting the patents held by Universal.

If everyone dreams of an invention that will be a money-making machine, Americans and particularly the practical citizens of Chicago have been peculiarly adept at inventing new and better ways of solving problems. The inventive strain has been a part of America since the Revolution freed the colonies of Britain's attempt to keep a stranglehold on all industrial technology. Certainly the make-do realities of frontier life demanded invention. In more modern times there have been in general two ways to go with an invention. One, patent it and use the patent to beat back all competition. Or, two, forget about patent law and use the invention to build a production and marketing organization that always stays one step ahead of the competition.

There's the classic tale of the Midwesterner who first came up with the amazing idea of putting chocolate-covered ice cream on a stick. He was well on the way to making a fortune, but he ended a bankrupt. Charging from one courtroom to another, he neglected his own business to the point that it melted away and eventually the lawyers' fees overwhelmed him. On the other hand, a century after Cyrus McCormick, farm equipment descended from his inventions is still being sold.

Carbon Petroleum, a man with categorical opinions on many subjects, chose the first route—the court. Perhaps by necessity. Up against the Standard Oils, the Shells, and the Sinclairs, it would not have been easy for Dubbs to go into the refining business. Rather, he set out first to sell his process on a royalty basis and finally to force the oil companies to beat a path to his door, royalty checks in hand. He had his basic patent and he had the millions of J. Ogden Armour behind him. He could hire lawyers and he did. Soon he put himself in a heads-you-win, tails-I-lose situation. He was suing his potential customers; he was making enemies where he needed friends. It wasn't too long before he got a reputation as a professional litigant, a man to be avoided.

In addition, in the cozy 1920s when big business was riding high, the major oil companies happily formed the Patent Club. It was just that, a club. If you were a member of the club, you had access to a pool of patents on petroleum-refining processes. Dubbs, of course, was blackballed.

And for Dubbs, disaster was ahead.

Jonathan Ogden Armour once said that just maybe, even probably, J. P. Morgan had more money than he did. But even so, Armour professed to believe that he had more power than Morgan, more power than any other man in the world. There was truth in the claim. Born November 11, 1863, in Milwaukee, where his father was building his meat-packing empire, J. Ogden was called back from Yale by his suddenly ailing father just after he had registered for his freshman year. The idea was that he had better begin learning about the management of the business; he became an errand boy for his father.

The early death of his brother, Philip D. Jr., in 1900 and of his father the following year (prostrate in the family mansion on Prairie Avenue and dying of pneumonia, the senior Armour protested, "Here I am, just think of it, ordered about by women") made J. Ogden the principal heir to the Armour fortune and the head of Armour & Co.

Prior to World War I, Armour & Co. was doing a half billion dollars a year. Even today, that volume would rank the firm among the corporations on *Fortune*'s list of the 500 largest. Military demand and skyrocketing prices during the war greatly increased Armour's volume and profits. Before the war was over it was said to be doing a billion-dollar business. And the Armour family owned all of the common and voting stock, although bonds and preferred stock were sold to the public. J. Ogden also found himself the head of the Armour Grain Co. Armour grain elevators dotted the prairies and the company was a major grain dealer. Armour

controlled a vast fleet of refrigerated railroad cars, and until
the 1922 antitrust consent decree forced the meat packers
to get out of the grocery-products business, Armour & Co.
was a factor in supplying the nation with fruits and vegeta-
bles. In short, J. P. Morgan might dictate in Wall Street, but J.
Ogden could pretty well dictate what the nation ate and
how much it paid to eat.

J. Ogden was not the dedicated businessman his father
was. Or his brother Philip. As one living member of the
Armour family says, "Philip was aggressive and eager about
business. He enjoyed getting up at five o'clock in the morning, driving to the office in a coach behind handsome horses,
and putting in a good twelve-hour day. But the way it has
always been told in the family, J.O. was not in that line. I
don't think he ever expected—or wanted—to run Armour &
Co. He wanted to be a second-son country gentleman. His
father really ran the company almost to the day he died.
Then at age 38, J. Ogden suddenly had no choice, he had to
take over."

If Armour was a gambler, a long-shot player, it could be
said that gambling was part and parcel of the business that
was thrust upon him. Inventory speculation is the name of
the game, even today, in the meat-packing business.

The companies still in the business buy fresh meat in huge
quantities, millions of pounds. That's inventory. And that's
the gamble. Fractions of a penny, multiplied by millions, can
make the difference between kingly profits and disaster
when the packers resell the dressed meat. In P.D.'s day, and
even J. Ogden's, the gamble could be hair-raising. The puz-
zling term "meat packer" dates from a time when companies sold all the fresh pork they could in a matter of days,
hoping for cold weather, and packed most of the rest in salt,
i.e., salt pork.

At the close of the Civil War, P.D. had pulled off an amazing coup. The Union Army had been existing on salt pork
and the price had doubled and tripled and quadrupled as
demand increased and profiteers hoarded supplies. If others

thought the bloody war would drag on forever, P.D. saw victory approaching in the leadership of those two citizens from Illinois, Grant and Lincoln. P.D. scurried off to New York and smilingly agreed to sell civilian and army purvey-ors salt pork to the full extent of their needs and greed, signing firm contracts. The price was $60 a barrel. After Appomattox and the collapse of prices, he filled the con-tracts at a cost to Armour & Co. of less than one-third the contract price. As P.D. told friends at the time, he was a bull on the Union, but a bear on pork. The profits were tremen-dous.

In the closing year of World War I the situation was not much different. Meat prices were out of sight and demand unlimited. Armour & Co., it was rumored, was making money faster than any other corporation in the United States. But in J. Ogden's judgment, victory for the Allies was not yet in sight. Instead of selling, like his father, he bought. J. Ogden's birthday, November 11, 1918, must have been grim even as he celebrated the Armistice. Going into a se-vere postwar deflation, Armour & Co. lost millions on its high-priced inventories and the harsh recession of 1921–22 was no help.

J. Ogden made still another costly mistake in judging the outcome of the war. His gambling guess was that the war had bled the British Empire so badly that Great Britain's economic power would crumble—and that Germany would rise from the ashes to achieve new economic strength. As the head of an international corporation—Armour & Co. had been selling grain to Europe for decades—J. Ogden was no stranger to the sophisticated world of international fi-nance and he felt he could make a killing in foreign-cur-rency speculation. Accordingly, he bought German marks and sold, or shorted, the currency that had ruled the world for two hundred years, the British pound sterling.

Armour, of course, was off by more than a quarter of a century and one world war.

What with the staggering inventory losses and the failure

of the deutsche-mark connection, it was the Armour empire
that was crumbling even as the twenties began to roar. J.
Ogden maneuvered frantically to shore up his defenses. The
corporation was reorganized to make possible the sale of $50
million worth of bonds and $60 million in preferred stock.
The numbers were mind-boggling for those years. At one
point, Chicago, New York, and Boston banks furnished $63
million through short-term notes. J. Ogden, the man who
felt that he might be as rich as J. P. Morgan, was in the hands
of the bankers. In addition to the corporate financing, Armour borrowed $20 million from the banks on a personal
note.

And in 1923 the bankers forced J. Ogden to give up the
presidency of Armour & Co. F. Edson White, a veteran
Armour officer, was made president and J. Ogden accepted
the title of chairman of the board. In a public statement,
Armour said that everything was as it should be, that White's
appointment and the addition of three bankers to the company's board of directors were all part of a planned move
toward making Armour & Co. more of a "public rather than
a private family corporation."

Now J. Ogden was no longer the country gentleman, over-
seeing an empire from his $10 million one-thousand-acre
estate north of Chicago, dabbling in this or that intriguing
venture. He needed money, big money, fast. And right
there in Chicago was the Board of Trade, a place where a
man could make millions, almost overnight. After all, his
father had done it, breaking the great Leiter wheat corner.

J. Ogden chose to go the other way. He did not attempt
the classic corner in the manner of Joseph Leiter. But he did
plunge into the wheat market, buying and buying vast quantities of wheat. The reports are inconsistent, but it seems
clear that he owned at least 10 million bushels of wheat at
the height of his buying spree. At the high tide of the 1925
market on the Board of Trade in January of that year,
Armour's commitment represented more than $20 million
worth of wheat.

But the tide was running against Armour. He was overextended, a depression that would not sustain high farm prices was settling in over the Midwest farm belt even as the rest of the country prospered, and Armour was up against a tough-minded group of Board of Trade veterans determined to break Armour's mini-corner and profit on the short, or down, side of the market.

Armour lost. Disastrously. The La Salle Street legend is that he lost a million dollars a day, day after day, for as many as ninety days. That seems impossible. But it is certain that Armour was trapped, forced to sell but unable to sell, while equity vanished and debt piled up. There were no buyers. Each day the price of wheat took another sickening plunge and Armour could only watch as he fell into a final bankruptcy.

Many Chicagoans, after the fact, believe that Armour managed to lose $90 million and more in the wheat speculation. A longtime friend of two generations of the family says, "I was always told that the $90 million figure was too low, that actually J. Ogden lost more than $100 million for the family and the meat-packing firm on the wheat speculation alone and another $50 million through the Armour Grain Co."

In any event, the newspapers of the early 1920s commonly placed a value of $150 million on the family holdings of Armour & Co. common stock. And that was gone along with vast interest in such as the Continental Bank and the Milwaukee Road. The moneymen, led by a Boston banker, Frederick H. Prince, moved in to salvage their loans. (Forty years later, Prince's son, William Wood Prince, was to lose control of Armour, profitably, in a bitter, three-cornered proxy fight. The Greyhound Corp. was the winner and now owns Armour & Co. Much to Chicago's dismay, Greyhound pulled Armour's headquarters out of Chicago and moved the offices to its own recently adopted home city, Phoenix, Arizona.) Perhaps realizing a lifelong ambition, J. Ogden settled in England with what was left to him. But inside of two years he was dead. At age 64, he died in his suite in the Carlton Hotel after a long bout with typhoid fever and pneumonia.

There was nothing left when the Continental Bank settled his estate. In fact, there was a net deficit of $1,805,000. The great meat-packing company was gone. The luxury estate, Mellody Farm, was gone. (Armour liked the sound of the name. The strange spelling is accounted for by the fact that Armour actually named the estate after the original Irish owner of the acres. Mellody Farm is now the campus of Lake Forest Academy, but the bell system in the kitchen of what used to be the main house still reads: Mr. Armour's bedroom, etc.) The personal fortune of his wife, Lolita, was also gone, and various members of the family had lost millions.

J. Ogden was the father of one daughter, also Lolita, later Mrs. John J. Mitchell, Jr. He had no sons. With his downfall, control of the company gradually slipped from family hands. Laurance H. Armour departed in 1926. Andrew Watson Armour, Laurance's brother, left in 1929, and Lester Armour, son of P.D. Jr., resigned the following year. In 1931, P. D. Armour III gave up his vice-presidency at age 37 after the board of directors elected a non-family veteran officer as president. He said his resignation was the greatest disappointment of his life.

In the process of settling J. Ogden's estate and selling off anything that was worth a dollar, including Derbyshire and "Armour" sterling silverware and 450 pieces of "solid" goldware, valued in total at $300,000, the Continental Bank came across 500 shares of something called Universal Oil Products. There were only 1,000 shares outstanding and the bank officers determined that at the moment the shares had no known value. This was 1928 and Carbon Petroleum's company, having long since lost its subsidies from Armour, was doing more for the benefit of lawyers than it was for stockholders. In a grand gesture, the bank handed the UOP stock over to Mrs. Lolita Armour and told her she might as well have the pretty piece of engraved paper as a token of the fortune (one estimate was $8 million) she had lent to her husband and lost.

Three years later, the oil industry admitted defeat in the matter of the UOP patents, old, improved, and new. A group led by six majors paid a cool $25 million to be shut of UOP lawsuits and to obtain clear rights to Dubbs's better methods. Dubbs got a check for $3,500,000 and Mrs. Lolita Armour's piece of "worthless" paper brought in $12,-500,000.

The six leading companies in the UOP deal were Shell, Standard of California, Standard of Indiana, Standard of New Jersey, the Texas Co., and Phillips Petroleum. Over the years, UOP has been reincarnated several times. For nearly three decades the ownership was in a special trust, with the profits going to joint research in petroleum technology. In 1959, the trustee sold the company to the public, 2,900,000 shares at $25 a share, or $72,500,000. (Mrs. Armour would have taken in $36 million.) At the time, royalties on patents held by the company were pumping out revenues, almost pure profit, of something like $18 million a year. The company headquarters is in Des Plaines, a Chicago suburb, but in the 1970s California's Signal Industries bought UOP and then in the merger madness of the 1980s Signal was swallowed up by Allied Corp. Hidden somewhere in an $8 billion oil-and-gas conglomerate, UOP still makes a bundle out of its patents (6,000) and its petroleum engineering projects.

In the early 1930s, with General Motors selling for $2.50 a share and automobiles for $1,000 and less, Mrs. Armour's $12,500,000 was really something. She was back in the realm of the big rich after her money was wisely invested. She built herself a new mansion on the Chicago lakefront and shrewdly salvaged something else from her husband's estate. The bankers were still trying to unload Mellody Farm, the Lake Forest estate, but were finding no buyers in the midst of the Great Depression. The furnishings of the house had long since been sold at auction, so the bankers made no objection when Lolita asked permission to scrounge for anything that might fit her new home. She and her carpenters removed a 15th-century Italian mantelpiece and the roomful of wood paneling that went with it. It all fit very nicely in her new library.

Lolita's good fortune didn't materially help the rest of the Chicago Armours, except for her daughter, also named Lolita. But before J. Ogden's disaster quite a few Armour millions had been spread around the family. Laurance Hearne Armour, grandson of one of P.D.'s brothers, did much for the family fortune by marrying Lacy Withers in 1911. Lacy was the granddaughter of A. H. Pierce, better known as Shanghai for his acquisitiveness in building up his cattle ranch and his herds. Shanghai's vast Texas acreage has since been divided in half, one half run by Laurance Armour, the other by Chicago's John Runnels family, related to the Witherses by marriage. It turned out that the cattle ranch was sitting atop one of the richest of Texas oil fields. Newspaper gossip had it that Lacy was the largest single shareholder of Texaco in addition to receiving fat royalty checks from Texaco for pumping oil out of the ground.

Laurance's brother, Andrew Watson Armour, and Lester Armour did very well in Chicago banking. Lester's second wife (1949) was Alexandra Galitzine Romanoff, but the two most prominent Armours in Chicago in a later generation were the children of Lester and his first wife, Leola Stanton. Thomas Stanton Armour became president of Mitchell, Hutchins & Co., a highly successful Chicago and New York investment banking and brokerage house. Vernon Booth Armour served for years as a partner in William Blair & Co., perhaps Chicago's most prestigious local investment banking house, and earlier as a partner in what is now Smith Barney, Harris Upham & Co.

Carbon Petroleum Dubbs died in 1962 at age 81 in Santa Barbara, California, in still a third house that oil built. Some few of the older residents of Wilmette remember that Dubbs was elected president of Wilmette village and in 1932, just as he was finishing his mansion in the suburb, succeeded in persuading the village board to ban the construction of gasoline service stations within the village borders.

"These confounded filling stations destroy property values," said Carbon Petroleum.

II

FIELD

Having reached a point in life—he was 45 in 1986—that no doubt entitled him to a philosophical thought or two, Marshall Field announced himself certain of one thing. Setting specific goals, he said, is a sure way to make yourself unhappy.

Nevertheless, Field, who carries the weight of Roman numeral V after his name as well as the responsibility for one of America's larger fortunes, does have a few general goals.

He would like it said at the end of his life that he made a contribution, that he left a few things, perhaps even society, better off.

And, toward that goal, if closer to home, he would like to add to the fortune he inherited.

It is possible that when he said setting goals is a prelude to unhappiness Field was thinking of the Chicago *Sun-Times*. He had inherited, and repeated, vows made by his grandfather and his father: someday the *Sun-Times*, founded by Marshall Field III, would take first place in Chicago away from the long-dominant Chicago *Tribune*. In 1983, Marshall, under pressure from his half brother, Frederick, had agreed to sell the *Sun-Times*. It was an action that many Chicagoans, including some of Marshall's friends, equated with desertion.

With four children of his own, including Marshall VI, Field rejects the idea that the old, often true saw—shirt sleeves to shirt sleeves in three generations—should ever be stretched to apply to the Field family. In fact, as he has said with variations on a number of occasions, "The only real tradition in my family is that each successive generation should not blow it. If you can leave the family fortune a little bigger than you found it, that's what counts."

Equipped with a healthy sense of humor and ironic insight, Field has also noted from time to time that he is tight with his money. "People kid me about the pain it causes me to give anything away," is one way he puts it, "and that hurts me because it is true."

The tightwad image may be carefully cultivated, a reflection of a problem of the very rich. Legions of people assume the very wealthy have so much money that they are delighted to scatter it around. Field's grandfather learned about this curious thinking firsthand when he enlisted in the Army as a private at the start of World War I. His barrack buddies took it for granted that Field could lend unlimited amounts of money and that he didn't really want to be repaid. Years later, meeting the problem, he assigned an employee to check out the stories in the supplicant letters he constantly received. In an entire year the employee found only one person who was telling the truth about his scheme for making money if he only had a little of Field's cash for start-up capital.

It is probably equally true today, as a 19th-century multimultimillionaire once said, that a man who has $10 million is just as well off as someone who is rich. In either case, the well-endowed are only human; small change is real; big money is something else. Five million dollars is a chess piece to be moved after careful thought to the most advantageous position on the board. With great equanimity, Field could make the decision, for example, to approve the sale of World Book, the encyclopedia company that for years was the money cow in the Field Enterprises empire. He did just that in 1978, exchanging World Book for $120 million to be employed elsewhere. But paying $16 for a steak in a restaurant appalls him unless the $16 is on the bill of someone who is patronizing one of the two restaurants of which he is a part owner.

Field can be openhanded if he is not picking up a tab and if real money is involved in a worthwhile endeavor. When a few years back Chicago's great Field Museum of Natural History faced extraordinary over-budget costs for remodeling to make it easier for handicapped people to get around, Marshall immediately pulled out his checkbook and took care of the problem.

The Field Museum goes back to Marshall Field I, the man who built the original fortune from pennies, establishing a department store that over the years made his name familiar far beyond the Midwest. In the 1890s and the following decades Marshall Field became as much a title as a name in Chicago and today Chicago people say Marshall Field's as often as Field's when they refer to the store. Until the corporation was gobbled up in the midst of the merger mania, the New York Stock Exchange recognized the power of the name by listing the stock under the "M's" rather than the "F's." A man who appeared in the newspapers and magazines of his time as cold, austere, devoted to his business, Field I was approaching 60 when he donated $1 million toward the establishment of what was first called the Field Columbian Museum but is now world-renowned as the Field Museum of Natural History.

The museum opened in 1894 on a wave of civic pride and enthusiasm for education and progress following the remarkable success of the World's Columbian Exposition held in Chicago to mark the 400th anniversary of the discovery of America and to proclaim Chicago's arrival as the nation's second-largest city and as the capital of the Midwest. An-

other donation by Field I of enduring benefit to Chicago and
the nation was the land, valued at the time at $300,000, he
gave to help a struggling Baptist college. Subsequent millions from John D. Rockefeller launched what became the
University of Chicago on its way to greatness, but Field also
gave the university additional donations in cash and land.
One piece of land was used by the university as an athletic
field and was, of course, to Field's embarrassment, called by
the students Marshall Field.

Marshall Field I, like an astonishing number of entrepreneurs over the years in the United States, was very rich as a
very young man. Unlike the supposed all-American heroes
of Horatio Alger, he made it from rags to riches pretty much
on his own and not through the kindly intervention of a
wealthy man. In fact, when he was just 20 years old, Field
refused just such an offer.

Given the time and place, Field was not born to poverty.
He was the third of four boys in a family of six children (three
others died in infancy, a more or less normal mortality record for rural America in that period). The place was a farm
outside the village of Conway, Massachusetts. The time was
August 18, 1834. In later life, Field saw no reason to try to
trace his ancestry back to noble beginnings; after all, he was
Marshall Field. However, others agree that the family name
goes back to Alsace and landed gentry called De la Feld, that
it traveled to England with the Norman invasion and was
changed to Field in later centuries as France became the
great enemy. The Field family that could have been Marshall's was apparently established on these shores by one
Zechariah Field, who first settled in Hartford, Connecticut,
in 1630 and later moved on to Massachusetts. The land
owned by Marshall's parents, John and Fidelia (Nash), was
hilly but still productive enough to allow a third son the
unusual privilege of attending school through age 17. But
the farm obviously could not support families that might be
generated in adulthood by six children. Naturally enough,
the farm would go to Chandler Field, the eldest son. That

left Joseph, three years older than Marshall, Marshall, and Henry, seven years younger, nowhere to go except out into the wide world.

Somehow Marshall immediately chose the right road. He found a job as a clerk in a dry-goods store in Pittsfield, Massachusetts. The proprietor, of course, had a prize. Field was endowed with an excellent and active brain. He was used to dawn-to-dark work on the farm. If the testimony of successful men can be believed, luck had little to do with their eminence. It wasn't that they happened to be standing on the right street corner at the right time. It was all talent and hard work. Conscientious application to the task at hand was, in Field's mind, the royal road to success. The harder you worked, the more you learned. As surely as the sun rises, your employer would recognize and reward your devotion to duty. If thrift was a matter of necessity on the farm, it was an article of faith for Field. A proper young man would avoid all frivolities and save his money; squandering a nickel or a quarter might seem innocent enough, but saving that much a day could amount to thousands of dollars in just a few years and found a fortune. Field worked hard and studied. He took notes. He knew the inventory carried in the store precisely and he learned the whys and wherefores of purchasing and profit margins. It turned out that he was a salesman, good with people and particularly with the ladies, in spite of his normally aloof manner.

But older brother Joseph had left relatively settled New England for Chicago and had sent back alluring reports of the hustling, bustling, growing West where real estate values and populations doubled almost overnight and fortunes were to be made.

With perhaps only one remarkable exception in his entire life, Field was not given to impulsive acts and it was not impulse that moved him to abandon what seemed to be a certain if modest career in the Pittsfield dry-goods store. He felt he had learned all he could after nearly four years of diligent labor, he was about to turn 21, and he trusted the judgment of his older brother. Field gave notice to his employer and remained resolute in his decision to uproot himself and venture West even when the proprietor made the offer that would have delighted any Alger hero. If Field would stay, he would be made a full partner in the business.

In spite of that turndown, Field's employer gave him an excellent letter of recommendation, testifying to his character and integrity and most prominently to his business talent. When Field arrived in Chicago in 1856 the city was officially not as old as he. It had been an important Indian meeting place and trading center for centuries with its water passage between the Great Lakes and the Mississippi River system. The city had been incorporated only in 1837. Field joined a population that stood at about 80,000, but may have been 81,000 the day after his arrival as thousands poured into Chicago from the Eastern seaboard and from Germany, Scandinavia, Ireland, England, and France. And from the South. In those days leading up to the Civil War, the land of Lincoln (and Douglas) was a magnet for hopeful blacks as well as whites. If Field's migration was on the face of it a gamble his judgment was correct. By the time of the World's Columbian Exposition nearly four decades later and the span during which Field built his fortune, Chicago's population had grown to more than 1,200,000. Chicago may have had a big-city look to the 21-year-old Field and it is certain that the city's activity was impressive. But when Field arrived Chicago was also a raw frontier city of wooden buildings and mud streets. It was not until the 1850s that Chicago began the performance of a minor miracle, lifting itself out of the mud. Wooden and later brick buildings were elevated two and three feet and new streets laid down over the mud. George M. Pullman, later the sleeping-car king, became an instant hero in 1861 when he succeeded in raising the city's major hotel, the four-story brick Tremont House.

Whatever Marshall thought about the city, he went along with his brother Joseph's plan, not at first successful, to land a job for him at what was then Chicago's largest dry-goods store, Cooley, Wadsworth and Company. Four years later Marshall Field was a full partner in the firm, then Cooley, Farwell and Company. (John Farwell was the founder of Chicago's best, "old money" family; in the 1970s, Francis Farwell became a senior partner of Chicago's top-ranked local investment banking house, William [McCormick] Blair & Co. Farwell Smith, a descendant of McCormicks and of Percy H. Smith, a builder of the Chicago & North Western Railroad, and son of Hermon Dunlap Smith, former chairman of the country's largest insurance brokerage firm, Marsh & McLennan, was a well-established Chicago investment banker before he went off to Washington to serve in both the Ford and Carter administrations.) Field had come to Chicago with the nickels, dimes, and quarters he had saved from his Pittsfield job and during his first year with the Cooley firm he saved half of the $400 salary he was paid. One way he pulled that off was saving the price of a room; he slept in the store. Inside of another four years the name of the firm was Cooley, Farwell, Field and Company and Field was then ready at the pleasant age of 30 to move on and run his own show.

First off, Field made a pass at some of the McCormick reaper money, but Cyrus wasn't interested. Field turned to Potter Palmer, then the proprietor of the dry-goods store that had been and was the chief competitor of the evolving Cooley, Farwell, Field emporium and the aggressive store that Field had really wanted to work for when he first came to Chicago. Increasingly Palmer had become interested in Chicago real estate and his dream of bringing to the city a hotel to rival anything New York City had to offer. As matters evolved, Palmer was delighted to turn the active management of his retail store and wholesale business over to Field, a young man Palmer had long since spotted as a comer. This was 1864, and the 30-year-old Field had enough money and credit to buy into the Potter Palmer firm for $260,000. It says something about Field's character and talent that John Farwell, instead of writing Field off as a deserter, lent Field $100,000 to help swing the deal. Farwell's generosity was especially noteworthy in that Field not only deserted but also took along with him another accomplished young executive, Levi Z. Leiter. Later on Leiter became so wealthy from the Field holdings and from astute investments in Chicago real estate that he was still rich after he bailed out his son, Joseph, when that dilettantish young man, a gambling friend of Frederick "Bet a Million" Gates, attempted to corner the wheat market in a battle with Philip D. Armour and lost disastrously. Nearly $10 million of Leiter money evaporated in the wheat pits of the Chicago Board of Trade, but even today the Leiter family, long dispersed to Washington, D.C., and other world capitals, still owns important real estate in Chicago.

After only eight years in Chicago, Marshall Field had it made by most standards; if his name was not in lights it was up there over the most handsome store in Chicago: Field, Palmer and Leiter.

In 1867 the firm rang up sales of $9 million, establishing itself as the largest in the city. Two years later, with Palmer traveling in Europe for his health and for the sake of his wife's cultural ambitions, the name and the organization changed again; Field and Leiter were equal partners in Field, Leiter and Company, but Field's two brothers, Joseph and Henry, were both junior partners. Not long after he first got Marshall settled in Chicago, Joseph moved on to Sioux City, Iowa, and then to Omaha, Nebraska, where he did well in banking. Reversing course completely, he went off to Manchester, England, where he functioned for years as the chief importer of woolens and other European goods for the Field store. Over the years, Marshall Field acquired a reputation not only for "giving the lady what she wants" but also for anticipating what the lady might want. Joseph, a shrewd judge of fashion as well as price, should share in that reputation. He made one other notable contribution to the merchandising operation. In 1893 he sent his son Stanley to

Chicago, and Stanley was the last of the family to function in the top management of the store.

"Awe" and "respect" are the two words that contemporary writers most frequently used to describe the way people viewed Marshall Field in later life. (There were also numerous references to his cold blue eyes.) But even though, or because, he was arriving in the upper reaches of the Chicago business world when he was barely out of his 20s, Field was already on his way to becoming a living legend, according to Stephen Becker in his book *Marshall Field III.* Becker has this to say: "Even his penny-pinching was viewed with awful respect; Andrew MacLeish (the poet's father), who had worked for Field and who in 1867 took charge of Carson, Pirie's retail division,* complimented Field on his wage scale: 'Not even a Scotsman could live on that.' They said Field was shrewd; so he was. Honest; so he was. Cold; so he was. He was incorruptible. He was rectitude personified. He was the sharpest merchant in the United States, but the customer was always right. He never made a shady penny. If Marshall Field said no, Marshall Field meant no. Absolutely straight. No vices. A handsome man."

When it comes down to it, any entrepreneur, any businessman who charts a new course, is a gambler. Field gambled on Chicago and on his abilities as a merchant. Only once in his life did he act on impulse, without careful study and diligent preparation. And, from his point of view, it was a big mistake.

Field was never one for large social gatherings, although he could be most charming and even outgoing in a small group of his peers and particularly when a one-on-one situation called for an effort. In the late winter of 1862 he did agree to attend a party given by a friend and there he met

---

* The MacLeish name was never added to the corporate name of Carson, Pirie, Scott & Co., but the family was instrumental in building the department store into a chief competitor of Field's. John T. Pirie, chairman of the firm in the 1950s, was the last of the four families in top management. However, the MacLeish family retained a large stock interest in the company into the 1980s.

Nannie Douglas Scott. Bachelor Field was 28 years old, Nannie Scott, 23, quiet, pretty, and accomplished.

Visiting friends in Chicago, she hailed from a place called Vernon Furnace, a village in southeastern Ohio. Her father was a representative of a slowly vanishing breed, the prosperous local manufacturer best typified in the 18th and 19th centuries by the local flour miller. He owned an iron foundry in what was then known as the Hanging Rock Iron Region of Ohio. The king of his village, he had prospered mightily with the coming of the Civil War. (Marshall Field chose to ignore the war except for its effect on his business—cotton goods were hard to come by—and was able to do so without damage to his reputation even though it would appear that he was a prime candidate for military service.) In Vernon Furnace, the Scotts lived well in a large brick home, participated in the society of nearby Ironton, a small city on the Ohio River, and sent daughter Nannie off to Troy, New York, to finish at Miss Willard's School for Young Ladies.

At his friend's party Field was charming, charmed, and smitten—and alarmed to find that Miss Scott was leaving in the morning for Ohio. The next day Field appeared at the railroad station to see Nannie off. On a wild impulse he leaped aboard the train as it was pulling out, joined Nannie, and proceeded to propose marriage. Nannie, described then and through her life as girlishly romantic, accepted. Field hopped off at the next station to hurry back to the store, an act that should have given Nannie second thoughts but didn't.

Later, the superstitious might have concluded that the marriage was ill-starred. After Marshall had paid a visit to Vernon Furnace and been found acceptable, it was agreed that the marriage would take place on a Thursday in June of 1863 in Ohio. Monday of that week, with caterers and an orchestra hired from Ironton, and classmates of Nannie's arriving from Chicago and the East, Jennie, the prettier, vivacious sister of Nannie, the belle of the large Scott family, came skittering down the main staircase of the house to join a tea for Marshall and the gathering clan. Unbelievably, a large brass-and-crystal chandelier fell as she passed underneath. Horribly burned by the flaming kerosene that lit the chandelier, Jennie was dead the next day. There was a funeral at Vernon Furnace instead of a wedding and the marriage was postponed.

But Nannie and Marshall did marry and they had children, first Lewis, born in 1866 but dead as an infant, then a second son and princely heir, Marshall Field II, born on April 21, 1868, and finally Ethel Newcomb, born in 1873. The consistent story was that Nannie Field, having escaped from Vernon Furnace, was unhappy almost from the beginning of her marriage. Apparently Field's dash aboard the train to propose was just about the last exciting, happy, romantic impulse he had in him. At a time when Field's elegant store was one of the few public places a proper lady could visit unescorted, Nannie was not satisfied being Mrs. Marshall Field, seeing to the children, the house, the servants, and attending women's teas and formal dinner parties. However, she did serve competently as hostess for the necessary entertaining the Fields did in a city where position in the business world defined society.

Later on it was Field's habit to arrive at his store promptly at nine in the morning and to leave as promptly at four in the afternoon. He knew how to pick competent subordinates, and he delegated all but final authority, although with his extraordinary memory he never missed or forgot a detail. Seven hours a day at the store was sufficient, and as the years went by Field had an empire outside the dry-goods business to attend to. But in the early years of his marriage Field was building his business and he did face at least two crises that demanded full-time attention for long periods. Perhaps he can be excused at least partially for the standing charge, not uncommon then or now, that he neglected his wife and his family for the sake of business.

There was the Great Chicago Fire, "Mrs. O'Leary's fire," of 1871 that wiped out more than half of the cracker-box and

wood-frame city and did not spare the impressive brick
Field building, erected by Potter Palmer, on State Street at
Washington, even though Field was on deck all night long
directing efforts to save the store. What Field and his men
did save were the store records and the most valuable merchandise. Within a few weeks he was back in business, having immediately bought and cleaned out one of the few
buildings that survived the fire and could meet his needs in
any fashion. A railway horse-car barn, it was a couple of
dozen blocks south of the central shopping district, but the
makeshift store did a roaring business what with the goods
Field's wagons had saved from the burning store and the
new supplies he had coming in from the East. More than
that, the firm was loaded with insurance. (Although a number of insurance companies went broke as enormous claims
were filed, a national boom in property and casualty insurance dates from the Chicago fire.) And if Field, the prudent
Yankee, needed a lesson, he had learned it well in the old
Cooley, Wadsworth days; the Panic of 1857 just a year after
Field went to work in Chicago had ruined a number of
retailers, left owing large bills to suppliers but unable to
collect from their retail customers. But not Cooley, Wadsworth. Cash on the barrelhead was the rule there, and while
Field, the shrewd merchandiser, might allow a lady of quality to take a dress home and think about it and while he
would allow anyone to return any product without question,
he would not extend credit. (A century later Marshall Field
& Co. was still being chary of credit sales; the store's principal form of credit was being polite when customers with
good addresses failed to meet a monthly billing in full. And
even after the modern credit-card mania Field's credit policies remained for years far more stringent than those of
other major stores.) Between what Field, Leiter and Company had in the till and with cash from new sales Field had
no money problems even before the insurance companies
paid off.

The question was not whether Field would rebuild and go

on, but where. Potter Palmer was determined to make State Street the great street of Chicago; he had bought up large tracts along the street south of the Chicago River but the street was a black ruin. Disastrously, Palmer's dream hotel that was to anchor a magnificent State Street along with the Field store had opened only thirteen days before the fire. And just before the fire, Field, bent on building a bigger and better store on his own land, had been negotiating for property that was not on State Street but a block over on Wabash Avenue. After the fire Field panicked the business and real estate community by throwing up a new building on the West Side of the city, blocks from State Street. Obligingly, customers and the retail trade followed Field to the West Side. But even though sales were quickly running at a $20 million clip it was only a temporary move. In a few years Field, Leiter and Company was back doing business on the old stand at State and Washington.

But then disaster once again. During a November night in 1877, a fire in the Field store destroyed all but the shell of the five-story building and all the merchandise. Field was reduced to doing business from a nearby, rented hall. Strangely enough, he had difficulty making up his mind what to do next. And he made what for him was a mistake. While he temporized, rival Carson, Pirie agreed to lease the new building going up on Field's longtime site. It cost Field three-quarters of a million dollars to purchase the land and the building. That included a $100,000 payment to buy Carson, Pirie out of the lease. Among other things it had to be painful to Field to arm a competitor with $100,000 in cash to be used against him.

Meanwhile, Levi Z. Leiter, as shrewd as Field in his own way, a tiny man, always busy, had seen great opportunity in the disaster of the 1871 fire. With Field following his lead, Leiter made major purchases of Chicago real estate at what could be called fire-sale prices. And if real estate is the foundation of almost every great and enduring fortune, Marshall

Field's purchases at the time and later on built a second fortune for the family outside the merchandising business.

Like most strong-willed entrepreneurs, Field did not relish partners. Subordinates, yes; subordinates who were competent and talented—and Field was a good judge of talent—and who marched to orders. Over the years, Field rewarded his officers, if not his help, and a number became rich men after Field granted them stock in the company. But once he was established and secure Field wanted no one around in a position to challenge his authority. Harry Selfridge was the great example. Known as "Mile a Minute" Harry, Selfridge rose from stock boy to general manager of the store in less than ten years during the 1880s. A dandy, bubbling with energy and ideas, ambitious, Selfridge had the nerve to ask Field for stock and a partnership. Field swallowed that one, but when Selfridge after another ten years of success at the store suggested to Field that the name of the store be changed to Field, Selfridge and Company, that was too much. Field refused, Selfridge offered his resignation, generously suggesting that he would stay on until the end of the year to allow Field time to make adjustments. Field gave him until the next day to pack up and depart. Happily, Selfridge departed with a million dollars, the value of the stock Field had given him, and went on to found what was to become London's famous Selfridge store. (Among other alumni, Montgomery Ward clerked for Field's.)

In the history of business the falling out of partners is almost as frequent as divorce. The reasons are many, ranging from personalities to disagreements over basic policy, e.g., to risk the firm's capital in an attempt to expand or to maintain a comfortable little business. Typically, the disagreement ends with one partner agreeing to buy out the other under a formula of one kind or another. Usually there's a fascinating footnote, with variations. The partner who remains with the business goes on to millions and a national reputation while the partner who pulls out dribbles away his money in obscurity, always with the knowledge eating at him that the stock he traded for $100,000 has increased in value to a million or ten million dollars. The reverse often occurs. One partner departs with his cash and watches his former friend slide into bankruptcy.

Field's partners and associates departed one after another over the years, but if their wealth never matched Field's, they uniformly, like Selfridge, did well. With Levi Leiter, Field made the typical offer. He would set a price and Leiter could buy Field out or Field would buy Leiter out at that same price. After some thought Leiter agreed and was astonished at the bargain figure Field came up with.

On the face of it, Field was taking a long gamble. But he knew Leiter was not a bold man. More important, Field knew that Leiter was increasingly and profitably involved in real estate and that his socially ambitious wife had her eye on the government swirl in Washington. Even more important to Field's plans, Field had quietly lined up the support of the firm's top executives; if Leiter, a man with a quick temper, difficult to deal with, took over, he might lose the firm's best people. When this came home to him, Leiter passed up the chance to buy Field out, accepted Field's bargain-basement price, and quietly left with his millions.

This was 1881, the firm was generating a profit of more than $2 million a year, and it was far more than a retail store. Like predecessor firms and other major stores in Chicago, Field was also a wholesaler. In fact, for a long period the wholesale operation appeared more important, even to Field, than the dry-goods store. The McCormick reaper, the Deere plow, and the Armours, the Swifts, and the other meat packers of Chicago had created great wealth out there on the plains. Towns and cities had sprung up as the railroads pushed across the country from the Chicago hub. Every village had its general store. Even in the larger towns very few establishments were equipped to do their own buying. They bought their goods from Field and others, but Field became the dominant wholesaler in the Midwest. Beyond that, he established and made an additional profit on a network of companies which manufactured the goods he sold to himself and to other stores. He owned factories or had manufacturing arrangements in the Far East and the Middle East, Australia, Germany, Italy, Spain, as well as the United States. Fieldcrest Mills, today an independent and separate public company with $100 million in sales in bed clothing and towels and still a supplier to the Field stores, is one offshoot from the early Field wholesale-manufacturing operation. Another is Chicago's famed Merchandise Mart, once the largest office building in the world and still an international display center for manufacturers and designers of household furnishings. After World War II, the Mart was purchased from the Fields by the Joseph Kennedy family at what turned out to be a bargain price and it became a not insignificant part of the Kennedy fortune.

If Field was reticent, even shy, he did not believe in ostentatious displays of his accumulating millions. He rode to the store each morning in a hansom carriage, but walked the last blocks so people would not see him driven to work. He built a $2 million twenty-five-room mansion for his family, but told the fashionable New York architect he had hired he did not want any frills. Field was only 39 years old when the mansion—some thought it looked more like a fortress than a house—was built. It was located on the South Side, less than a couple of dozen blocks from the central business district and the store. The mansion was a measure of Field's wealth and confidence and the success of his empire. It was completed only two years after the Great Chicago Fire and in the year of one of the country's periodic panics, as recessions or depressions were then called. Important wealth was represented in the vicinity of the Field house on Prairie Avenue. George Pullman was one neighbor. For decades and well into the 20th century the Prairie Avenue mansion was officially home base for the wandering Field family even though it often stood empty for months except for a complement of servants. Meanwhile, wealth was moving north, north of the business district and the Chicago River. The

South Side was and is the most naturally attractive sector of Chicago's long lakefront, but by the turn of the century railroads were busy on lines that had pushed through the South Side to the center of the city. Smoke from a booming industrial plant and a terrible stench from the stockyards and slaughterhouses floated over the area. Not far away was the Levee, a rough, tough district of poor immigrants, bars, and brothels.

Nannie Douglas Scott never seems to have been happy. Perhaps, having made some contact with a different world at Miss Willard's School, the romantic young woman found little to excite her in raw, bustling, commercial Chicago. Perhaps the death of her first child left a mark that could not be erased by the polite lunches, teas, and dinners she attended or gave in the gray mausoleum. Certainly, Marshall Field did not provide the marriage Nannie wanted. He was always described by his contemporaries as handsome, a fine figure of a man, correct in all things, courteous, soft-spoken. Business associates spoke of his brilliant analytical mind, his grasp of detail, his memory, and the respect he inspired. There's a near-void where words like "warm," "jovial," "outgoing," "pleasant" might be used. Apparently Field kept his distance from people except when the occasion seemed worth an effort. Dinner parties he attended infrequently and reluctantly. His preferred entertainment, particularly in later life, was poker at the Chicago Club or a friend's house. George Pullman and Philip D. Armour were regulars but the stakes the millionaires played for would not frighten players in an average suburban Saturday-night poker game. Field could become ecstatic at winning twenty dollars in a night although he disliked himself for his addiction to the game.

Other than giving Field a daughter and a son and heir, Nannie Field seems to have left little in the way of a positive impression on her life and times. In a city where wealth and position might have stepped off the latest train from the East or might have been created by last year's back-room deal in railroad stocks, the position of the wife of Marshall Field in Chicago society was as solid as diamonds. She did not exploit her position and she did not choose to challenge the ambitious reigning queen and pioneer feminist, Mrs. Potter Palmer.

Nannie Field's one real splash in Chicago society was the Mikado Ball, a major effort on Mrs. Field's part in behalf of her children. Marshall II was 17 years old and Ethel was 14 in 1886, the year of the ball. More than four hundred young people attended; favors were designed by James Whistler in London and handed out along with blossoms from Japanese trees. An orchestra played Gilbert and Sullivan, and scenery from the New York production of *The Mikado* (or perhaps only copied from it) was shipped in for atmosphere. The final cost of the party was reckoned at $75,000, a pretty penny for no-frills Field in 1886.

Perhaps even more so than now, Americans in Field's day and in a raw Midwestern city like Chicago were fascinated by the ancient and superior culture of Europe. But before the jet airplane shrank the world, only the rich could afford to taste London and Paris. It is easy to understand that instant millionaires like Field could afford the cost of touring Europe with the family. What's difficult to understand in the 1980s is how businessmen could afford the time. New York was a long overnight journey from Chicago by train and Europe was a week or more away by steamer. A month on the Continent was routine for rich Chicagoans. Having done her duty by Field and Chicago society, Nannie Field expanded the annual safari to the Continent. Traveling with or without the children, she soon became an expatriate. Her routine was Paris in the spring, the Mediterranean coast and southern France in the winter, and England almost anytime in between. The rumor in Chicago, enhanced by the explanation that she traveled for her health, was that Mrs. Field was floating from art gallery to museum to cathedral in a drug haze. But it is less than probable that Nannie was a full-blown drug addict. In her time a goodly part of American womanhood, rich and poor, dissatisfied with the kitchen and bedroom status of women, got through the day with a little help. The patent medicines available everywhere for everything from headache to "female troubles" were based on alcohol and opium and were freely available.

The evolution of the Field family was curious. Marshall II went off to Harvard at the appropriate time, but did not put in the appropriate number of years needed for a degree. Instead, at age 22, in the fall of 1890, he married Albertine Huck, the beautiful 18-year-old daughter of a well-to-do Chicago brewer. Young Marshall apparently had no interest in following in his father's footsteps at the store and there's no evidence that the father made the classic attempt to force the son into the business. (Later, Stanley Field, the son of Joseph Field, the brother who went to Manchester, England, to handle imports for Field, reversed the family transatlantic migration and came to Chicago. He became a companion and perhaps substitute son for Field and rose to important executive positions in the store.) On New Year's Day 1891, three months after the marriage of Marshall II, 17-year-old sister Ethel also married. Ethel and her new husband, Arthur Magie Tree, the son of a Chicago judge and well-traveled diplomat, promptly took off for England. Marshall and his new wife followed on and the two Chicago families leased neighboring estates in Warwickshire.

At this point it could be said that the Field family was no longer resident in America. The patriarch was living a lonely life in Chicago, rattling around in the Prairie Avenue mansion, but his wife and two children were established in England and on the Continent. And then there were grandchildren. Marshall II and Albertine were prolific. However, the firstborn, a son and heir to the name, died in October 1892 after only thirteen days of life. But on September 28, 1893, another son, also christened Marshall, arrived during one of the couple's visits to the Prairie Avenue house. Henry and Gwendolyn followed, but a fourth child, a boy, also died in a few days.

If Field was a distant husband and father, he was an enthusiastic grandfather. Secure in his position and his millions, he increased and extended his trips to Europe to spend time with the grandchildren and welcomed family visits to Chicago even though his business interests had increased tenfold over the years. Legend had it that in the 1890s, before the income tax, his real estate holdings made him the largest taxpayer in the United States. (A factor there may have been that Field, straitlaced, honest by his own lights, paid his taxes.) Eventually he was a major stockholder and often a director of some thirty large corporations. The list included a number of the booming Midwest railroads, banks in Chicago and New York, the Pullman Company, McCormick's International Harvester, and the United States Steel Co. Field was the power in the Chicago business community; the city's business and financial leaders did not throw their weight to one side or another of a civic or business issue until Field's opinion had been sought. When George Pullman, fond of the bottle and of young women and possessed of a Victorian passion for Clara Barton, founder of the American Red Cross, let his great car-building company slide to the brink of bankruptcy in the years following the Pullman factory strike and the tragic Haymarket riot, it was Field who stepped in. In what seemed a matter of days and with a few miraculously simple decisions, Field had the company back on its feet. When Charles Schwab and the powers of Wall Street put together U.S. Steel in the hopes of monopolizing the steel business, they came out on the short end in a battle with Field. Field had no objection to bigger and more powerful business trusts. In fact, he went along with the prevailing business thinking of the time: trusts would eliminate the "ruinous" competition that periodically precipitated bankruptcies, unemployment, and financial panics. The issue between Schwab and Field was a matter of geography. Schwab wanted a major new expansion mill located in Pennsylvania. Today, Gary, Indiana, the great steel-mill town, is testimony to Field's power and negotiating ability. Whether or not

Field was merely boosting Chicago (and his retail business), he was correct from a business standpoint; the Chicago district, closer to the modern-day big users of steel, grew to outproduce the Pittsburgh district.

For the most part, Field was a very careful, conservative investor, and real estate was his big outside thing. (His will instructed his trustees to concentrate investments in real estate.) Field could scarcely miss once he decided that Chicago would grow and prosper in spite of the devastation of the Great Chicago Fire of 1871. In the decade of the 1880s the city's population doubled as immigrants from Europe and other seekers of livelihood and fortune poured in. (Shortly before his death at age 97 in 1981, Chicago patriarch and investment banker William McCormick Blair told friends and colleagues that the 1980s would boom. The eighties were great the last time, he said.)

Through the 19th century Chicago had plenty of competition for the title Queen City of the Western Territory. Cincinnati, St. Louis, Indianapolis, Milwaukee, and a number of now obscure towns along the Mississippi were convinced at various times that they would become the largest city west of the Alleghenies. Wheat, corn, cattle, and the thinking of the New York and New England financial crowd, many of whom migrated to Chicago, helped the Windy City.

Chicago is located astride a minor continental divide. In the days before white settlers drove the Indians from their homelands, Chicago was a meeting and trading ground for the local tribes.

When Louis Jolliet, an explorer and fur trader, came to the area 300 years ago, he found the two great waterways of North America: the Mississippi River to the south and west (via the Des Plaines and Illinois Rivers) and the Great Lakes to the north and east. Between these systems was the swampland Jolliet named the Chicago Portage and others called Mud Lake. During the spring rains, shallow-draft vessels, including Indian canoes, could traverse the swamp, going from the Des Plaines about eight miles to Lake Michigan.

Transportation was a vital consideration, but even more pressing was the havoc wrought by flooding, notably periodic outbreaks of cholera, dysentery, strep infection, and typhoid fever. The epidemics understandably aroused civic indignation and in 1836 aggressive, infant Chicago began building the Illinois (for the Illinois River) and Michigan (for Lake Michigan) Canal. It was a commendable feat, some 100 miles of canal when completed in 1848.

Water transport for cargo and passenger vessels was then possible with the Erie Canal all the way from the Hudson River through Chicago to New Orleans. Chicago thrived.

The I & M Canal also reversed the flow of the Chicago River to an extent, after it was deepened and widened. Subsequently, it was supplemented by the much larger Chicago Sanitary and Ship Canal which, since its opening January 17, 1900, has effectively reversed the flow of the Chicago and Calumet Rivers. (The I & M waterway was closed in 1914.)

The newer, wider canal not only encouraged commercial traffic but, as the priority in the name indicated, was most beneficial in allowing Chicago to flush its growing sewage and pollution down the river system instead of into Lake Michigan, which supplies the metropolitan area with water.

Predictably the towns and cities downstream loudly objected to the dumping of Chicago's waste in their waters. The Great Lakes cities objected to the diversion of Lake Michigan water via the north channel of the Chicago River and the Calumet River south of Chicago. Both were flowing out of the lake. Locks installed at all three streams greatly reduced the amount of water being taken out of the lake.

As a consequence of pressure from down-river residents, the pollution problem was attacked by the Metropolitan Sanitary District of Greater Chicago with the design and building of tunnels and reservoirs that would carry off and store sewer overflow. Under Phase I, in the 1980s, four tunnel systems totaling 110 miles were under construction. Phase II will add 21 miles of tunnels and was designed primarily for flood control. It also will eliminate the 15 percent of pollution from combined sewer overflows not reached by Phase I. Sewage and rainwater alike will travel through huge tunnels to reservoirs hundreds of feet underground to be processed when conditions permit.

The processing will take place in the three largest sewage treatment plants on the West Side, and four other smaller plants in the western and northern suburbs.

As the railroad age blossomed and the importance of canals diminished, foreign, Eastern, and Chicago money pushed rail lines west and south of Chicago. More important to the city's future, New York and New England financiers chose northerly routes along the Great Lakes for the rail network, making Chicago the premier rail hub rather than, for instance, more centrally located St. Louis. Mounting hostility between the North and South was a factor, and the Civil War impeded traffic on the Ohio River and the Mississippi, securing Chicago's position and channeling millions of dollars to the city. Significantly for Chicago's growth in commerce and industry, the city was safely in Yankee territory even though the city had its quota of Southern sympathizers. The war also destroyed north-south traffic on the Mississippi River while the rush westward after the war did far more for Chicago with its east-west rail lines than its position as the transfer point (by canal and river) between the Great Lakes and the Mississippi River system had done or would do.

Occasionally Marshall Field did depart from his conservative real estate and blue-chip investment philosophy. Once he and Levi Leiter put up the money to develop a lead and silver mine at Leadville, Colorado. The gamble made a million dollars for the partners. In 1892 Field lent Samuel Insull $250,000, having correctly judged that Insull possessed unusual organizational and financial abilities. Insull used the money to buy chunks of stock in the ailing Chicago Edison utility and with Field's backing took over control of the company. Forty-two years later when the bottom dropped out of everything in the Great Depression and it became evident that Insull had put together a vast utility empire with watered stock, bonds, and other "Chinese paper," it was Stanley Field, representing the family, who told Insull he was fired. (The Fields were the largest stockholders in the company. Reorganized as Commonwealth Edison, the utility prospered mightily through the decades until trapped by inflation and high interest rates in the late 1970s and early 1980s.)

Strangely enough, Field was a Democrat, but he did not make his politics public and refused all suggestions that he run for office or accept political appointment. Field's adherence to the Democratic Party would seem to be a matter of pragmatism. As a major importer, he supported free trade against Republican protectionism. He must have been appalled by free-silver, cheap-money Populism and the emotional oratory of William Jennings Bryan, but even as a cash-on-the-barrelhead merchant he could see that the strict gold-standard principles of sound-money Republicans could be bad for business. War was certainly bad for business, Field felt; he was not enthusiastic about the war between the states and he used his influence to counter the "manifest destiny" nationalism of McKinley Republicanism that sent the country galloping into the Spanish-American War.

At the same time, what angered—and frightened—Field was the unrest and protest among the big and increasing immigrant population of Chicago—the strikes, the street riots, the overtones of European socialism and anarchism. Marshall Field & Co. trucks were available to supplement police vans, Field was instrumental in raising money to recruit and equip a stronger National Guard, and eventually it was Field as much as anyone who prevailed upon Washington to establish Fort Sheridan to the north of the city with a complement of Regular Army troops as a safeguard against insurrection.

On another social front, Field came fairly late in life to philanthropy. Although he was criticized over the years as a tightwad, the pattern is not unusual for men who have piled up millions on their own—the earlier decades are devoted to making the money, the latter years to giving some part of it away. Even so, Field was only 44 years old when he entered upon what was apparently his first public, or publicized, project in the good-works category. He was a reluctant but still founding member of the corporation for the Chicago Academy of Fine Arts. And 50 when the money was raised to make possible a grand opening in 1884 of what by then was called the Art Institute of Chicago. Chicago has always had more than its share of art collectors, and the backbone of the institute's opening exhibit was paintings loaned by Chicagoans. That included Millet's "Harvest Moon." Owner: Marshall Field.

It may have been a defensive ploy, but Field argued with more than a little justice that civic improvements should be supported by the generality of the people in a city. A handful of wealthy people should not put up the money and dictate the cultural and social direction of the metropolis. But as he grew older Field mellowed under peer pressure. If it was Rockefeller's millions that really built a failing Baptist academy into one of the world's great educational institutions, the University of Chicago, Field's support was crucial in the earliest days.

All told, Field donated twenty-five acres of valuable land to the fledgling university, and in 1890, along with five other Chicago leaders, he put his name on the articles of incorporation for the university. Two years later he contributed $100,000 to the building fund—on condition that the trustees raise a total of $1 million within ninety days. With Field's mighty prestige behind the fund-raising campaign, the Chicago business community anted up the necessary money within Field's deadline.

The contribution of less than half a million in land and cash did not exactly put a strain on the Field family bank balance. But the big one for Field came right on top of his help for the university.

Chicago had decided that this young, burgeoning country should celebrate the 400th anniversary of the discovery of the Americas by Christopher Columbus with the staging of a world's fair. One way and another the great Columbian Exposition celebrated the 401st anniversary.

With the usual delays in such projects, the Columbian Exposition of 1893 was organized like other world's fairs with the idea that it would pay for itself, and surprisingly the exposition was one of the few then or now that did finish in the black. In the summer months of 1893 an astonishing 28 million admissions were recorded at the gates as people from all over flocked to see the marvels of the age—and the dancer Little Egypt. Marshall Field was the largest stockholder and contributor of capital to build the 600-acre fair. Hometown boosterism was certainly a factor in Field's support for a Baptist university; his motivation for backing the Columbian Exposition was even more direct. Not only would the Exposition focus world attention on Chicago but it would also attract thousands of visitors to the city and to the city's largest and best department store.

While the fair was in progress a number of people started talking up the idea that some of the wonders assembled in Chicago ought to be retained and housed permanently in a grand building. Field agreed to put up $1 million and again attached a condition. Others would have to raise an additional $500,000. (Over the years the conditional gift has become almost standard practice, and not necessarily as a result of Field's thinking that good works should be supported by the community, but for the very practical reason that once it is known that Rockefeller, Ford, Mellon, or Field money is behind a project other people think there's no need to contribute.)

Chicago raised the money and the Field Columbian Museum opened on June 2, 1894. Now the Field Museum of Natural History and one of the great institutions of its kind in the world, the museum benefited from additional Field millions.

Field was then approaching his 59th birthday. Nearly six feet tall, a handsome man with a strong jaw, a full head of hair and a flourishing mustache, Field was at the height of his power and prestige. To his embarrassment and distaste, he was often urged to run for public office or to accept government appointments. Nominally a Democrat, he very possibly could have become at the turn of the century the Democratic nominee for President of the United States, backed by those party members who, like Field, deplored the populist demagoguery of William Jennings Bryan and also the reforms and the imperialism of Theodore Roosevelt. (Field publicly opposed the Spanish-American War.)

Acknowledged as one of the leading businessmen of the country, Field found his fortune piling up. The sales of the store and the wholesaling operation were estimated at $35 million in 1895. Field's real estate holdings were vast. His stockholdings in nearly thirty major U.S. corporations were so large that a newspaper reporter once asked him if he dominated those companies. He denied it, but in addition to his stock ownership, he was a director or officer or both of many of the corporations.

In 1900, on the Fourth of July, Field did the classic for the hometown boy who makes good. He went back to Conway, Massachusetts, to lay the cornerstone for a free public library, his gift to his native village. A year later he returned for the dedication and paid for a dinner, music, and fireworks for everyone.

But if Field had done it all and become one of the nation's outstanding men, it could not be argued that he was among the happiest. For years he had spent most of his time alone in the mansion, his wife, his children, and then his grandchildren 5,500 miles away.

On February 23, 1896, Nannie Scott Field died in Nice during an excursion to the South of France, where the February weather was certainly better for an ailing person than

Chicago's. Having been absent from Chicago and Field for the greater part of twenty years, she was brought home to be buried in Graceland Cemetery.

If there was gossip in Chicago about Field it was underground. For years his admiration for Mrs. Arthur J. Caton was open and public. The Catons lived around the corner from the Field mansion. Delia Spencer Caton was a beautiful young woman, and Field often appeared at parties and other functions with the Catons and sometimes went on vacation trips with them. Arthur Caton, a wealthy lawyer, died suddenly in November 1904 during a trip to New York City. Eleven months later, on September 5, 1905, Delia Caton and Field were married in St. Margaret's Church in London. She was 50 years old; Field had just passed his 70th birthday.

By all accounts it was the happiest time of Field's later life. But it was to be brief. The bride and groom were in New York City when the great tragedy of his life began to unfold. Back in Chicago, his son, Marshall Field II, had shot himself, the bullet entering the abdomen. Field hired a private train and ordered the engineer to put on all steam to take them home.

At Mercy Hospital, Marshall II survived a lengthy operation and for a time it appeared that he was rallying and would live. But on November 27, after five days in the hospital, the heir to the Field fortune died. The surgery and the medicine of the time were not equal to the internal damage he had suffered.

The official statement was that Marshall II had been cleaning a pistol when it accidentally discharged. But almost no one believed that. Marshall II seemed to prove the folk belief that sons of dominant, self-made men are failures. From childhood he had not been well, he had gone to Harvard because Harvard was one of the universities where sons of the wealthy went, and by design or otherwise he had not entered the family business and instead, except for a devotion to wife and children, had occupied himself with a miscellany of more or less meaningless activities, mainly in foreign countries. He was 37 years old, an age that causes any number of persons to ask what the meaning of life is.

All that, plus family reticence—the elder Field flailed with a cane at the packs of reporters and photographers that hounded him from railroad station to hospital to home and told them they should be ashamed of themselves—and police statements that an investigation was underway, only fueled rumor.

Soon a better story than suicide began making the rounds. Actually, it was said, young Field had been shot, or stabbed, in one of the brothels in the honky-tonk section near the Field mansion. Preferably, the brothel was the one operated by the Everleigh sisters with their $15,000 gold piano and their gold-plated clientele. Gossip even supplied a murderess, a Spanish woman, never further identified.

Marshall Field III, 12 years old at the time and playing in a nearby room with games received on his recent birthday, always said he heard the shot. And always that the shot was not accidental.

His grandson, Marshall V, insists he would rather believe the more romantic brothel tale.

The newspapers of the time had it that Marshall I never smiled again after his son's death. At least not within range of reporters or photographers.

Prior to Field's new marriage, his circumscribed social activities centered on lunch with his peers at the Chicago Club, his low-stakes poker games, occasional visits to a racetrack, infrequent dinner parties, and the Sunday-morning breakfasts he liked to provide a few close friends, including the Catons, at the Prairie Avenue mansion. That and, remarkably, golf, a game he was so addicted to that he tried to play three times a week, summer or winter.

After Field and Delia Caton were married, Field's passion for golf continued. On New Year's Day 1906 he journeyed a half hour by train to the Chicago Golf Club, located near suburban Wheaton. Opened in 1893–94, the course was the

first eighteen-hole layout in the United States (the East
Coast had a number of nine-hole courses and one aberrant
twelve-hole course). Then and now, Chicago Golf's membership was made up of dedicated golfers from the top rungs
of the city. Field's foursome included Robert Todd Lincoln,
the President's son and a prominent Chicago lawyer (his
name remains a part of the title of a leading Chicago law
firm, Isham, Lincoln and Beale); nephew Stanley Field; and
James Simpson, a senior executive of Marshall Field & Co.
and later chairman.

They played with red golf balls because there was snow on
the ground that New Year's Day. Along the way Field told
Stanley Field that he intended to change his will the following week when he returned from a brief trip to New York to
attend a directors' meeting. He was going to double his gift
to the Field Museum from $8 million to $16 million.

The next day Field found himself with a sore throat and
the beginnings of a head cold, but he persisted in his golfing
routine of recent years. He played twice that week and the
following Monday evening boarded the Broadway Limited
with the new Mrs. Field for the trip to Manhattan. As the
train rolled eastward Field felt worse and worse, and a telegram was dispatched to Pittsburgh to have a doctor meet
the train there. But after the examination he decided to go
on to New York, where he was staying at his favorite hotel,
the Holland House. In New York a battery of doctors put him
in the hospital. Stanley Field arrived from Chicago and then
Dr. Frank Billings, Chicago's leading physician and surgeon
and a friend. Billings agreed that Field was suffering from
severe pneumonia, then almost certain death for a 71-year-
old, and on Tuesday afternoon, January 16, 1906, Field died.

Not counting trust funds already set up, the fortune of the
merchant, as he preferred to be known, amounted to an
estate valued in 1900 dollars at $120 million. In a day before
inheritance or income taxes, the bulk went in trust to Marshall Field III along with instructions that the money should

continue to be invested in real estate and conservative stocks.

In only seven weeks Marshall III had suffered through the death of his father and his grandfather. Very shortly he was to undergo another experience commonly considered a significant trauma for a child. After his father's death, his strong-willed and protective mother let it be known that she had definite plans for the Field heirs. The wealth of her sons, said Albertine, should be employed for the greatest good of "their countrymen" and she hoped that they would grow up to be politicians, fulfilling the highest of "patriotic ambitions."

Having said that, Albertine promptly packed up the three children and departed Chicago for England, where she apparently intended to live permanently. At least she bought a house in London and put the children in school. Inside of two years she married Maldwin A. Drummond, the second son in a distinguished British banking family who had been, in the English tradition for second sons, assigned a career in the Army. The marriage gave Albertine additional entrée to royal and aristocratic society, and the Drummonds entertained lavishly in London until they moved to the ancestral home in Hampshire.

Actually young Marshall, Henry, and little Gwendolyn may have suffered less by being transplanted to England than the children of a modern American executive transferred, say, from Baltimore to Chicago. The millionaires of the United States with their new or newly inherited money were eager to sample and join polished and sophisticated European society, and the Fields were not an exception. The first Mrs. Marshall Field had lived for years in Europe. Her daughter Ethel had married Arthur Tree, a member of another distinguished British family, and after a divorce had married a British naval officer. Albertine and Marshall, traveling for pleasure, spent a greater part of their time in England and had many friends there. With Ethel and her two young sons in England an aunt and cousins were nearby.

When the time came, the Drummonds had no difficulty in entering Marshall and later Henry at Eton. With the help of or in spite of the playing fields of Eton—in later life Marshall thought Eton overemphasized team sports—Marshall began to grow out of the effects of rheumatic fever that had made him a "sickly" child. What Marshall certainly did gain from Eton, and later Cambridge, was an educated gentleman's sense of history, literature, and philosophy along with something of that particular British brand of noblesse oblige. That last reinforced his mother's belief that a responsibility to society came with the Field wealth.

Still, life for Marshall III at the time was a young man's dream. Occasionally moody, he was most of the time open, friendly, secure, and at the same time modest. He enjoyed the eating and drinking clubs of Trinity College, the house parties at his mother's and at other country estates, a wide circle of mostly wealthy friends, male and female, and bridge, chess, and the sports that appealed to him—hunting, fishing, sailing, and, most of all, riding.

One incident offers something of the flavor of Marshall's life at the time. His interest in riding and horses extended to the racetrack, where once his bets paid off to the tune of several hundred pounds. With that bounty in his pocket, he took off for the Continent and the Monte Carlo Casino. In the tradition of such escapades, he came back to England on money cabled from home.

Nevertheless, Marshall did his share of studying and he did pass his final examination (in history) at Trinity College. This was early in 1914, war clouds were building over Europe, and as Marshall said years later, an era was ending.

For Marshall an era was ending in more ways than one. He was approaching his 21st birthday and that meant among other things that he would become a trustee of the Field estate with a duty to participate in the management of the estate's investments. (At his grandfather's death Marshall was tagged, incorrectly, by the newspapers as the world's richest boy. Marshall I's complicated and detailed 20,000-

word will actually parceled out control of the fortune over decades. Albertine, the daughter of a well-to-do Chicago brewer, was given the income from a $500,000 trust and $500,000 outright on top of what she was left by her husband. At one point she felt it necessary to petition the trustees for more money for the education of her children.)

In addition to being declared an adult by law and by his grandfather, Marshall in 1914 had to deal with the fact that his mother had developed cancer. The surgery of the day was ineffective, and Marshall spent the summer of 1914 at the Drummond country house to be with her.

Then there was Evelyn Marshall. She was the daughter of a wealthy New York businessman, and Marshall had met her in London during her travels. Albertine's illness limited the usual round of summer parties, but the lovely and charming Evelyn was a guest. Herewith the kind of coincidence found only in a romantic novel. In August 1914, Great Britain declared war on Germany. It was time for Evelyn and other touring Americans to go home. Marshall thought of enlisting in the British military as most of his Cambridge classmates were doing. But at that early stage of the war the military was open only to British citizens. Family duty called; he was wanted in Chicago to begin his education in finance and money management. Evelyn's father was a director of the Cunard Line, and the two young people sailed for New York on the luxury liner *Lusitania*.

Not too long afterward the engagement was announced, and Marshall Field III and Evelyn Marshall were married by a Roman Catholic bishop in the Marshalls' midtown Manhattan home on February 8, 1915. (The Field family had become nominally Catholic with the marriage of Marshall II to Albertine.)

Settling down in Chicago after a lengthy honeymoon, Marshall received increasingly alarming reports on his mother's condition. In August, Marshall and Evelyn sailed for England. The ship was in mid-Atlantic when a wireless message informed them of Albertine's death.

The pulls on young Marshall were many and conflicting, imposed by a mother who had raised him as an English aristocrat but impressed upon him his responsibility to Chicago, the United States, his family, and his grandfather's fortune. His brother Henry had joined the British Army with the relaxation of regulations. His sister Gwendolyn was living in England with Aunt Ethel, now married to Captain, later Admiral, David Beatty. Marshall was living in Chicago with his bride at 1200 Lake Shore Drive, moneyed society having deserted the South Side for the Near North Side, where, for instance, mansions of various members of the McCormick family had turned Rush Street just north of the Chicago River into what amounted to a McCormick compound. Initially, officers of the Continental Bank and other trustees of the Field estate were inclined to patronize this Field youth with the British accent that he never quite lost. But they ended by being impressed by his relative maturity, quick mind, and apparent devotion to his grandfather's city.

Nevertheless, Marshall IV was born in New York City (on June 15, 1916) and was only a few months old when his father, acting out his sympathies for the British, attempted to enlist in the U.S. Army. His history of rheumatic fever caused the peacetime Army to reject his application. When the official U.S. declaration of war against Germany did come on April 6, 1917, Field was not at work in Chicago. He was in South Carolina playing polo.

Of course, it would not have been strange if Field had spent all his time in such pleasures as playing polo. What he did next involves elements of the problems and privileges of the very rich that Field had to live with all his life. He used clout to get himself into uniform. Hurrying home from South Carolina, he called upon a family acquaintance who happened to be commanding officer of the First Illinois Cavalry, a remnant, in that still relatively informal time, of the military units that traditionally have been formed by good men and true in times of national stress. The good colonel ignored Field's physical history and swore him in then and there. As a private.

Afterward Field told a reporter: "I am enlisting because it is my personal conviction regarding myself and myself solely. I am not moralizing over what other people should do. I felt I ought to do my bit. My wife, after some reflection, agreed to my enlistment. Because I don't know enough about military matters to be an officer, I enlisted as a private. I chose the cavalry because I believed this organization was more likely than others to see service, and because I considered it the most distinguished of the Illinois organizations. The fact that I like horseback riding and have done a great deal of riding may have had something to do with my enlisting in the cavalry."

It was a statement typical of Field throughout his life—honest, straightforward, modest, and a little naïve. Field did his training at Fort Sill, quickly became a lieutenant, and moved on to Camp Logan outside Houston, where his Battery B was dubbed the "Millionaires' Battery" because Field and half a dozen other wealthy Chicagoans were officers.

Millionaires' Battery or no, the military marked Field in one way for the rest of his life. The military's enforced intimacy with a miscellaneous mass of people is a shock for anyone, and it certainly was for Field, more used to lords and ladies than to ordinary folk.

It was particularly painful to Field to discover that enlisted men, and officers too, thought of him as an easy mark. Naturally openhanded and generous, Field was quite willing to lend a man something to tide him over until payday. That is, he was. Some people were not gentlemen. Field was embarrassed and hurt that he had to defend himself from those who tried to take advantage of him. The lesson is one learned early or late by most rich people and fairly or unfairly earns many a reputation as a miser. Field certainly was not transformed into a skinflint, but he remembered and was afterwards more cautious in his dealings with people.

As for World War I, Field's battery landed in France in

mid-June of 1918 and saw two months of combat with an artillery regiment before the Armistice. Field came out unscathed as a captain.

In a bit of cruel irony, Marshall's younger brother was not so lucky. Henry had enlisted in England in 1915 with the relaxation of military regulations and had served with the Navy air crews that floated barrage balloons over London. Back in the United States in 1917, he was determined like Marshall to enlist. But first, having had some throat trouble, he decided it would be a good idea to have his tonsils removed. The tonsillectomy spawned worse trouble, a severe infection.

On July 8, 1917, during surgery to drain what was described as an abscess in the heart cavity, he died. He was only 21 years old. He was also a recent bridegroom. Just five months before his death, Henry, tall (six feet two inches), handsome, and a happy sort of healthy fellow, had married Nancy Keene Perkins, a member of a first family of Virginia and a niece of Nancy Langhorne, later Lady Astor.

When Marshall's war was over he made a long detour to Rome and then returned to Chicago and his family, which now included two children, Marshall IV and Barbara, born January 6, 1918, in New York while Field was in training at Camp Logan. (During some months of her pregnancy and Field's training, Mrs. Field lived in a suite at the Rice Hotel in Houston.)

In Chicago, Marshall's immediate and primary concern in 1919 was the affairs of the estate. The greater part of the fortune had been split three-fifths to Marshall and two-fifths to the younger son, and Henry's death had raised questions. The trustees and Marshall filed several friendly court suits to make sure they were proceeding correctly. But at age 25 early in 1919, he was also thinking of an active career for himself.

Following a path not uncommon for young men of wealth, Marshall became a bond salesman with the respected securities house of Lee, Higginson & Co. Persistence, he said later, was the key to success for a salesman.

From bond salesman Field moved on to investment banker. Backing a young (32) and successful commercial banker and investment banker, Charles Glore, he was by 1921 a principal in Marshall Field, Glore, Ward & Co. He had wanted to call the investment banking firm simply Marshall Field & Co., but a very profitable deal for the estate in 1917 had deprived him of the legal right to that designation. Although the estate retained a healthy chunk of common and preferred stock in Marshall Field & Co., the store had paid the estate $10 million for the exclusive right to the name, Marshall Field & Co., and the goodwill attached thereto. In any event, *The Bawl Street Journal,* Wall Street's annual outrageous parody of itself, immediately dubbed the new firm Jesus Christ, Tom, Dick and Harry.

Investment bankers finance corporations through stock and bond issues, and very shortly the Field firm opened an office in New York, where big money, old money, and international money circulated. And where Evelyn Field was at home.

It did not take much persuading to get Marshall, with his international background, to move to Manhattan, and he established the family on the East Coast with a bang and flair. Temporarily leasing a Morgan partner's town house, Field ordered up a mansion of his own—built on not one or two but four lots at Sixty-ninth and Seventieth streets. At the same time he set about duplicating something of what he had loved in England. He bought 1,800 acres on a North Shore Long Island peninsula jutting out into the Sound. It took an army of workmen five years to shape Caumsett, as Field called the estate from a local Indian name, to Field's wishes. In the end there were seventeen major buildings on the estate, not counting the baronial main house and such incidentals as kennels for the hunting dogs, a bathhouse beside the swimming pool, and dockage for the fifty-foot yacht the family used for pleasure and also used by Field to commute to Wall Street. Terraces, formal gardens, and lawns were landscaped by a Scot.

In the tradition of the English country gentleman and in keeping with his own character, Marshall attempted to run the estate on a profit-making basis. He bred and raised horses and cattle (Guernseys), and he operated a farm and a dairy and grew exotic flowers, including orchids, in greenhouses.

If anyone doubted that Caumsett was serious business for Field—and later on he was viciously attacked as a light-minded, misdirected playboy—there's a court record that says otherwise. Producing meticulous records, Field beat the government in a court trial and again on appeal when the Internal Revenue Bureau disallowed business deductions Field claimed for the operation of Caumsett and hit him for $300,000 in back taxes.

It is difficult for ordinary mortals to believe that anyone could play as hard and work as hard as Field did in the decades that followed his move to New York. The estate on Long Island was in Jay Gatsby country, and the parties at Caumsett and elsewhere were numerous. Field raced horses in Kentucky, Maryland, New York, and New England. Later on there was a "vacation" home in Maine and a 13,000-acre plantation in South Carolina for hunting (quail). (Supposedly one of the few immodest statements he ever made was to call himself a good shot.) Field played tennis on his outdoor and indoor courts at Caumsett and belatedly took up golf, becoming a respectable country club player in a short time. At one time he served as a director of no fewer than twenty-three corporations, ranging from the Chicago & North Western Railroad to an Italian corporation.

He was serious about investment banking and his firm. International finance was what interested him most. Typically, through the Roaring Twenties, when others were speculating profitably in Wall Street's great bull market and coining money in often suspect deals and manipulations, Field had his money in blue-chip stocks and utilities.

Through all this, his play and his moneymaking activities, Field never abandoned Chicago, and he spent an unbelievable amount of time (to a jet-age businessman) on the overnight trains between New York and Chicago.

On top of everything else, Field was an extraordinary father, obviously something that had to do with the vacuum in his own boyhood after the deaths of his father and grandfather. Then, too, he had that supreme quality demanded of any parent. He was for the most part patient in all his dealings with others, but especially with his children and his children's friends. His own children numbered three in the 1920s after the birth of a daughter, Bettine, in 1923. Field played any kind of childhood game with them and also taught them over the years everything from riding to chess.

If ordinary mortals wonder how Field could work in long vacations too, it should be remembered that there was always a butler, a chauffeur, a secretary, a lawyer, a governess, a manager, at hand. (When Field first moved to New York he hired a young Northern Trust banker, George Richardson, to be his representative on the board of the estate, and Richardson served for thirty-five years, at least an equal of Field in decision making and certainly the man who took care of the details.)

Moving into his 30s, Marshall had the world by the tail and the world was good. But it was not enough. In fact, it appeared that things were too easy for Field. Where was the challenge, the purpose, in life? Field's reaction was to step up his social activities—more hunting and fishing trips, more partying, and eventually more drinking, something that was almost a duty in many circles during the Prohibition era. (Among other things, Field learned to fly, although he always maintained that things mechanical baffled him.) Marshall, often absent, and Evelyn drifted apart. On August 4, 1930, Evelyn was granted a divorce on the grounds of incompatibility, in Reno, then the divorce capital of the country.

One of Marshall's things was riding to the hounds in England and there he met Audrey James Coats, a brunette stunner who had been widowed in 1925 and was an adornment of the hunt and racing society. Less than two weeks after Evelyn's divorce was final, Marshall and Audrey were married.

In late August of 1930 the stock market's attempt to rally from the disasters of Black Tuesday and Black Thursday 1929 had failed miserably and the country was being hammered by the first body blows of the terrible years of the Great Depression. On paper Field had lost millions, but his huge fortune was still a fortune. His honeymoon with Audrey was something out of F. Scott Fitzgerald. Off to Africa they went for big-game hunting in Kenya. The retinue included professional pilots to fly the two airplanes Field had purchased to ferry the party from place to place. But the expedition was plagued by accidents. After the lighter of the two planes was damaged and after surviving three crash landings in the larger plane, the Fields gave up. They hiked for two days and rode in a truck to reach civilization and a commercial airport.

In 1932 Field voted, as he had in 1928, for Herbert Hoover and the Republican ticket. In not too many years he was being excoriated along with Franklin Roosevelt as a traitor to his class and at least as a pink tea liberal. Indeed, years after his death when his conservative son was head of the family and the empire, there were some archconservative Lake Forest businessmen who believed "that Communist" was still alive and in charge of the most public of the Field holdings, the Chicago *Sun-Times*.

Certainly Field did undergo a transformation in his later years. His enemies created a Rasputin to account for Field's fall from grace. This was Dr. Gregory Zilboorg, perfectly fitted for the role. Zilboorg was a brilliant, highly educated Russian Jew who in 1917 had served as a very young man in the brief, relatively moderate government of Russian revolutionary leader Aleksandr Kerenski. After Kerenski was overthrown by Lenin and the Bolsheviks, Zilboorg came to the United States, completed the necessary work, and established himself as a psychoanalyst in Manhattan. Field became Zilboorg's patient in 1935. The analysis was brief by Freudian standards, lasting only one and a half years, but the testimony of the patient indicates it was quite helpful; Field felt better about himself.

It was not exactly weird in a world of breadlines and bankruptcies that Field should have had questions about the life he led, half as a hard-drinking playboy, half as a hard-working manager of the family money. In 1933, the year Franklin Roosevelt closed the banks to save the system from collapse, Field was 40 years old.

Months before Field took to Dr. Zilboorg's couch five times a week, the marriage to Audrey, a lady more given to fun parties than to social issues, ended in divorce after less than four years. Little more than a year later, Field and Ruth Pruyn Phipps were married in the Pruyn family apartment in River House, then just about the best address in Manhattan. The ceremony was attended only by family and a few close friends.

She was old money, a member of a Hudson River Dutch family and a family that had taken public service seriously. She was also the divorced wife of Ogden Phipps, a member of a family little known to the public except for its racing stables but one of the richest in the country. With the marriage came Ruth's two young sons. With the marriage also came a number of new friends, well-to-do if not wealthy by Field standards, concerned with the plight of the country, intellectual and accomplished supporters of Franklin Roosevelt's New Deal as the best of options.

Dr. Zilboorg aside, it is not surprising that Field swung away from the archconservative views of a grandfather who had entertained the preachments of "Social Darwinism"—the fittest had indeed survived and prospered. If it was a time when leading owners of American coal mines urged Roosevelt to nationalize the mines, it was also a time when a multimillionaire of Republican background could decide that the Wagner Labor Relations Act of 1935 was good. In any event, the seeds of a new direction for Field were there. His mother had talked to him of the duties of wealth, and he could not have been unaware during his Eton and English years of the British tradition of public service. After World War I he had served as a national leader of an effort to help returning servicemen and their families, and child welfare had always been an interest, if not the priority interest that it became in the late 1930s.

Of a multitude of business ventures, Field probably displayed more enthusiasm for the Marshall Field Garden Apartments than any other, involving himself from start to finish in every phase of the Chicago project. The start came in 1927, at least a decade before anyone thought of calling Field a do-gooder. As with all his business ventures, Field hoped to make money, but the apartment complex was an experiment designed to prove that it was possible to make a decent profit on well-built low-rent housing for low-income families. By that standard, the project was a failure; to cover escalating costs, rents had to be boosted above the preconceived level, but more than a half century later the buildings, in a tumbledown area, provide sturdy housing, primarily for blacks.

Social historians as well as real estate developers still take note of the forty-three-story office building at 135 South La Salle Street in the heart of Chicago's financial district. The real estate people point to it as proof that a well-designed and well-built office building, properly maintained, can still attract excellent tenants in spite of the proliferation of modern buildings. Social historians offer it as an example of courage and commitment. Planned in the prosperous late 1920s, the building was pushed through to completion in 1931 and 1932 depression years. Field and the family trustees, although determined to make a profit in the long run, saw the building as a means of providing jobs in a stricken city and hoped the building would attract the offices of new businesses rather than take tenants away from older buildings.

In spite of his mother's belief that he should enter upon a political career, Field did not exhibit an interest in either an elective or an appointive office. Never equipped with a large ego, Field might serve on the board of an organization he found worthy, but in general his way was to support organizations with money, time, and influence (for example, he worked with hospitals, homes for deprived children, research efforts in race relations and in the causes of juvenile delinquency). At the same time, in the mid-1930s, Field was relieving himself of business ties that demanded his time. In 1936 he gave up an active role in the Chicago investment banking firm of Field, Glore and Co. (later Glore, Forgan and Co. and active as an independent firm until the 1960s, when it disappeared in a succession of ill-conceived mergers). In two years he resigned as a director of two dozen corporations and a number of business-oriented organizations.

If there was a new Marshall Field, he had not exactly turned his back on the pleasures of life and the style of living available to him. It wasn't until 1936 that he bought the 13,000-acre plantation in South Carolina where hunting for quail and riding were the great attractions. He had a six-bedroom apartment on Park Avenue, a summer home in Maine, and an oceangoing yacht. He was also taking a new and greater interest in opera (Wagner), symphony (Mozart), and painting, both as a collector and as a museum supporter.

Field's new directions made him a happier man; his third marriage was good and enduring, he drank far less, and he found satisfaction in a number of the causes in which he involved himself. By the 1936 election he was an open supporter of the Democratic Party, although he could not stomach Roosevelt whole (e.g., he opposed the attempt to pack the Supreme Court). As an investment banker, he had been most interested in financing European projects, and as his voice retained a trace of a British accent, so did his viewpoint. He was alarmed and repelled by the scent of Franco, Mussolini, and Hitler and the growing threat of a European war. Early on, he attempted to raise money to ship wheat to Spain in support of the forces of the Republic opposing Franco's takeover. Later he was the vigorous president of a national committee that brought thousands of children out of Spain and other parts of Europe.

If many of Field's peers in business and society first embraced Franklin Roosevelt as the man to save the Republic from chaos and even revolution, they were soon disenchanted and heaped upon "that man in the White House" blame for social unrest and all the ills of the country. Field, jolted by the Depression disaster, took a long look at the myths, prejudices, and beliefs he had taken for granted. In the end, he welcomed change and new ideas. Not unreasonably he felt that he was privileged and that privilege carried with it obligations to society.

The idea for the newspaper *PM* was one that immediately appealed to Field when it was presented to him by Ralph Ingersoll and Louis Weiss in 1939. Weiss was a prominent and brilliant Manhattan lawyer with a passionate devotion to equal justice under Anglo-Saxon and American constitutional law, and for years, both before and after 1939, he was a friend and adviser to Field. Ingersoll was a stranger to Field until Weiss heard Ingersoll was looking for money to start a newspaper of a different kind, checked him out, and made the introduction.

Ingersoll, a member of a respected Connecticut and New York family, started out to be a mining engineer and pursued that career briefly after getting an engineering degree at Yale. But after a lengthy trip through Mexico he sat down and wrote a book about the country and opted for a writing career. In New York, Ingersoll worked for a Hearst newspaper and *The New Yorker*. He then joined Time Inc., where Henry Luce, one editor-owner who relished divergent opinion as long as it came with brilliance, very quickly appointed him managing editor of *Fortune*. Ingersoll made a success of that struggling magazine of capitalism and Luce moved him up to vice-president and general manager of Time Inc.

In 1938 Ingersoll left Time Inc. to launch his own enter-prise, a Manhattan daily newspaper that would crusade and tell the truth, or the truth as Ingersoll saw it. To preserve the paper's independence from outside interests, it would not carry advertising. It would stand on its own feet and make a profit, Ingersoll thought, solely on circulation revenues; it would sell for five cents at a time when newspapers sold for two and three cents. Editorially, it would be run by Ingersoll and the working staff and its news columns would reflect the biases of the staff. Above all, Ingersoll promised, it would be against "people" who push other people around, little peo-ple or nations.

Field was immediately taken with the whole idea, the commitment to crusading for a better society and the prom-ise that the enterprise would make money. On the basis of a brief presentation by Ingersoll and the recommendation of Louis Weiss, Field invested $200,000 in what on June 18, 1940, became the newspaper *PM*.

Immediately *PM* was controversial. For openers, its for-mat was radical. Printed on paper several grades above stan-dard newspaper stock, it was tabloid in size and stapled together. Stories were continuous, no jumps to page 27. Photographs and graphics were emphasized; it looked more like a magazine than a newspaper. Talent was in evidence everywhere, in the sports department as well as in Washing-ton coverage.

Beyond its radical appearance *PM* was openly pro-labor and a militant supporter of F.D.R. and the New Deal. Its crusades, as it went along, touched raw nerves in the busi-ness community. It was a time when opinion was both more polarized and divided, if anything, than it is in the 1980s. Robert Taft, a deity in the conservative wing of the Republi-can Party and later on, in 1952, as senator from Ohio the loser to Dwight Eisenhower for the Republican nomination for President, could appear on the same platform with Nor-man Thomas, the perennial presidential candidate of the

Socialist Party. What united left and right was opposition to intervention in Europe's looming war.

Once *PM*'s curiosity value waned, the paper's circulation plummeted. Amateurish blunders by its own circulation department did not help. Worse, Captain Joseph Patterson's New York *Daily News* blackmailed news vendors around the city into boycotting *PM*, a tactic reminiscent of the earlier newspaper circulation wars of Chicago in which the Chicago *Tribune* of Patterson's cousin, Colonel Robert McCormick, was an enthusiastic participant.

By early fall of 1940 *PM* had regained substantial readership after almost disappearing, but circulation was still less than half the 200,000 Ingersoll figured as the break-even point. Continuing losses generated panic among the original backers Ingersoll had rounded up, and some were no doubt disabused by what they read every day in the paper.

After all, the stockholder group included Philip Wrigley, head of the William Wrigley chewing-gum company, and John Hay Whitney, later Dwight Eisenhower's ambassador to England and still later owner of the New York *Herald Tribune*, along with a sprinkling of other conservative businessmen and lawyers.

Very early on, William Benton, the advertising executive (Benton & Bowles) and later the major stockholder in Chicago of the Encyclopaedia Britannica, had decamped. At the least it looked as if Ingersoll would lose some backers. Among the others there was little disposition to pour good money after bad, and it began to look as if *PM* would not last out its first six months.

Marshall Field was almost alone in his belief that the experiment should have a longer chance to prove itself. To the board and then to the stockholders Field presented a proposition. He would buy everyone out for 20 cents on the dollar and agree to underwrite the newspaper for a "longer" period of time. That was fair enough in that the stockholders stood to lose 100 cents on the dollar. Once Huntington Hartford, the peripatetic heir to the A&P fortune, and Whitney accepted the offer, the rest of the stockholders quickly followed, and Field, the Chicago multimillionaire, still a large stockholder in his grandfather's store, owner of office buildings and real estate, 47 years old, a handsome man, shy and gentle in most personal relations, now a thoughtful and consistent liberal on economic and social issues, became a Manhattan newspaper publisher.

Publisher is not the right word. Then and later, Field declined to exercise control over *PM*. It was the concept or ideal that Field supported. As he said at the time and on a number of other occasions, democracy thrived on free competition of ideas. He saw a need for an unfettered, controversial, and liberal daily newspaper; to have dictated editorial policy and operating procedures would have subverted the mission.

For sinking his money, perhaps $5 million and more before the experiment was over, into *PM* and letting it run wild, Field was depicted in some quarters, both in print and otherwise, as a do-gooder dupe at best. But his approach to the enterprise is not at all uncommon in the business world and his grandson follows the same practice today. The investor, whether a billion-dollar conglomerate or an individual, makes the important go/no-go decisions, signs on the best possible people, and lets them run—or hang themselves.

In the era in which *PM* was born and lived for a time, with the leftover social turmoil of the Great Depression, World War II, and the emergence of Russia as a world power, it was enough to be anywhere left of center to be branded in some circles as Communist. Raucously liberal, *PM* easily qualified for the label and was viewed by many as a slick version of the *Daily Worker*. There was some substance to the charge. At a time when a small group of well-disciplined Communist Party members in both New York City and Washington carried on a continuing campaign to gain control of the American Newspaper Guild units, *PM* without a doubt had some real live Communists on the staff. (Very early Ingersoll deliberately recruited a Communist, certified by Earl Browder, the Party's frequent presidential candidate, on the theory that *PM* should not boycott any shade of opinion. The reporter did not last long.) On a newspaper that took a stand and encouraged opinion in its news columns, it is probable that the motivation for some stories and the slant within them might not have stood up to a jury trial. But in general the paper was merely militantly liberal. On the issue of the time that divided wheat from chaff, Party-liner from liberal, Stalin's pact with Hitler, *PM* was pure, continuing to support intervention against Hitler. But in 1946 James Wechsler, a former labor reporter and a man of liberal persuasions who later became editor of the New York *Post*, resigned with three others in disgust over the paper's tolerance of Russia's march into Eastern Europe. (In a statement, Wechsler hoped the resignations would not embarrass Field, "an honest and courageous American.")

In 1944 *PM* managed to emerge from red ink, helped possibly by the fact that Red Russia was now a winning ally, muting the Communist issue. But the paper was only breaking even and soon it was back losing money.

By 1948 Field was running out the string with *PM*. He allowed a new group to come in as investors and managers, and *PM* became the New York *Star* for six months. On January 27, 1949, the *Star* folded; a study of the paper's outlook had convinced Field that it would take ten years, $10 million, and a lot of luck to turn the paper into a self-supporting entity. (Ralph Ingersoll died in 1985, the multimillionaire publisher of a string of conservative newspapers.)

Anyway, Field was occupied happily elsewhere.

Even as he was involved in the berthing of *PM* in New York, Field was thinking Chicago and another newspaper. An internationalist by his education in England, he had long been alarmed by the truculent isolationism of Colonel Robert McCormick's Chicago *Tribune*. McCormick served tea in his secure office in the Tribune Tower and warned visitors that the British were plotting to come down through Canada and conquer the United States with the help of Eastern seaboard radicals. Field had the idea that Hitler was the threat to an unprepared country.

As a liberal, Field was disgusted with McCormick's ultraconservatism and savage attacks on Franklin Roosevelt. The *Tribune*'s front page was decorated with the American flag and a cartoon in color that usually exposed the latest trickery of that man in the White House aimed at pulling down the Republic. The front page also proclaimed that the *Tribune* was the world's greatest newspaper, and McCormick had the paper delivered far and wide so that the deluded readers of such as the New York *Times* might be enlightened.

When Roosevelt ran for his third term, the Colonel daily urged right-minded voters to remember that there were only so many days left to save the Republic. When the Roosevelt vote was counted, the afternoon Chicago *Times* ran this headline: "Only 52 Days Til Christmas."

The *Times* supported Roosevelt and was nominally a Democratic paper. But it was one of four afternoon papers, and a tabloid with a limited circulation that did not include many of the rich and powerful. In the morning there was no answer to the *Tribune* and the Colonel's fulminations.

If there was a place for a liberal and pioneering newspaper in Manhattan, if Field could convince himself that *PM* was making a worthwhile contribution to democratic debate, the need for a solid, mainstream newspaper in Chicago as an alternative to McCormick's pathological view of reality was overwhelmingly evident.

In the late months of 1940 Field began to think seriously of challenging the *Tribune,* and in early 1941 he talked to a number of advisers and friends about how best to go about it. By then the overriding motivation was not the wish to counter McCormick's attacks on the New Deal and anything tainted with liberal thought. Rather it was Field's mounting concern with the Colonel's violent opposition to any of Roosevelt's efforts to aid England or France and to prepare the United States against the probability of war with Hitler and the Axis. Encouraged by various prominent Chicagoans (e.g., Adlai Stevenson) and by Roosevelt, Field and his aides explored the possibility of buying one of the existing papers in his hometown, the Chicago *Daily News* or the *Times.* Very quickly Field decided to go all out with a brand-new paper that would present its own image. That was the more difficult and more costly approach. Field paid top dollar to assemble an editorial, advertising, and circulation staff. Naturally enough, there were cost overruns, mistakes, conflicts, and chaos. A problem for years was the contract Field agreed to at an exorbitant cost to have his paper printed on the presses of the Chicago *Daily News.*

But the wonder was that in less than six months Field was in business with a respectable product. A promotional contest was held to choose a name for the paper and the winner was the Chicago *Sun,* although Field allowed that he liked another nominee, *The McCormick Reaper.*

As misfortune decreed, the timing of the appearance of the *Sun* hardly could have been worse. The first editions were dated December 4, 1941. Three days later, with the Japanese attack on Pearl Harbor, McCormick became an all-out supporter of the military effort against the Axis. Of course, things would have gone better, particularly at home, if it hadn't been for the bumblers and pinkos in Washington. The critical shortage of rubber was Washington's fault, for instance, and had little or nothing to do with the fact that the Japanese move into Southeast Asia had cut off supplies of natural rubber.

The *Sun* was a handsome, full-sized newspaper, well written and edited if at times uneven. The presentation editorial in the inaugural edition emphasized that the *Sun* was a Chicago paper (even if Field was involved with that New York experiment), that it would present the news "fairly and honestly," with its opinions confined to the editorial page (hello, McCormick). Further positioning itself at a distance from the *Tribune,* the *Sun* said it supported the Roosevelt administration, and would continue to do so as long as the administration merited trust. And, the editorial said, "the *Sun* believes the best interests of Chicago, of the Midwest, and of America can best be served at this moment by the complete defeat of Adolf Hitler and everything he stands for."

The language was mild, gentlemanly, as Field preferred, but the *Sun* was staking out its own territory, very definitely contrasting its attitude with that of the *Tribune.*

But the *Sun* had a lot of growing up to do, both as a business organization and as one that could produce a consistent newspaper. Field spent the greater part of his time in Chicago and at the *Sun.* He was, however, again placing his trust in the people he had hired, and some of them, including his top command, were less than satisfactory. For the most part Field limited himself on the editorial side to making gentle suggestions that the paper ought to examine the city's problems (e.g., the transit system) and make responsible recommendations for improvements.

On the business side he sat in on the conferences where the major decisions were made and went along even when it came to slashing staffs, something that occurred only too frequently. Field must have had ambiguous feelings about the firings. He wanted a great newspaper and was willing to spend to get it, but in spite of what his enemies said, he was also a businessman and he hoped to see the *Sun* stand on its own feet and make a profit. At the same time, he was by the account of those closest to him a compassionate man and the mass firings must have pained him. (Much earlier he had made a speech that produced headline stories, derision, and proof in the minds of enemies that he was a soft-headed do-gooder. He did say in the speech that he didn't give a damn about his money. In context what he said was commendable and said to make a point. At a time when German millionaires had thrown in with Hitler, Field was saying he would rather lose his fortune than save it by supporting fascism.)

The *Sun* was costing Field plenty. Inside of six months and once initial excitement died down, the *Sun's* circulation sank to a respectable but disappointing level of little more than 200,000. And it was losing about half that many dollars each week. But in 1942 the paper's circulation began to inch up slowly and some small gains in advertising were achieved. This despite *Tribune* pressure on news vendors and advertisers.

Except for an occasional belittling reference, the *Tribune* did not stoop to recognize a rival in the *Sun*. After all, the *Tribune* was all-powerful; it could destroy by direct attack or simply by denying its pages to the enemy of the day. Somehow Robert M. Hutchins survived as president of the University of Chicago even though a McCormick edict lasting more than four years ruled that his title could be used in the *Tribune* but not his name.

When McCormick decided that the *Sun* was not going to set gently, the *Tribune* opened up in midsummer of 1942 with an attack that is probably unbelievable to anyone not familiar with the *Tribune* of the time. World War II was on and Marshall Field was "a slacker," an editorial said, and continued:

"Field is of an age to volunteer. [Actually, he was approaching his 49th birthday.] He cried for war before it came. Now that it has come, he lets [others] do the fighting while he skulks in his clubs, night and otherwise. No one would suggest that he is indispensable to *PM* or to anything else. The term to fit to him and to all the herd of hysterical effeminates is coward."

Two days later the *Sun* came back with a beautiful one-sentence reply at the top of its editorial page: "You are getting rattled, Colonel McCormick."

A reply that a wider audience might have understood came later from the American Legion Post that represented Field's World War I field artillery unit. In a letter approved by vote of the Post, the Legion recalled that Field had volunteered as a private in 1917 even though he had a wife and two children at the time and that he had served effectively and courageously with his unit through a number of front-line battles in France. In fine, the Legion approved of Field as "a soldier, a man and a gentleman."

It could be noted that McCormick had earned his colonelcy as a behind-the-lines staff officer in France. It could also be noted that Field's son, Marshall Field IV, already married and a father, had enlisted immediately after Pearl Harbor and at the time McCormick's slacker editorial appeared young Field was under Japanese fire in the South Pacific.

Marshall Jr., as he was properly identified while his father lived, rated an IQ even higher than that of his father. And he took a more serious attitude toward his schooling. Straight through from elementary school on, he earned top marks; at St. Paul's preparatory school a gold medal for scholastic achievement went to him, and at Harvard, class of 1938, he graduated *magna cum laude* with a degree in English literature. In the summer after his freshman year, Marshall IV took a look at the real world. When he might have been touring Europe with Harvard friends, or at least enjoying Caumsett and the sporting society of Long Island, he shoveled slag into an open-hearth furnace at the Republic Steel mill in Buffalo. (Hiding his identity, he used the name Mike Farley.)

A quiet, even shy young man, conservative in most things, Marshall IV married immediately after his graduation from Harvard. His bride was Joanne Bass, the daughter of a former governor of New Hampshire. For a number of reasons, including the obvious need to equip himself to manage the Field estate someday, Marshall decided on the law and picked the University of Virginia law school, a popular alternative of many Ivy League graduates. In June 1940, he was graduated, third in his class and president of the class, and very properly off on a course that would have qualified him for the top rungs in the profession. He clerked for a federal judge with the promise that he would later join Justice Stanley Reed at the U.S. Supreme Court.

But then came Pearl Harbor. Volunteering for the Navy,

Marshall was assigned to officer candidate school at Northwestern University. One of many "90-day wonders" in those hurry-up mobilization days, he was commissioned and dispatched to the West Coast to join the USS *Enterprise,* then the only American aircraft carrier still in service in the South Pacific. Aboard the *Enterprise* as a gunnery officer during the Battle of Santa Cruz off Guadalcanal on October 26, 1942, Field was blown from his gun turret and knocked unconscious for an hour, but was not seriously injured. In all, Field managed to get through twelve important battles in the Pacific before earning shore duty in late 1944.

September 28, 1943, was a day of significance in the Field family. On that day Marshall III turned 50 and with his signature on a document he finally came into full control of his grandfather's estate. Estimates at the time put the value of the estate at $90 million. Whatever Field felt about reaching the half-century mark, an outsider would have found his status princely and good. He was in excellent health. He was handsome by any standard, his hair now beginning to silver, his face still strong. Unaccountably there was a look of sadness about the light brown eyes when his face was in repose, but he was happily engaged.

The *Sun* was making progress and he enjoyed his outside activities. He was a trustee of the New York Philharmonic Society and the Metropolitan Museum, as well as of the Illinois Children's Home and Aid Society. The Field Foundation, established in 1940, was making grants to a number of projects Field considered worthwhile outside the conventional charities. The greater part of the money went to help disadvantaged children and blacks. Although the foundation was designed primarily to systematize Field's giving, Field nevertheless continued to give personal money when an idea or situation struck him.

If *PM* was still a gnawing problem in New York, Field had Ruth, their children, and his grandchildren. The generations were slightly mixed up. On his 50th birthday, Field and Ruth's daughter Phyllis was just a few days from her seventh birthday, and Fiona was five years old; the youngest of Field's three children by his first marriage, Bettine, was 20, and still at home. Then there were his son's children, Marshall V, two and one-half years old, and Joanne, one year old.

During World War II, Field was the central figure in two home-front battles of national significance. One was ironic, even amusing considering the conflicts in political philosophy. Conservatives, out to get a traitor to his class, the man who was putting millions into that Communist rag *PM*, succeeded in stirring Congress to adopt the "Marshall Field amendment" to the tax code. The idea was to limit the number of years that an individual could write off losses on an enterprise against income. Field's lawyers, anticipating passage of the amendment, very quickly turned Marshall Field, the individual, into Field Enterprises, Inc., a corporation. After all, Field was in business. Any number of politically conservative millionaires must have been outraged to discover that one day they would no longer be able to write off the expenses of the farm or the racing stable.

The second battle was fought in behalf of the Chicago *Sun*. The Associated Press, then and now the strongest wire service furnishing news reports to newspapers and other media, was organized as a co-op, or as critics said, a club. Newspapers were elected as members of the AP. And members blackballed competing newspapers. With Colonel McCormick standing guard, the AP was one club that Field could not join. The *Sun* was dependent for day-to-day coverage around the world on either the United Press, more sprightly than the AP but less inclusive, or Hearst's much smaller International News Service. At the instigation of the *Sun*, the U.S. Department of Justice risked political backlash and a freedom-of-the-press fight and filed antitrust charges against the AP. It was an open-and-shut case that was nevertheless fought through for two years to the U.S. Supreme Court. In 1945 the AP became a commercial enterprise open to any buyer, including the *Sun*.

There was an ironic twist here, too. Both the United Press

and International News Service lost customers to the AP and eventually the two were merged to become United Press International.

As for the Marshall Field amendment to the income-tax laws, Field would have incorporated anyway. In any event, between the amendment and Field's new status as full heir to the Field fortune an idea was emerging. In part to assure the *Sun*'s future, Field would build a communications corporation that would be profitable overall.

Simon and Schuster, Inc., with its pioneering Pocket Books division, fit the plan. The publishing house was in the black, and Pocket Books, low-priced for a mass market, especially appealed to Field and his interest in education and young people. Field signed an agreement to buy Simon and Schuster in 1944.

Field employed a small staff of investment specialists to comb the country for likely investment opportunities. In 1945 the staff came up with one that really appealed to Field, World Book Encyclopedia. Again it was a profit-making firm, and this time the product was targeted specifically at helping to educate young people. With its Childcraft series it started with preschoolers, while the encyclopedia could be used by students through college. Field was happy to put money into World Book to improve quality, to finance installment sales of the encyclopedia, and to expand the sales force. The volumes were sold door-to-door; the more salesmen to ring doorbells, the higher the sales. With the postwar baby boom, general prosperity, and keen national interest in education, World Book evolved into a prolific cash cow for Field Enterprises, more profitable over the decades than any other Field property since the first Marshall's store. (By the late 1970s the school-age population was declining and householders were increasingly wary of opening the door to strangers. World Book, by then an international corporation with editions in Europe and Japan, was sold to Scott & Fetzer, a specialist in door-to-door sales. In the future, the capital could be employed at a higher rate of return elsewhere.)

With the end of World War II, Marshall IV came home, and home was Chicago. Without any urging from his father he opted for newspapering, not the law. No doubt there was also recognition on his part of a duty to the family and the family's fortune. In the best tradition, young Marshall set about learning the newspaper business. In 1946—he was 30 years old—Marshall started out at the *Sun* working a delivery truck, loading stacks of papers aboard the truck, tossing them off to news vendors. After that he made the rounds of the various departments of the paper and moved on to successively more important management positions. In four years he was publisher. Later generations of Fields were able to take an objective and humorous view of their power and position. In a remark typical of him and of Marshall V, he said the distance between the tailgate of a delivery truck and the driver's seat was shorter if you owned the truck.

By the time Marshall IV took over the paper Field Enterprises had a number of other good things going for it. Back in 1941 his father had approved one idea for making money out of *PM*. The paper produced a lot of good feature material, articles and photographs, that never saw print. With that as a base, *Parade* was born as a modern-day supplement, or magazine as it was called, for Sunday newspapers. Once the war was over, *Parade* became a very successful publication. (Another successful publication was an early television guide.)

Of particular note was Field's purchase in 1945 and 1946 of radio stations WJJD in Chicago and WSAI in Cincinnati. KOIN in Portland and KJR in Seattle were added a decade later. Then all four were sold. Over the years Field Enterprises flirted, alternately hot and cold, with radio and television. In hindsight the corporation would have been millions ahead if it had stayed with radio after 1945 and expanded into television. Right after World War II, in the infancy of television, Field could have had TV franchises for his radio stations for the asking. Only much later did the Federal Communications Commission see monopoly in the common ownership of newspapers and radio and TV stations. Particularly the early TV stations turned into antennas with a cash register attached. And after a period when it was feared that television would kill radio, the value of most radio stations plunged but then doubled and tripled. In the 1960s Field Enterprises spent lavishly to start a UHF station, WFLD (W-Field), in Chicago, sold it off, then bought it back in a package of five UHF stations from Kaiser Broadcasting, and then in 1982 and 1983 put WFLD and the other stations on the block at handsome prices.

The fluctuating Field interest in radio and television was due in part to concern for the bottom line and at various times to a belief that television particularly was an entertainment industry—show business. For years the central idea was to build a strong and respected newspaper, something not exactly akin to comedy shows and bang-bang series.

With the *Sun* making progress but still losing money, Marshall III thought he could improve his position against the *Tribune* by buying one of Chicago's afternoon newspapers. What he really wanted was the Chicago *Daily News*, owned by Frank Knox, candidate for the vice-presidency on the 1936 Republican ticket with Alfred Landon but serving as Secretary of the Navy under Franklin Roosevelt during World War II and therefore suspect in Colonel McCormick's eyes. Purchase of the *Daily News* would have extricated Field from his expensive printing contract with the paper, and given the *Sun* a permanent home and Field the leading newspaper in the afternoon field. When Knox died in 1944, Field was ready to buy the paper, but he politely declined to bid higher than an offer made by a syndicate formed by officers, editors, and employees of the *Daily News*. John S. Knight (Detroit *Free Press*, Akron *Beacon Journal*, now Knight-Ridder newspapers) was not bothered by the niceties of the situation, put in a higher bid, and as the owner of the *Daily News* became Field's new landlord.

Three years later, with the death of another owner, Field bought the Chicago *Times,* acquiring its building, presses, debts, and circulation. The afternoon *Times* was a lively paper and it supported the Democratic Party. Often good at the journalist craft, the *Times* was nevertheless a tabloid more in the tradition of the New York *Mirror* or the New York *Daily News* than of the New York *Times.* (Nevertheless, for years the *Tribune* with its conservative pose carried more sex, crime, and fire stories than any other newspaper in Chicago.) For some months Field continued to publish two newspapers with a combined Sunday edition, but that only proved a way of increasing his deficits.

In February 1947 the two papers were merged and the Chicago *Sun-Times* appeared on the streets as a morning tabloid.

The new *Sun-Times* was an anomaly, independent but hewing to an intellectual liberal line, serious about the news but a tabloid. The tabloid image was hard to shake, and the paper kept trying to talk about itself as a "modern size" newspaper. It was an attractive newspaper, and numbers of people did like the convenient size. Content was not really the problem. A banner headline reporting a triple murder on the *Tribune*'s front page was diffused on a full-size *Tribune* front page carrying a dozen other stories; the same headline on the relatively small front page of the *Sun-Times* screamed and affronted many who might otherwise have been readers.

However, the *Sun* and the *Times* retained the greater part of their previous readers and advertisers, and the *Sun-Times* was moving into the black when Marshall IV took over as publisher in 1950. If anything, Marshall IV was more deeply committed to the newspaper and to Chicago than his father. He was a legal resident of Illinois, whereas his father retained a New York residency even after he began spending the greater part of the year in Chicago. While Marshall III put his own money into the paper to keep it afloat, his son plowed back most of the *Sun-Times* profits once the paper was earning money. On the part of Marshall IV, this was a carefully measured policy designed to improve quality and generate growth without extravagant spending that would have sunk the paper in red ink again.

The decision to turn the paper over to his son had to be difficult for Field. As he said on a number of occasions, he knew and admired the fact that his son had "a mind and a will" of his own. Marshall IV's independence and determination reminded his father of the family founder, Marshall I. Field knew where his son's independent bent would take him. Marshall IV was decidedly a conservative on political and social issues. That is, by the standards of his father. Brilliant, a man who asked questions and absorbed facts, Marshall IV was, however, even more distant from the Colonel McCormick brand of extreme conservatism. He was more or less a Dewey-Eisenhower Republican, a supporter of the liberal wing of the Republican Party.

His father, profoundly distressed at the death in 1945 of Franklin Roosevelt, the President who could carry the country with him when liberal issues were at stake, could write an editorial suggesting, after the Republican Party won a majority in the Congress in the 1946 elections, that Harry Truman should step aside for a Republican appointee. It was an embarrassingly naïve idea based on the logic that unified American leadership was vital in a world struggling to recover from the devastations of World War II.

The elder Field could also hope that General Dwight Eisenhower would run for the presidency in 1948 on the Democratic ticket, assuring a Democratic victory. Or that he would run as a Republican and assure the dominance of GOP liberals.

As matters turned out, the *Sun-Times* was one of a handful of newspapers to support Truman in the 1948 elections. Truman's astonishing victory over Governor Thomas Dewey of New York was savored at the *Sun-Times* with special delight in that the rival *Tribune* committed one of the journalistic blunders of all time, headlining a Dewey victory in its early edition. Field and the *Sun-Times* could also relish the victory of Field's friend and fellow aristocrat Adlai Stevenson in the race for governor of Illinois and of Paul Douglas in the contest for the U.S. Senate.

But by the time the 1952 elections came around, Marshall IV had been editor and publisher of the *Sun-Times* for two years. Six months before the party conventions the paper vigorously endorsed Eisenhower as candidate and President on the Republican ticket. In a letter later that year, the senior Field wrote to his son: "When the editorial leadership of the paper was turned over to you, I was certain that you would assume an independent and direct attitude, and this you have done."

If Marshall III was a convinced and determined liberal, his love for children was real, and for his own children deep. Marshall IV was the heir, and his father would not stand in his way when he wished to make the newspaper the focal point of his career even though that meant muffling the paper's liberal voice.

The letter was sent in early October to Marshall IV at the *Sun-Times* and written to him as editor and publisher of the paper. It was carried in the Letters to the Editor column, without the complimentary closing "With my best love, Dad."

"Dad" said he understood and respected Marshall's endorsement of Eisenhower, but he wished to clear up the confusion in many minds between "my position on this campaign and yours." He had hoped that Eisenhower might blend the liberal element in the Republican Party into the "ascendancy" and that no matter who won, the official gains of the past twenty years would be furthered. But as the campaign developed he had had stronger and stronger doubts that Eisenhower could realign the GOP. On the other hand, he was in "complete agreement" with the positions taken by Adlai Stevenson.

If the letter was intended to blunt the *Sun-Times*'s endorsement of Eisenhower, the effect was not noticeable in

the election results. If it cleared up one confusion, it created
another. People who did not know the elder Field found it
difficult to understand how father and son could differ in
private and public over such a major issue without an angry
confrontation and possibly the exercise of power. But Field's
quiet and reasonable presentation of both sides of the question together with his own conclusion was exactly in character.

The 1952 election aside, Field continued his involvement
with the affairs of Field Enterprises and his various outside
activities. Except for Dr. Edward Sparling, the president,
and the faculty members who walked out of the YMCA
Central College of Chicago rather than accept limitations on
the enrollment of blacks, Field had as much to do as anyone
with the establishment of Roosevelt College, now an important urban university.

Field did take longer and more frequent vacations, enjoying the extended time with his wife. He spent most of the
summer of 1953 with Ruth, their daughters, and her two
children touring Europe by automobile, but in the following
year he suffered his first real health problem since his childhood. A tiny cancerous growth on one lung was removed
successfully at Johns Hopkins Hospital in Baltimore, but at
age 61 recovery was slow.

By 1956 Field was in trouble again, suffering fainting
spells from time to time. And this time it proved to be
cancer of the brain. By mid-October, in spite of his wish to
do what he could to help Adlai Stevenson in his second try
for the presidency, Field was in New York Hospital, where
an operation relieved pressure on his brain but was a hope-
less exercise.

Conscious only intermittently, Marshall Field III died on
November 8, 1956, little more than five weeks after his 63rd
birthday.

With his two divorces Field had not been a communicant
in the Roman Catholic Church for years, but a priest was
allowed by the family to perform the last rites of the Church

as he lay dying. Funeral services were held at the St. James Episcopal Church in New York City and at the Episcopal St. James Cathedral in Chicago.

The fuzzy liberal had lost something like $5 million on *PM* and spent four or five times that much to get the Chicago *Sun* on its feet. But before his death published reports put the family fortune at more than $165 million, a very businesslike accomplishment.

Field had also picked his lawyers wisely. During his lifetime members of the family had been well taken care of. Field Enterprises went to Marshall IV intact, and a trust provided that control of the empire would pass on to Marshall V and his half brother, Frederick W. Field, born in 1952, two years after Field's second marriage, to Katherine Woodruff, a member of a prominent banking family in Joliet, Illinois.

Marshall IV had always made his goal clear. He wanted to see the *Sun-Times* return a respectable business profit and he wanted to beat the *Tribune*. In 1959 he sold *Parade* magazine to the New York *Herald Tribune* for $11 million and then used the capital to help in the $24 million purchase of the afternoon Chicago *Daily News*. Like his father, he had admired the *Daily News,* and with that paper in the corporate family he would have the *Tribune* surrounded. Among other things, advertisers could be offered a joint rate package, an advertisement that would run in the *Sun-Times* and also reach the basic reader of the *Daily News,* the more affluent suburban resident. (The *Tribune* later responded by buying the Hearst afternoon newspaper and turning it into a tabloid called *Chicago Today.* The effort cost the *Tribune* millions before the paper was closed.)

In 1958 the *Sun-Times* had been moved into a new home, a sparkling modern building on the Chicago River designed to give the impression of a ship. It had been built with the idea that someday it would house two newspapers, and very shortly Field moved the *Daily News* into the building, saving costs particularly in that the *Sun-Times* presses could print both the morning and afternoon papers.

In the 1960s the *Sun-Times* was making money, two, three, four million dollars a year. But that was a subsidized profit in that stockholder Field was not taking any money out of the paper but putting the profits back into improvements. And by normal corporate standards it was a very narrow profit for a $100 million operation; a slight swing in revenues could have plunged the paper into the red once again and threatened its future. In hindsight it could be said that a major opportunity was missed. Every new expenditure was scrutinized, closely budgeted, and held to the minimum. A bold investment program might have paid off handsomely. Colonel McCormick may have gone to his reward (April 1955) in a place where he would not be infuriated by labor unions, Democrats and New Dealers, foreigners and unruly minorities, but the men who found themselves in charge of the *Tribune* strove to keep the paper, with all its eccentricities and prejudices, exactly as the Colonel might have wanted it. (McCormick had no children. Members of the family who might have succeeded him earned his displeasure and were excised. An analysis of the Colonel's will indicated that, deliberately or otherwise, McCormick had diffused power in the Tribune Company so that it would be difficult for any one person to fill his shoes.) The *Tribune* was being preserved even to an occasional McCormick-like outburst that did violence to the reader. When McCormick's successor as publisher, Don Maxwell, went to the hospital, a friend, knowing that Maxwell was a Civil War buff, sent him the best-selling novel *The Carpetbaggers*, by Harold Robbins. Actually it was a novel of corporate maneuverings, many of which took place in the bedroom. Shocked at the sex, Maxwell ordered *The Carpetbaggers* stricken from the *Tribune*'s list of best-sellers and the purging of the list henceforth of similarly offending books.

It was not until the 1970s that the *Tribune*, evolving slowly under a new breed of managers and professional newspapermen, moved into the 20th century. Eventually the Colonel's hallmark was erased—the American flag that had decorated the front page, the slogan that proclaimed the *Tribune* the world's greatest newspaper, and the daily front-page cartoon. Today the *Tribune*'s editorial page, in the masthead space where newspapers often call attention to a proud heritage by listing the founder and successors of note, merely announces that it was founded on June 10, 1847. The Colonel has disappeared. For the *Sun-Times* the competition is tougher than it was for decades and much tougher than it was when Marshall Field saw the need for an alternative morning newspaper in Chicago.

There was a special and tragic reason for the cautious, step-by-step approach to investment in growth at the *Sun-Times*. Using an old-fashioned phrase, *Time* magazine put it this way: ". . . after the death of his father in 1956 and a series of bone-wearing negotiations with other publishers, [Marshall IV] suffered a nervous breakdown that hospitalized him for six months."

More accurately, Field was a manic-depressive. As he grew older the alternating periods of mania and depression appeared and became more pronounced. Electric shock and the drugs available at the time had an ameliorating effect but could not fully control the psychosis.

Trustees of the Field estate and professional managers of various entities in Field Enterprises were generally in charge. Necessarily their approach was conservative. Formally and informally, they were forced to act in a fiduciary capacity; their first duty was to avoid mistakes, their own or Field's.

They were unable to prevent what was probably the worst mistake in the history of the Field family, the purchase in 1959 of the Chicago *Daily News*. Marshall III had coveted the *Daily News* and so did his son. On a high, Marshall IV persisted in spite of almost unanimous opposition within the organization. The *Daily News* was only marginally profitable, the outlook for metropolitan afternoon newspapers was not promising, the paper had been weakened by a management focus on cost cutting rather than improvement, and the price tag was excessive by any standard.

Ironically, the purchase did initial damage to the *Daily News*. Under Field management, efforts were made to improve the *Daily News*, but in the main the paper and its Republican editorial outlook went unchanged. Nevertheless, a number of conservative subscribers were outraged to see their fine old newspaper taken into bed with "that Communist," Marshall Field III, and his sensational tabloid. Mistaken as all that was, the *Daily News* lost a notch or two in prestige.

Marshall IV was only 49 years old when he died suddenly and inexplicably on September 18, 1965. Suffering from viral infection, he died of congestive heart failure, alone in the bedroom of his duplex apartment on fashionable Lakeview Avenue.

When his will was filed in probate court, his personal fortune, aside from Field Enterprises, was estimated at more than $25 million. His six children were the principal beneficiaries.

Marshall V, born May 13, 1941, and Joanne, born November 1, 1942, were children of his first young marriage. That marriage ended in divorce in 1947. His second marriage, to Katherine Woodruff, lasted from 1950 until 1963. There were three children, Frederick Woodruff, Katherine, and Barbara. Fourteen months before his death, Field surprised family and friends and married Julia Lynn Templeton, the 23-year-old daughter of a Chicago businessman. A daughter, Corrine, was three months old at Field's death. Not included in Field's will by name, his widow received the third of the personal estate provided by law. The rest was divided among the children.

But then there was the wealth of Field Enterprises. Roughly 20 percent of Enterprises was held by the Field Foundation. Following the terms of a trust established by Marshall III, the remaining 80 percent of the stock in Enterprises was to be divided equally among direct male heirs when they reached the age of 25.

At the time of Field's death, Marshall V was 24 and Frederick 13.

Immediately after his father's death young Marshall moved to Chicago and began preparations to take over the family business, or businesses. As a teenager he had set his sights on the Chicago *Sun-Times*, but at Harvard he had opted for a broad education. His degree was in fine arts, and even while he was still in college he had begun to collect early American painters. (His first purchase: "Lion Pride," by Edward Hicks, 1780–1849.) However, he did spend a summer in the editorial department of the Boston *Globe*.

In Chicago, Field put himself in the hands of the executives and editors who had been running the empire and agreed to a five-year training program that included stints in the more than twenty divisions and subdivisions of Field Enterprises. He sold books door-to-door for World Book and worked on the copy desk of the *Daily News*.

Always impatient to get on with the job at hand, Field ended the five-year program after four years. In 1969 he became publisher of the *Sun-Times* and the *Daily News*. It was a title that had not been used since the death of his father. At age 28, Field was the youngest publisher of any major newspaper in the country. But more important to the strength and longevity of the empire, Field had become a member of the board of directors of Field Enterprises and the "family" trustee on the four-man board of trustees that still held final power. Not only did he have 40 percent of the voting stock in Enterprises but as the family trustee he was entitled to an extra vote in case the four trustees voted in a two-two tie. With a long life ahead of him he was in full control, for all practical purposes, of one of the largest privately owned corporations in America, one that was ringing up sales of more than $200 million a year and churning out profits of something like $10 million annually. Or rather he would be until his half brother Frederick reached 25 and became an equal partner.

Chairman of the board, a title he held after 1972, was the position Field liked. He had all the information he needed to keep tabs on the multiple operations of Enterprises but he was relieved of detail. As with his grandfather, his idea was to hire the best people and let them run with the ball. But they had best not fumble. Under Marshall V turnover at the top was frequent.

As Field has said any number of times, tradition in the Field family demands that each generation not only make a contribution to society but also and most important leave the family fortune bigger than it was. Traits in the family, he adds, seem to skip generations. He likens himself to the first Marshall and to Marshall III. Marshall I, of course, created the fortune, while Marshall III broadened and increased the base. (Marshall IV sold the last of the family holdings, pre-ferred stock, in Marshall Field & Co., the department-store chain, in part to raise cash for taxes to settle his father's estate, but Marshall V retains a sentimental attachment even though the stores have passed not only out of family control but out of the hands of Chicagoans; in 1982 BAT Industries, the London conglomerate, acquired Marshall Field & Co. through its U.S. affiliate for $310 million.)

As for his political and economic views, Field says he is more liberal than the first Marshall but less liberal than the founder of *PM* and the Chicago *Sun*.

In any event, it would have been easy for Field at age 25, or 30, or 35 to forget about family, duty, and tradition and to walk away, leaving instructions for the mailing of his divi-dend checks. Instead, he's in the office, at the desk, as in-volved as the chairman of any corporation. He has put his stamp on the corporation and he has not ducked the tough ones.

For instance, it was Field's judgment that set the corpora-tion off on a vigorous new entry into real estate with the sale of World Book for $120 million and ultimately the acquisition of the real estate holdings and expertise of the old-line Boston real estate firm of Cabot, Cabot & Forbes.

And it was Marshall who walked into the city room of the Chicago *Daily News* on Friday, February 3, 1978, to announce the decision—a tragedy to the editors and reporters who filled the room and still considered a tragedy by citizens of the city—that after 102 years the end had come for the *Daily News.*

Field had agreed to pump an extra $2 million into the *Daily News* and had put James Hoge, the brilliant young editor of the *Sun-Times,* in charge of a two-year drive to revive the afternoon newspaper. The two-year trial was not yet over but the bottom-line result was only too evident. Back in the 1950s something more than 600,000 copies of the *Daily News* were sold each weekday. Now circulation was little more than half that. The paper had lost nearly $22 million in less than four years and was losing in 1978 at the rate of $11 million a year. It was up against too many hard facts of modern metropolitan society, the central one being that there was no way to deliver timely news to an electronic home in the suburbs in the afternoon. The suburban subscriber had been the *Daily News*'s strength; as the six o'clock news came on the television screen the subscriber in the suburbs was reading a paper that had gone to press before noon—and had been delivered twenty miles by costly truck.

Actually, the *Tribune* struck the final blow. Years before, Colonel McCormick had insisted on printing late-afternoon editions of his morning paper so that they could be put aboard trains leaving Chicago for delivery in New York, Washington, and other outposts of civilization. In 1974 the *Tribune* gave up on its own afternoon paper, *Chicago Today,* but attempted to cover the afternoon market by printing a still earlier edition of the *Tribune.* Then in 1977 the announcement came that the *Tribune* was killing the earliest editions. That dumped an impossible burden on the *Daily*

News. Alone it had to support the cost of a daytime distribution network throughout the city and the suburbs.

June 1, 1977, was a date approached by the executives of Field Enterprises, Inc., with more than a little apprehension. On that date Frederick (Ted) Woodruff Field, Marshall's half brother, reached his 25th birthday and under the terms of the Field trust assumed full control of his interest in the corporation. And his interest was equal to that of Marshall's. The lawyers had been at work, and there was a lengthy document setting out the details of the corporate mechanism as it would exist. But that only emphasized the fact that Ted Field was now an equal—his stock gave him as many votes as Marshall and the votes would elect six of his representatives to the board of directors along with Marshall's six.

The apprehension in the ranks was based on a fear of the unknown. Ted had grown up in Alaska, and at a half dozen or more schools and colleges, under the care of his mother, Katherine Woodruff Field Fanning, and he was living in Newport Beach, California. His most obvious interest, one that occasionally got him in the newspapers, was racing cars. He owned a stable of Indianapolis-class racers and entered them in races around the country with professional drivers at the wheel. It is a million-dollar-a-year sport usually supported by large corporations with an automobile-related product to advertise. Young Field also risked his neck frequently, getting behind the wheel himself in Grand Tour events. However, in 1984 he tired of the sport and, announcing that he was not going to drive anymore, handed the cars over to his lead driver. By then the 31-year-old Ted had settled on a career: he was going to make movies, another risky enterprise that could eat dollars at a 200-mile-an-hour clip. Hollywood reported that he had money in a number of turkeys but that he did well with *The Return of the Nerds*. Similarly, Ted was supposedly making money on California real estate, but his fling in a chain of barbecue restaurants called Four Guys from Texas did not sizzle.

Marshall, more at home with his art collection than in a race-car pit, did his best to keep his half brother informed about the affairs of Field Enterprises, but from the beginning Ted let it be known that he had little interest in the dynasty. In public the Fields insisted they were happy brothers, but that may have been because they were not speaking.

Giving brothers 50-50 power over assets worth nearly half a billion dollars may have been the only way, but it was hardly practical. As one corporate insider once said, Marshall's first question concerning a proposal tended to be: how much can we lose? Ted's first question was: how much can we make and how fast?

Matters started to come to a head in 1983 when Marshall and his professional managers decided the time had come to turn a nice profit on the UHF television stations owned by Field Enterprises. They succeeded in selling WFLD for $140 million, WKBD in Detroit for $70 million, WLVI in Boston for $47 million, and KBHK in San Francisco for $23 million, while scrapping an unsuccessful entry in the Philadelphia market.

Question: what does a corporation do with $280 million, a greater part of it profit, when there are only two stockholders? And one of them is eager to get his hands on money to finance motion pictures?

Something that is not exactly smart is to take the profits into the corporation where they will be taxed, and then pay them out in dividends to the stockholders, at which point they will be subject to personal income taxes. Very quickly the lawyers converted Field Enterprises, a corporation, into Field Enterprises, a partnership. Ted now had $140 million in his pocket, minus a portion for Uncle Sam, but enough to establish his standing with anyone likely to lend money for a motion picture.

There was more of the cash where that came from, and Marshall was now willing to raise the money if it would rid him of his partner even if it meant selling the *Sun-Times* and giving up the family pledge to battle the *Tribune.*

When Marshall announced the decision in 1983 to dissolve the corporation and put the *Sun-Times* up for sale, money was talking. "Three generations of the Field family have been proud and privileged to be in the newspaper business," Marshall said in a formal statement. "Had this decision been mine alone to make, I probably would not have taken this action."

Marshall's critics focused on that word "probably." It was Ted's fault, but maybe it wasn't. Maybe Marshall would have dumped the newspaper anyway.

There were those who said Marshall could have gone to the mat with Ted. But in the end that would have meant a public brawl in the courts, unless Ted backed down, and Marshall would have had no standing in the courts against his 50-50 partner. In fact, the shoe was on the other foot; in any given transaction, then or in the future, Ted could always sue Marshall for mismanagement of the estate. Finally and obviously, Marshall could have paid off his half brother with cash or property and kept the *Sun-Times.* When it came down to it, Marshall opted to sell the paper and keep Cabot, Cabot & Forbes. Marshall I had instructed his heirs to stay with real estate; compared with the newspaper business, it was safe, the tax advantages were many, and the returns on capital easily outstripped anything that could be hoped for from the *Sun-Times* in the foreseeable future.

In January 1984, Rupert Murdoch, the transplanted Australian, owner of some eighty newspapers and magazines in the United Kingdom, Australia, and the United States, a billionaire, and a fighter, became the owner of the *Sun-Times* after paying the Fields $90 million-plus in cash.

There was an irony here. Later on Murdoch put together a spectacular $2 billion deal with Denver oilman Marvin Davis to buy six television stations. One of the stations was the old Field station, WFLD-TV, in Chicago. For the third time the *Sun-Times* and WFLD were corporate bedfellows, only this time current federal rules on cross-ownership, designed to keep any entity from controlling local information, demanded that Murdoch get rid of either the newspaper or the television station.

Very quickly Marshall Field was back in the newspaper business. For $30 million he bought Pioneer Press, the prospering string of suburban newspapers built up over twenty years by Time Inc. but later seen by Time Inc., with its magazines and huge stake in cable television, as an almost frivolous diversion. Field was chairman of Cabot, Cabot & Forbes and watching the firm's first major entry into Chicago real estate. In addition, he was chairman of his own private company, called Old Mountain Co., a catchall for any project that caught his fancy, including the hotel he owned on Jupiter Island not far from the Field family villa at Hobe Sound, Florida, where he keeps his fishing boat. At times it appeared that Marshall, the holder of a fine arts degree from Harvard and the collector of paintings, was more interested in raising money for the Chicago Art Institute than anything else.

Back in 1910 Frederick Pepper ran the carpentry shop at Marshall Field & Co. He and his men kept the store shipshape and were prepared to build partitions, counters, and just about anything that might be needed. In the 1980s the Pepper Construction Co. still did carpentry work for the Field stores, but under Frederick's grandson, Richard, it was a major construction company with contracts that often totaled more than $300 million in a single year.

The company has done work as distant as Saudi Arabia. However, Chicago is the place as far as Richard Pepper is concerned. "You can reach the world from Chicago," Pepper says, "but by itself our county, Cook County, has a larger population than any one of the states except for six, and only a handful of countries in the entire world have a gross product larger than that of the Chicago metropolitan area. We come in there right after the United States, Russia, the Western European countries, and Japan."

That's one large reason Marshall Field V chooses to remain in Chicago. Chicago opportunities are as great as any for the Field Corp., Field Publications, and the Old Mountain Co.

It would make sense for Marshall's Boston-based real estate company, Cabot, Cabot & Forbes, to undertake a major project in Chicago, and Marshall got just that underway in the late 1980s.

Rather obviously Field was out to build a conglomerate. He had Pioneer Press under his wing along with *The Weekly Reader,* a publication with 8.5 million school-age readers, plus educational publications acquired from Xerox and the Field Book Club, aimed at children but one of the very largest book clubs.

Chicago has spawned its share of conglomerates, many of them of huge size. Beatrice Foods was in the $10 billion class before the financial people began to chop it up in 1985. It owned everything from Coca-Cola bottling companies to a window-blind firm and was selling in ninety countries, including mainland China. The company history traces back to a local dairy in Beatrice, Nebraska, and the name should be pronounced (but isn't) the way the Beatrice villagers do: Bee-atrice. Consolidated Foods is another.

The late Nathan Cummings, a multimillionaire, an internationally known art collector before his death, and among other things a partner of Colonel Henry Crown in the purchase way back of the Empire State Building, put Consolidated together.

One of the early, major Cummings acquisitions was the Kitchens of Sara Lee. Charles Lubin was a neighborhood baker on Chicago's South Side when he created Sara Lee and the frozen-bakery-products industry. Later on Cummings fired Lubin as head of Sara Lee even though Lubin was the genius behind the operation and even though Sara Lee was named for Lubin's daughter. In 1985 new management dropped the prosaic name Consolidated Foods and renamed the whole corporation for Lubin's daughter. By all

counts Lubin was a happy man. He had cashed in his Consolidated Foods stock for a few millions and had invested a big
chunk of it in Gus Swift's meat company just as it was being
converted into a modern conglomerate called Esmark, a
corporate restructuring that soon doubled and tripled and
quadrupled the price of the stock. CFS Continental, Inc.,
originally a supplier of coffee to restaurants and hotels, was
built into a billion-dollar distributor of foods and supplies to
the food-service industry by the Cohn brothers, Robert and
Alvin.

Chicago has always provided fertile ground for the
growth of wealth—and industries. The railroads, for instance, and the country's number one airline, United. Motorola, Zenith (carving out a niche in computers), and Admiral (Japanese-owned) survive if in different form from the
city's concentration of consumer electronics and appliance
companies. Printing was always big in Chicago; the big Donnelley, Cuneo, and Hall plants made family fortunes, and
hundreds of smaller printers did well even after economics
sent many printers to low-wage areas.

From patent-medicine days on, Chicago has been headquarters for an impressive group of pharmaceutical companies, G. D. Searle (Enovid, Ovulen, Dramamine, Metamucil,
and, until it was sold, NutraSweet), Abbott Laboratories ($3
billion worth of drugs and health-care equipment), Baxter
Travenol (the creator of intravenous techniques and the
largest supplier), and American Hospital Supply (the largest
hospital supply company, now merged with Baxter Travenol).

The Kempers made millions in insurance and so did W.
Clement Stone. During his lifetime Stone's positive thinking
not only built an international company but impelled him to
give away more than $150 million.

That was Stone's standard giving plus what he contributed
to a range of favored projects—e.g., attempts to rehabilitate
criminals and to forecast the future by reading tree-ring
cycles. A multimillion-dollar contribution to Richard Nixon's

campaign did not get him an appointment to the Court of St. James's as he thought he had been promised. It was a disappointment; Stone felt he could have done much in a quiet way with his power of positive mental attitude to help the British regain their power.

Railroading, along with a very profitable real estate and lumber deal, created Chicago's first millionaire, William Ogden. Selling stock to farmers along the right-of-way to raise capital, Ogden got the Galena and Chicago Union Railroad rolling in October 1848, although its tracks ran only ten miles west of Chicago, something like 150 miles short of Galena on the Mississippi River across from Iowa. Much later he merged the Chicago & North Western Railroad with his Galena and Chicago, and it was Ogden who drove the golden spike at Promontory, Utah, in 1869, symbolically joining the Union Pacific and the Central Pacific (later part of the Southern Pacific) to complete the nation's first transcontinental rail network.

The Chicago & North Western Railroad stretched to the West Coast in the usual zigzag, hodgepodge fashion when Ben W. Heineman took it over in 1956 with the thought that something could be done with a railroad that habitually lost money running through sparsely populated states like South Dakota and Wyoming even though it also had a continuing headache, the job of providing commuter service to the north and northwest suburbs of Chicago.

Born in Wausau, Wisconsin, Heineman arrived in Chicago in the unpromising year of 1931 at age 16 with his mother after the untimely death of his father. The University of Michigan accepted him at that age, and he went on to graduate from Northwestern University's law school. After practicing law in Chicago for a number of years, with time out for government service during World War II, Heineman headed up a group that took over the old Minneapolis & St. Louis Railway Co. This was 1954. Heineman continued a corporate law practice, but he also served as chairman of the railway company. In that capacity he got a firsthand look at the merger and acquisition game and at how money-losing companies can be turned inside out to create something new and profitable. The railroad became MSL, Inc.

Two years later Heineman moved over to the Chicago & North Western where he became chairman, chief executive officer and largest stockholder and set off on a spectacular run. He was able to pump real money into modernizing the road and he started building an industrial company within the corporation. Eventually he sold the railroad to its employees at a bargain price and the stock very shortly made many of them, executives, conductors, engineers and trainmen, wealthy, depending on how much stock they had subscribed to.

As for Heineman he reorganized the industrial companies as Northwest Industries and went on building. By 1980 Northwest had sales of $2.6 billion and profits of $172.2 million. Among other things, Heineman was a member of the First National Bank's prestigious board of directors and the holder of 101,000 shares of the bank's stock, then worth more than $2 million.

Heineman's story is one that keeps happening in the city where the winds of opportunity blow along with the winds off the prairies. In fact, his story is still unfolding in a new chapter. The 1980 and the 1982–83 recessions did not help Northwest Industries. Worse, the great OPEC oil squeeze wrecked for the time being the start in Northwest's family of companies. This was Lone Star Steel, a Texas company generating $750 million in sales, primarily from the sale of steel pipe used in the petroleum industry. When oil drilling came close to a halt in the 1980s, so did Lone Star.

Already past retirement age, Heineman sold out—to young William Farley. Heineman had his millions, his house in Door County, Wisconsin, on the shores of Lake Michigan, and an eighty-foot sailing yacht rigged with enough electronic controls so that he and his wife could sail it without a crew. And Farley, a Chicago builder for the era extending into the new century, had his hands around a billion-dollar empire that he would shape to his vision.

III

PRITZKER

Maybe it was worth only a couple of million dollars, an incidental property in the world of Jay Arthur Pritzker even then, twenty-odd years ago. Pritzker was talking to a newspaper reporter about the family interests and he had been asked about 200,000 acres of forest and farmland the Pritzkers owned in Arkansas and Louisiana. He brushed the question aside; the land did not really rate a mention.

There was nothing creative to be done with 200,000 acres of rural land. You could sell off trees to timber companies, rent the agricultural land to farmers, pocket a profit and pay the taxes. Where was the fun in that?

At the time the Pritzkers were deep into something that was fun, and Jay was delighted to talk about it.

A few years earlier, in 1957, Jay had had a business appointment in Los Angeles. Typically, he also had business matters of some importance to attend to in Chicago, and the night before his Los Angeles appointment his work kept him busy well into the evening. The solution was a flight to California aboard the red-eye special. That dumped him at the Los Angeles airport at six-thirty in the morning, "too late to get some sleep, too early to do anything." Wandering around, killing time, and as usual exercising his ever-active curiosity, Pritzker found himself in a hotel where there was a coffee shop. In spite of the name of the coffee shop, Fat Eddie's, the breakfast Pritzker had was excellent. And he was impressed with the customers and with the evident quality of the hotel; accommodations around the airports he had seen were second- and third-class highway motels. By the time breakfast was eaten, the Pritzker business brain was percolating despite the rigors of the red-eye special. A first-class airport hotel, travelers caught for the night, and more important, business travelers calling on the companies that often clustered around an airport. Pritzker headed for the hotel desk and elicited the name and address of the hotel's owner. He now forgets the particular business reason he had for visiting Los Angeles that day, but he does know that before the trip was over he was talking deal to the man whose first name was on the hotel: Hyatt Von Dehn, a swinger in California real estate. "I wrote out a few notes on what we might offer and a few days later Von Dehn called and accepted my offer."

It was a typical Pritzker operation: intuition signaled opportunity, a quick look at the books confirmed the basics— supposedly Jay is a world-class sprinter when it comes to reading a financial statement—an offer was made, and accepted, all done with a speed that would frighten and horrify most businessmen, lawyers, accountants, and master's degree graduates of business schools. Over the years the family has done any number of multimillion-dollar deals on the basis of a handshake or a few written sentences. Jay, a third-generation lawyer, is of the firm opinion that lawyers will "drive you up the wall by thinking up ways to complicate things."

The Pritzkers paid $2.1 million for the Los Angeles Hyatt and immediately set about turning Jay's vision of "first-class" airport hotels into reality. Number two in the chain was built from scratch at Burlingame, California, near the San Fran-

cisco airport. By the 1980s the Hyatt name was on 109 hotels
in the United States and around the world; the Pritzker
family either owns them or operates them under a management contract. And the airport concept is no longer central
to Hyatt. In Chicago, for instance, the Pritzkers spent $30
million to build the Hyatt Regency O'Hare with its ten-story
atrium, glass elevators, and copper-colored glass towers just
off the airport. (When the Regency O'Hare opened in 1973,
corporate, political, and social Chicago turned out for a
seven-course, three-wine dinner with dancing to the Duke
Ellington orchestra. The grand-opening affair was done
twice, once on a Friday night, again on Saturday, with 750
guests invited to each shift.) But the company also built the
even larger, 1,500-room Hyatt Regency Chicago just off
Michigan in downtown Chicago and bought the Water
Tower Inn, upgrading it and renaming it the Park Hyatt. In
the 1980s, expansion was still going strong with the opening
of Hyatts in Oakland and Long Beach, California, and New
Delhi. The Pritzkers were among the first to realize that
there was opportunity for the hotel industry within the cities; every major city had its grand old hotels, and many not
so grand, all built no later than the 1920s, and every highway
had its Holiday Inn motel, and more. The spectacular hotel
architect John Portman played a part in this, and Portman
and the Pritzkers were significant factors in the changing
style of hotels in this country and all over the world. In 1966
the Pritzkers bought the Atlanta Regency, designed by
Portman, for $18.9 million. The architect's grandiose plans
had frightened investors and potential buyers. Who would
put money into a hotel that devoted thousands of the square
feet that should have been cut up into profit-producing
rooms, to air—something called an atrium? The Pritzkers
saw a showplace that might run close to 100 percent capacity and attract a continuing stream of restaurant and bar
customers. They also saw a need for new, quality hotel
rooms in a city awakening to a new day. It was another
Pritzker bet on their judgment and a typical Pritzker foray;

from start to finish, negotiations for the hotel dragged on for all of one and a half days. Very shortly the Hyatt Regency Atlanta was generating profits at a rate unheard of outside Las Vegas.

In 1975, when Hyatt Corp. (U.S.A.) and Hyatt International were still more or less growing boys, the international operation produced more than $2 million in profits. The $2,029,000 earned that year by the foreign hotels is one of the few hard numbers indicating the wealth of the Pritzkers. As billionaires and openhanded philanthropists, the Pritzkers recognize that they operate in a real world where their activities will cause comment and draw frequent media attention. They will talk with noteworthy candor when asked a reasonable question, but they do not seek publicity. And when it comes to business matters, they like to operate like, well, the Pritzkers. They are entrepreneurs; making deals, creative deals, is the name of the game for them. They are highly competitive (apparently against their own record) and they like to win, but sometimes they do lose. "You pays your money and . . ." Jay says, and means it. They are sensitive to failure and uncomfortable, to say the least, with what the executives of many public companies go through when faced with an angry group of stockholders and embarrassing questions at the annual meeting. Win or lose, they want the freedom to commit $10 or $50 million without checking it through a corporate bureaucracy or submitting to the red tape and formalities of stockholder votes and other delaying rules put upon public companies by the stock exchanges and the U.S. Securities and Exchange Commission. Not that they can't handle such complications and public disclosures; from time to time they have been through a wringer or two with everyone looking on, and what the public has seen is frankness, patient determination, and even refreshing humor.

In the earlier stages of building the world Hyatt chain, the family reluctantly decided to go public. Of the stock issued, outside investors at one high (or low) point owned two-thirds of the stock in International and half the stock in Hyatt domestic. The $2,029,000 profit was the amount reported to stockholders by Hyatt International for the year 1975. Not that any portion of that went into the family pockets; the stock did not pay a dividend. But eventually profits on that order and much higher returns would come to the Pritzkers when they succeeded in buying out the public stockholders and returning the Hyatt corporations to the comfort of private ownership. Actually, 1975 was a poor year for the hotel empire, on top of an even worse one in 1974, when several things went wrong at the same time for the domestic hotel corporation. "If my brother Don had been alive and running Hyatt, it would never have happened," Jay told *Business Week* magazine in 1975. That was high tribute to the abilities of Donald N. Pritzker, without a doubt a brother touched with the genius of the clan. Still, 1975 was one of the years of the special depression that swamped real estate developers and a year of recession for the general economy. Donald was the youngest of the Pritzker brothers and only 39 years old when he died. Overweight but apparently healthy, he suffered a heart attack while playing the vigorous Pritzker brand of tennis on a court in Hawaii, where he had gone to attend the ceremonies of the opening of a non-Hyatt hotel. When he died he had been chief executive officer of Hyatt Corp. for ten years and president of Hyatt International for nearly five years. (His death was one of two tragedies to strike the Pritzker family. Jay's daughter Nancy died of carbon monoxide poisoning in her garaged car at age 22.)

By 1978 the hotels were doing much better, and Hyatt International turned in profits of $3,441,360. At that point, the family stock in International alone was worth, on paper, as valued by the stock market, something more than $11 million.

Even so, International was a small part of the empire built by Nicholas J., Abram N., Jay, and Robert Pritzker and bolstered no little by Jack N. and a few other Pritzkers.

It all started with Nicholas J. He was brought to this country and Chicago in 1881 at age nine from Kiev and, of
course, went to work immediately. That is, he did about any
odd job he could find, shining shoes, selling newspapers,
anything. By the time he was a young man, he had qualified
as a pharmacist, not bad for an immigrant from the Ukraine.
That was not enough. He went on to attend Northwestern
University and work his way through the law school of De
Paul University, a Catholic institution that prides itself on its
long years of service to successive waves of immigrants. By
1901, when he was 29 years old, Nicholas founded the law
firm that is still home base for the family today, Pritzker &
Pritzker.

The law firm is equipped with a roomful of the standard
law books, but it has not accepted a client since 1936.
Abram, more often known as A.N., felt there was too much
of a chance of a conflict of interest: what if a piece of real
estate or a company the family was eying turned out to be
owned by a client of the law firm?

Abram and his brother Jack did quite well during the
Great Depression of the 1930s with the investments they
made in real estate at rock-bottom prices. It was a successful
formula that still works well for the Pritzkers and helped to
build a number of Chicago fortunes. Today the Pritzkers
continue to display a clairvoyance and a faith in themselves
and the future in their willingness to invest in what may
seem to most people a losing proposition. In the spring of
1983, Jay, a World War II Navy pilot and an aviation buff
from his earliest days, offered upwards of $70 million for
bankrupt and grounded Braniff airlines. To Jay, working
through Hyatt, the proposition looked good in spite of ruinous competition in a deregulated industry; after all, a full-
blown Braniff had earned more than $45 million as late as
1978 and there was a chance Braniff could soar once again.

By the time Abram, eldest son of Nicholas, born in 1896,
the guiding spirit and the patriarch of the family into the
1980s and his 80s, was growing up, the Pritzkers were rea-

sonably well off. Like everyone in the family, Abram started young and learned young. Equipped with a law degree from Harvard, he was practicing law and dipping into finance and real estate before he was 30 years old. Like hundreds of other fortune seekers in the Roaring Twenties, Abram jumped into the great 1920s Florida land boom. A real estate syndicate he had put together went bust when land values evaporated and the syndicate partners lost $320,000. Under no legal obligation, Abram paid off his partners and ended up, he says, with $3.20. That $3.20, exact to the penny, could be kidding on the square. Abram and his sons had a real sense of humor.

A.N. was 76 in 1971 and a widower for one year when he married Lorraine Colantonio, part owner and manager of a suburban Hyatt hotel. (Accompanied by the Pritzker sons and assorted members of the family, the bride and groom flew to Acapulco after the wedding ceremony for the opening of a Hyatt hotel.)

Just about to mark his 90th birthday on January 8, 1986, Abram told a *Sun-Times* reporter that he didn't have enough to do. "My sons think I should retire because I'm 90, but I like to work. That's all I like to do. I don't like to sit around on my can." Actually, A.N. had more than enough to occupy anyone; he was the overseer of the family's charitable contributions and his estimate was that the Pritzkers were donating $4.5 million a year.

As fate would have it, A.N. passed to his reward just a few days before his birthday.

As Abram's sons Jay Arthur, born August 26, 1922, and Robert Alan, born June 30, 1926, tell it, the name Pritzker appears on none of the family business enterprises except the original law firm, not out of a desire for secrecy but because they don't think anyone can spell Pritzker. To someone not familiar with either name, Pritzker doesn't seem that much more difficult than Hyatt, but the family thinks Pritzker Hotel would never make it.

Whatever the joking, family was and is the thing with the

Pritzkers. Much of the family feeling and character goes back to the founder of the American family, Nicholas. Born an Orthodox Jew, he rejected the strictures of his upbringing. Although Abram was not religious, he inherited a generosity of spirit from his father as well as his independence of mind. When Nicholas, a widower, died, he left all the ready money in his estate, $75,000, to the housekeeper who had taken care of him in his last years. In too many families that degree of generosity would have meant a bitter squabble and lawsuits. But Nicholas's sons approved of the grant before and after his death and over the years helped guide the housekeeper into investments that made her a wealthy woman.

The generosity of the family is surprising. For starters, A.N. was not religious, but he did belong to a synagogue and he supported it and other Jewish organizations. "I pay my dues," he once told a reporter. "Even if I don't go, there are others who want to go to synagogue and I want to make it possible for them."

Similarly, A.N. is not a Zionist, but he supported the idea of a homeland for Jews—to the tune of an amazing $500,000 a year. The family annually buys a half million dollars' worth of Israeli bonds and gives the bonds back to Israel, forfeiting the interest.

Pritzker thought that was "reasonably liberal." Israel was not his country. America, the country that gave him an opportunity, was, he said.

Hence, among other large contributions to Jewish and non-Jewish organizations from the family and from the Pritzker Foundation, the $12 million given in 1968 to the University of Chicago medical school. And therein an exception to the Pritzkers' general desire for privacy. The medical school was renamed after the family.

On the other hand, not too many people outside the school know about Robert Pritzker's gift in 1970 of $1.4 million to the Illinois Institute of Technology to establish a center for environmental studies. A graduate of IIT in engineering, Bob is the family's expert in manufacturing and the management of the manufacturing companies. A number of the companies the Pritzkers own would fall into the heavy industry, or "dirty," category, and it was Bob's pledge back in 1970 to clean up all the Pritzker plants beyond the letter of any laws.

In one other activity the family has projected itself into the limelight. In 1979 Jay established the Pritzker Architecture Prize, worth $100,000 annually, and meant to be in architecture what the Nobel Prizes are in other fields. (The 1983 prize, presented by Jay during ceremonies at the Metropolitan Museum of Art, went to the great Chinese-American architect I. M. Pei.) It could be said that the creation of the prize in architecture fits with the family's longtime practice of giving back something of what they have received. Planning for the prize began not too long after the death of the youngest brother, Donald, in 1972. One reason the Pritzkers bought the hotel that became the Atlanta Hyatt Regency, designed by John Portman, was that Donald was struck by the radically new architecture of the hotel. As A.N. said years later, after striking architecture had made dozens of Hyatt hotels instant successes and local landmarks, "Every hotel we have we owe to that one in Atlanta." No doubt the patriarch of the clan also had in mind the fact that the financial success of the Atlanta hotel encouraged the Pritzkers to expand.

When an ordinary person buys a car or a dress at a bargain price, it is a triumph, a cause for bragging. When a businessman picks up a company or a piece of property at a bargain price, it is commonly considered shady practice. Going back to A.N.'s entry into real estate with his younger brother Jack (Jack died in 1979 at age 75) in the late 1920s and especially during the years of the Great Depression, the Pritzkers did a lot of bottom fishing, picking up assets at bargain prices. But they have never been accused of stomping on anyone. They've been astute in recognizing values that others shied away from or did not see. They've salvaged enterprises that were headed for the rocks. In putting together their vast empire the Pritzkers have refrained, with minor exceptions, from the kind of corporate battles that have marred the business world in recent years.

The Pritzkers have their ethics and their standards, initiated by Nicholas and passed on by A.N. Robert may have been expressing the family's view of the world a touch more than reality when he once said during a lecture: "The American businessman has always been pictured as a materialistic dynamo with the social conscience of the saber-toothed tiger. This may have had some validity in 1890 but there's no truth to the concept today."

Jay accurately summed up the family's approach to acquisitions this way: "We go in and say, 'Here's what we'll do—A, B, C. If you like, fine. If not, that's okay, too.' "

From time to time the Pritzkers have been called wheeler-dealers. It is a term A.N. vigorously rejected. The inference is tricky deals pulled off for a quick in-and-out profit. The Pritzkers still own most of what they ever acquired over a span of a half century. If they've bought troubled properties, paying a bargain price, they risked their money and invested new money and their talent—to turn a bad situation around. A.N., Jay, and Bob talked over the years about the "fun" to be had in putting a deal together and building something on what was a shaky foundation. They used words like "creative" and "innovative." They also see themselves as engaged in some kind of sports contest.

A.N., who referred to himself as a "negotiator," went so far as to say the family might be engaged in the same sort of business game even if the profits went to charity. That may be an easy statement for someone who has already made millions. Jay is more realistic when he says simply, "We like to win."

A.N. liked negotiating, and in common with Jay he may have had a talent for reading a balance sheet and the fine print in a contract, but the more striking aspect of the Pritzker operation is their willingness to commit millions on

the basis of what might seem to be only intuition. Supposedly Jay devours and absorbs complicated financial statements the way lots of people devour a fast-paced detective
novel. "If we have bought a lot of things on just a handshake
or a paragraph or two," Jay says, his father always told him
that it is not a contract that makes a deal but how you
behave afterwards. Sounding the same theme, Bob holds
that he would much rather have a business relationship with
a man than with a piece of paper.

If all this sounds like strange behavior for lawyers, it was
and is the Pritzker way.

A.N., the son of a lawyer, a lawyer himself, and the father
of lawyers, allowed that he was ashamed of the fact. That
would seem to make Robert, the graduate engineer, his
father's favorite. Jay makes a distinction between business-
man-lawyers and lawyer-lawyers. The latter, he says, can
only complicate business.

The story of the Cory Corp. illustrates a number of things
about the way the Pritzkers operate. Still vigorous and interested in the family enterprises at 87 in 1983, A.N. was running things in 1941 when he bought Cory, a maker of coffee
percolators and small appliances, in partnership with James
W. Alsdorf. The agreement for the purchase of Cory was
submitted for checking to a leading Chicago law firm, and
A.N. recalled that the law firm "disagreed with everything
in the contract."

A.N. shrugged off the objections and the deal went
through as written. A quarter of a century later, Hershey
Foods, seeking diversification beyond its chocolate business,
offered to buy Cory. Alsdorf, for estate reasons, was eager to
sell. Cory was churning out a profit of $3 to $4 million a year
and A.N. couldn't see any reason to accept the Hershey
offer, but he went along. Since they had bought the company for only $25,000 in cash and a $75,000 note and had
already collected sizable profits, it was a good deal by any
standards. Hershey paid $27.5 million for the company. And

forty years later A.N. still couldn't see anything wrong with the original purchase agreement.

Typically, the Pritzkers negotiated a fine deal, put up money for the purchase and to finance growth and expansion, and lived comfortably with a partner, Alsdorf, who ran the company, for twenty-five years.

Once A.N.'s sons elected him chairman of the Pritzker Giveaway Committee. That was after the family rescued the developers of the Hyatt Regency Atlanta. When it appeared that the hotel would be a tremendous success, the developers came crying to A.N. He was going to make a mint; they were broke and owed the Pritzkers substantial sums. Was that fair? A.N. sympathized and made a deal that would have shocked many businessmen but only appealed to his sons' sense of humor. A.N. outlined the offer he made the developers this way: "If the hotel made X dollars, I'd tear up half of that year's notes, and if it made two times X, I'd tear up the whole note. They [the developers] never did pay a dime more [on the note]."

As for the Pritzkers' faith in people and a handshake rather than legal documents, there's a story of one of the Pritzker expansions into the lumber business. (At last count the family owned 500,000 acres of timberland in this country and Costa Rica.) A Portland, Oregon, manufacturer of wooden doors suggested a partnership with the Pritzkers; they had the money and the timberland, he had know-how. Jay flew to Portland—this was in the early 1950s when Jay was still in his twenties, legal age—and in three days worked out a partnership arrangement that included the purchase of a plywood mill. In 1965 a conscientious accountant, auditing the considerably expanded Oregon firm, asked to see the original partnership contract. He found that the agreement had expired in 1960. The Pritzkers never bothered to write up a new pact.

No analyst would ever accuse the Pritzkers of operating according to a business plan. They are all over the board: hotels, airlines, timber, real estate, mining, industrial manufacturing, magazines, musical instruments. They are clear about what they don't like: tobacco, alcohol, and pharmaceuticals and additives that might have unwelcome side effects. In spite of their stake in hotels, they refused the lure of Las Vegas and Atlantic City until well after the big public companies like Hilton and MGM went after the gambler's dollar.

Otherwise, the family seems to be guided only by intuition and the individual preferences of each member. Jay and Bob agree that the family is as close as a colony of bees. But that only makes for informality. Times when A.N., Jay, Bob, and members of a younger generation sat together around a table were rare. "We always know what the others are thinking," Bob says, and the family sense of humor pops through to make a point: "Some of my best friends are Pritzkers," he adds. Apparently an informal veto may be exercised when a deal is in the making. If Jay, the financial expert, likes a situation but Bob doesn't, or vice versa, the family bows out. The number one criterion for Bob, the operating manager, seems to be his sense of whether or not a company would be "fun" to run.

According to Jay, the family got into lumber by way of a "ridiculous fluke." Bertrand Goldberg, the influential architect (Marina City), got the Pritzkers interested in a far-out idea: the manufacture of a Goldberg-designed lightweight "plywood freight car." "Someone," Jay says, "suggested we buy a plywood mill. It was like starting a cookie factory and deciding you needed to buy a wheat farm." The freight car never rolled, but some people would consider the timber and lumber operation a sufficient reward.

Until recent years the public knew little or nothing of the Pritzkers, but the business and financial world has known them for decades. Over the years they've worked in harness with everyone from the Rockefellers' Chase Manhattan Bank to the Murchison family of Texas (oil and football) and the Crown family (General Dynamics, construction materials and vast real estate holdings). Public notice only increased the number of phone calls and letters flooding into the law office with merger suggestions and appeals for money. A joke Jay enjoys has him endlessly circling his home in the evening, unable to get off the car telephone long enough to rush into the house. Something similar might be said about the time the Pritzkers spend in jet airplanes. Another family joke has Jay's secretary refusing to tell a caller where Jay could be reached. Knowledge of Jay's whereabouts might be worth a million dollars. No joke, Jay and Bob have been surprised to find themselves stepping off the same airliner.

Overnight in 1973 the Pritzkers became very well known in some important circles where no one could spell their name. What for them was an almost incidental acquisition projected them into the media limelight. They bought *McCall's* magazine for $8 million from the communications subsidiary of conglomerate Norton Simon, Inc. Instantly the magazine, newspaper, radio, and television industries and all Madison Avenue scurried to find out who these guys from Chicago were. The deal was brought to the Pritzkers by J. Ira Harris, a young Chicago deal maker with Salomon Brothers who later picked up a cool $30 million for his stake in Salomon when that old-line Manhattan investment banking house sold itself to Philbro, the metals and commodities firm.

It was Bob, the engineer, who was most interested in *McCall's* even though brother Jay approved of the numbers. (Typically, the deal was signed and sealed in just three days.) When Bob was graduated from the Illinois Institute of Technology at the early age of 19, a professor told him that he had the makings of an excellent engineer but that he was almost illiterate. His response was to set about reading all the classics of literature, including the great poets. He is still a poetry buff, and the occasional writing he does for engineering journals shows a firm command of the language.

For years Bob and the family have had an interest in the National Textbook Co. of Chicago, a publisher of schoolbooks. That led them indirectly into a magazine venture that preceded *McCall's*. In the early 1970s Abra Rockefeller Prentice and her then husband, Jon Anderson, had made another in what had been a long history of attempts by various literary-minded people to establish a Chicago-oriented magazine in the Second City. Their *Chicagoan* magazine had its points but it never quite made it, and Abra, no doubt with a slight push from the trustees of her Rockefeller inheritance, finally decided to put the magazine up for sale. It was the Pritzkers who bought it—for fun and to give a friend at National Textbook a chance at something he had always wanted.

As Jay has said a number of times, the family has had its "clinkers," and it has usually dropped the clinkers or stayed in for the long haul. Many a wheeler-dealer or big-time conglomerate has learned the hard way that a little clinker not worth top-management attention can run up million-dollar losses as fast as a $100 million corporation. The Pritzkers stayed with the *Chicagoan* for eight monthly issues and then in 1974 folded it when no improvement was in sight. *(Chicago* magazine, published by WFMT, Inc., a non-profit good-music station, went on to build a noteworthy success from a base of program listings. It was at a time when local magazines finally came into their own around the country and were able to pull in national advertising. *Chicago* continues to put out 200- and 250-page issues.)

McCall's was something else. Almost an institution, *McCall's* was nevertheless having its troubles like other mass-circulation family magazines in the advancing age of television. When the Pritzkers bought it in 1973, it was only holding in there, barely above a break-even point. But at a purchase price of $8 million (only a "peanut" deal, Jay said, reacting in surprise and chagrin to the flood of New York and national publicity the acquisition brought forth), Jay thought money was to be made and, typically, the family turned the *McCall's* people loose to do what they wanted. The page size of the magazine was cut along with money-losing excess circulation and advertising rates and subscription prices were adjusted. Inside of one year, ad pages had blossomed to 1,012 from 892, and the magazine was on the way to years of healthy profits.

Among a half dozen investments that have gone sour for the Pritzkers over four decades and more, the one that may have hurt the most was their excursion into Wall Street. Realistically, their pride may have been hurt more than their pocketbook. In the 1960s the family put money into Blair & Co., an investment banking and brokerage house. A member of the New York Stock Exchange, Blair & Co. (not to be confused with William Blair & Co., one of Chicago's strongest investment banking firms) was small by Merrill Lynch standards but it had an excellent reputation. In the roaring bull market of the late 1960s, Blair & Co. was doing very well along with all of Wall Street. That was the trouble: as trading volume shot up, the Street was buried in a flood of paperwork and DK became the best-known initials in the business. That stood for Don't Know and meant that no one knew what had happened with a buy or sell order. The DK orders ran into the thousands, representing millions of dollars. In 1979 Blair & Co. went under, a victim of old-fashioned management, the "on the first tee by three" kind. The Pritzkers had misjudged people. They had also put in $800,000 and lost $800,000. There was no stepping in to turn things around over the long haul.

A family joke has it that someday the Pritzkers are going to form something called the Marmon Tabernacle Choir. That's because mail and phone calls meant for the Mormon Church keep coming in to the Chicago headquarters of their Marmon Group. The name goes back to the once-famous Marmon automobile. (Bob Pritzker is a car buff. For years he drove a 1977 Avanti, the advanced car Studebaker designed in a last-gasp effort to stave off bankruptcy. Once the Pritzkers took a look at the Avanti Motor Co., spun off from Studebaker, but Bob decided the automobile was a better buy than the company.)

Today the Marmon Group is one of the largest privately owned industrial companies in the country. Marmon dates back to 1953, when Jay picked up a small, struggling Ohio manufacturing firm, the Colson Co. Colson, with sales of less than $5 million a year, was making bicycles and industrial casters, those wheels on a swivel found under furniture, but in Colson's case made for such as hand trucks used in plants and warehouses. Colson had also had an unsuccessful try at manufacturing rocket parts. Jay handed the job of running Colson over to brother Bob, then just 27 years old.

Turning a troubled company around is the toughest job a manager can tackle, and any number of experienced executives have developed ulcers trying. The Pritzkers have been specialists in the art. To Bob it is fun, fun. And he has always operated in a sector of the battlefield where the fighting was fierce. Like Colson, most of the companies that became a part of the Marmon empire were included later on during the 1983 recession among the old-fashioned, dying "smokestack" industries, the metalworking companies. The smile that seems always to hover on Bob's face breaks out when he walks on the floor of a factory where metal is being bent and turned into useful products. A compact man who wears bow ties, Bob is equipped with a bubbling curiosity. He's a questioner—and a listener. The target of the questions may be a company president, a blue-collar worker, or a customer. The questions are not necessarily for his benefit. They get his people to thinking; often they generate a more efficient way of making a gadget or even an idea for a new product.

In any event, Bob made a success of Colson. He dumped the bicycles, decided the company didn't have the expertise to make rocket parts, and concentrated on the mundane caster business. Typically, he acquired several small companies with products that fit and, typically, he spent money on new plant and equipment to make Colson more efficient and competitive.

For years the Pritzkers let their entry into industrial manufacturing perk along quietly, adding a small company here or there when Jay felt the numbers indicated a good return on investment and when Bob thought the company would be fun. Meanwhile, there were plenty of opportunities in everything from financing movies to a partnership with the Murchison family of Texas in developing the country's largest industrial park, Centex Park, in suburban Chicago, to the manufacture of plywood and flooring. (The family's entry into that last was dramatic. In 1962 flamboyant financier Edward M. Gilbert had decamped to Brazil with most of the cash of the E. L. Bruce Company, the Memphis flooring company he had pyramided into bankruptcy. The First National Bank of Chicago, having lent the Bruce Company large dollars, found itself with the company in its lap. Looking for a way out, the bank called for help: would Colonel Henry Crown, so wealthy and so astute that Howard Hughes had once asked him to bail out TWA, or the Pritzkers salvage the Bruce Company? As far back as the 1930s and A. N. Pritzker's real estate ventures, the First National had financed the Pritzkers, and Jay responded to a call from Gaylord Freeman, later the First National's chairman. In Freeman's office Jay and Colonel Crown were each willing for the other to take on the challenge. Finally, Freeman suggested a coin toss. Calling heads, Jay won, or lost, as he later said. But inside of six years Jay had turned E. L. Bruce around and was able to sell the company at a profit.)

By 1974 the Pritzkers, putting one foot ahead of the other, as Jay characterizes it, had built Marmon into a family kingdom that would have been the envy of any number of companies listed on the New York Stock Exchange and the *Fortune* list of the 500 largest industrial corporations. Sales hit the $300 million mark. But the Pritzkers were only getting into gear.

In 1976 they pulled off a classic Pritzker acquisition. For only $72 million in cash and an issue of $88 million in preferred stock they acquired the Cerro Corp., an international copper-mining firm with major metal-bending and wire factories and sales of nearly $600 million. The timing was perfect. Cerro was limping in the profits department coming out of the 1974–75 recession, and Peru and Chile had expropriated its major copper mines. Most of the players in the corporate acquisition game look at profits and pay up for profits. The Pritzkers like to look at hard assets, and Cerro was loaded, not counting $160 million in working capital and more than $100 million owed to it by Chile and Peru. Earnings can roller-coaster up and down, Jay says, but a factory is a factory, real wealth.

Acquisitions, major and minor, came one after the other once Cerro was in the family. For instance, there was Hammond Organ, a $127 million mini-conglomerate (organs to work gloves) with problems the Pritzkers overlooked. American Safety Equipment, a diversified maker of seat belts, added $48 million in sales. Then another huge one. In 1981 the Pritzkers grabbed off Trans Union, a Chicago company with $1.1 billion in annual revenues.

For the Pritzkers, the acquisition was out of the pattern. Management of the old-line company opposed the purchase, but Jay persisted—and paid up to win. To complete the $688 million cash purchase the Pritzkers had to borrow more than $450 million at the high rates of 1981. Ordinarily Jay likes to look, make an offer, and walk away if there is opposition.

Not many years ago the Pritzkers would have been up against the center of Eastern seaboard power, the Chase Manhattan Bank, known as the Rockefeller bank, in attempting to force the Trans Union deal. With its main business being the leasing of railroad cars, particularly tanker cars, Trans Union goes back to John D. Rockefeller and the tanker cars he controlled before the historic split-up of his Standard Oil Co. under the antitrust laws. But the leasing business, generating large tax credits that Marmon could use, was one reason Jay liked Trans Union.

From time to time over the years the Pritzkers have found themselves with members of the public as fellow stockholders in Marmon. It has happened when it was necessary to issue stock in order to complete a deal. Marmon became public back in 1966 when it issued stock to buy the Fenestra Co., a major manufacturing firm producing metal windows and doors. Forced to make periodic disclosures of company operations and annoyed by the red tape generated by the lawyers of the U.S. Securities and Exchange Commission and the stock exchanges, the Pritzkers paid off their outside stockholders and were happily operating once again in a telephone booth by 1971. But the Cerro deal, necessitating an issue of preferred stock, took Marmon public a second time in 1976. With only the preferred-stock holders left, the Pritzkers did not feel themselves inordinately hamstrung but they were still required to divulge bare-bones statistics on Marmon's financial health.

The 1978 figures show that Marmon rang up sales of $1.4 billion and threw off a profit of $63.6 million. Of course, not all of that went into the Pritzker treasury. The preferred-stock holders were paid $11,250,000 in dividends. The Pritzkers are in for the long haul, so presumably they were not unduly disturbed when the 1982 recession caught up with their industrial company, or even that a company like Marmon, with its concentration in such products as gears, copper tubing, truck springs and axles, castings, and railroad equipment, was hit more severely than consumer-product companies. But the damage to Marmon was deep. In the early months of 1983, the first quarter, profits dropped 57 percent to $6 million from the $13.9 million earned in the first quarter of 1982, when the recession had already eroded profits.

That should have put some strain on the extended Pritzker empire with its heavy load of debt. But obviously it did not. When debt and new competition generated by the deregulation of the air lanes grounded Braniff International Airlines, Jay Pritzker, the old Navy pilot and longtime director of Continental Airlines, couldn't resist. Using the cash and credit of the Hyatt Corp., Jay ended up, after weeks of negotiations, owning 80 percent of a new Braniff at a cost of $70 million.

Braniff was a large gamble even for the Pritzkers at a time when major airlines were close to crash landings. Between recession and the turmoil of deregulation, Continental Airlines was in protective bankruptcy while Eastern and TWA flew from one financial storm to another. Originally based in Dallas, Braniff faced murderous competition from American and various regional lines. The financial pressure on the new Braniff was unrelenting; the takeover agreement signed by Jay demanded monthly lease payments of $2 to $3 million for the thirty jetliners Braniff would put in the air. On the plus side there was the thought that Braniff had once generated annual profits of $45 million (1978) and a streamlined Braniff just might regain that altitude. Meanwhile, the airline had huge losses ($161 million in 1981) that might be utilized as an offset against Hyatt's tax liabilities. There was also the possibility that Hyatt's superior marketing organization could generate new business for both the airline and the hotels as other airline-hotel chains have.

The Braniff deal was not typical Pritzker. Negotiations—involving banks, insurance companies, and other creditors, a bankruptcy court, and the Braniff board of directors—dragged on for months. Moreover, Jay kept upping his offer until he had doubled his original bid. (At one early point, an anonymous representative of the banks was quoted as saying of Jay, "He's trying to steal the goddamn airline.")

The Pritzkers have always known how to relax and have fun in spite of the terrific energy and long hours they expend on business. Over the years they skied in the better places—Aspen, where the family owned a condominium, and St. Moritz, where Jay and his wife, Cindy, liked to rent a chalet for the season. Until Jay was floored by a massive heart attack in his early 60s, a matter that was satisfactorily patched up with quadruple bypass surgery, the competitive spirit of the Pritzkers displayed itself on the tennis courts, with Bob trying his best to beat Jay and claiming it was only his nearsightedness that gave Jay the edge.

With both Jay and Bob into their 60s it may be time for them to slow down a bit. But then there's the example of their father. At age 79, A.N. had no hesitation when the Navy, putting on a public relations tour for leading business-men, asked if he'd like to climb in with the pilot of a fighter plane and be catapulted off the deck of an aircraft carrier. The records say that A.N., a chief petty officer in the Navy during World War I, was the oldest man to undertake that harrowing, jet-propelled ride.

In that *Forbes* assigned a fortune of half a billion dollars to A.N. and to each of the sons, it might seem that they might enjoy sitting around on their cans. But there is no indication that the Pritzkers will stop building and looking for new fun projects. If the pile of money is too great for joint checking accounts, the practice established by Nicholas Pritzker back before the turn of the century, there would seem to be enough money to spread around to the many members of the family, even to A.N.'s eight great-grandchildren.

IV

MacARTHUR

Not many people got the best of John D. MacArthur during
his long life. Years before he died in January 1978 at age 80,
MacArthur was ranked as one of the country's two billionaires, and it is possible that he would not have had to share
honors if there had been a contest for leading skinflint. He
himself was the authority for the statement that he had
more enemies per square foot than any other man.

There is no record to indicate that the victory of John Paul
Stevens over MacArthur was a factor in the later appointment of Stevens as a justice of the U.S. Supreme Court, but
certainly it was an achievement that should have been hon-
orably noted.

Over the years MacArthur battled the federal government, the insurance commissions of various states, his own
son, and a long list of miscellaneous people in the courts.

Some people might think that the late Carl Byoir came
out on top when MacArthur dragged him into court. Somehow Byoir, then the proprietor of one of the nation's largest
and most prestigious public relations firms, had managed to
get under MacArthur's very thick skin and MacArthur sued

him for libel. After Byoir's death, MacArthur agreed to settle
the suit for $1. Byoir's widow chose to pay off MacArthur
with a $20 gold piece, demanding $19 in change. Later
MacArthur claimed he had been had. His wife admired the
gold piece and persuaded MacArthur to buy a matching
coin so she could have a set of earrings made. MacArthur
complained that he had won a settlement but that it had cost
him $39.

There was nothing ambiguous about the victory of John
Paul Stevens and his colleague in battle, William O'Connell,
a public relations consultant and later president of the
United States League of Savings Institutions. Back in the late
1950s, lawyer Stevens and O'Connell worked with the old
Bellance Aircraft Co. and both owned stock in the company.
That was apparently a mistake in judgment for both men. By
1959 the light-aircraft-manufacturing company had fallen
on evil times and was badly in need of an injection of new
money if it were to survive.

Multimillionaire MacArthur, an aviation buff, was a likely
source of new capital, and negotiations led to an agreement.
But then MacArthur lost a degree of his faith in Bellance's
future and he backed away from the deal.

Stevens, the legal counsel for Bellance, took a look at the
circumstances and quickly decided that MacArthur had
breached a legal contract to the detriment of the company.
When MacArthur stubbornly refused to honor the contract,
Stevens hauled him into court. The case came to a bench
trial in Chicago in the early 1960s. After lengthy presenta-
tions by Stevens and the lawyers for MacArthur, the judge in
some disgust called a halt to the proceedings. There was
such a vast disparity, the judge said, between what Stevens
was telling the court and what MacArthur's lawyers were
saying that only sworn testimony from MacArthur could
clear up the issues. Declaring a twenty-minute recess, the
judge asked that the lawyers call MacArthur and pass along
his suggestion that he appear in court. When the attorneys
returned with word that MacArthur found himself too busy

in Florida with his real estate interests to come to Chicago, the judge exploded, recessed the trial again, and told the lawyers that his was no longer a suggestion but a court request. That, of course, did not impress MacArthur, but MacArthur's arrogance did impress the judge, who announced that, circumstances being what they were, he would rule on the basis of the facts then before the court.

No one was surprised when lawyer Stevens won a total victory. In character, MacArthur battled on, appealing to a higher court and again losing. In the end, MacArthur had to pay Bellance $1.7 million plus $500,000 to compensate for the interest Bellance might have earned on the money if MacArthur had paid up promptly in 1959.

O'Connell scored a nice double victory out of all this. With the troubles Bellance had had, the company's stock had long since fallen to $1 a share, and O'Connell owned a fair share of the stock at that price. When the court handed Bellance $2.2 million of MacArthur's money, the stock shot up to $4 a share and O'Connell cashed in. Entirely by happenstance, O'Connell had set his sights on a two-bedroom, two-bath condominium in Palm Beach Shores, Florida. What particularly attracted O'Connell, an ardent golfer, was the fact that the residential complex was built around the three golf courses of the Professional Golfers' Association National Golf Club. O'Connell took some quiet satisfaction in using what was in effect MacArthur's money to pay the owner-developer of the condominiums and the club for a condominium. The owner happened to be John D. MacArthur. In that Florida real estate has doubled and tripled and quadrupled in value since O'Connell paid $25,000 for his condo in 1966, O'Connell is one man who bears MacArthur no grudges.

Rather obviously, MacArthur, who often took doggie bags home, enjoyed his reputation as a ruthless, penny-pinching eccentric. Unlike Howard Hughes or Daniel K. Ludwig, the tanker tycoon and the "other" American billionaire before MacArthur's death (Ludwig has been known to take a swing at cameramen), MacArthur always made himself available to reporters and would even be interviewed by long-distance telephone—as long as the reporter was paying the toll. No question outraged him and he readily told or confirmed the outrageous. He met with reporters and others who might have business with him at a table in the coffee shop of the aging Colonnades Beach Hotel on Florida's Singer Island. As he said, the table, always equipped with a pot of coffee, a pack of Winston cigarettes, and a telephone, was good enough for him. Who needed a fancy office? He owned the 450-room hotel, of course, and lived there for most of the last sixteen years of his life even though he maintained his legal residence in Illinois, an out-of-character decision in that Illinois adopted a personal income tax. (In the early 1960s, MacArthur's home in Chicago was a two-story house, in the style of a mean suburban tract house, which he had built on the roof of one of his insurance company buildings.) A reporter who got a glimpse of the two-bedroom apartment occupied by MacArthur and his wife, Catherine, in the Colonnades, found the paint peeling and the plaster in need of repair.

No one could guess MacArthur's reaction, especially when the subject was money. His one-word reply to an appeal for money from Billy Graham was "Baloney." In 1972 MacArthur kicked the Professional Golfers' Association out of his Florida club when the PGA refused to go along with an increase in the $40,000 a year the association was paying for office space and other privileges. MacArthur changed the name to the John D. MacArthur National Golf Club, not out of egotism, but because he could save a few dollars. On the various club signs his three initials were substituted for PGA. Years before, when the MacArthurs did live in a handsome house in the Chicago suburbs, near Libertyville, Mrs. MacArthur would drive for miles to cash in on supermarket bargains, particularly when specials were offered on MacArthur's Winstons. (It was bad enough that the butler once spilled soup in his lap. MacArthur got rid of the suburban house when he came home unannounced one night and found the servants having a party and drinking "my booze.")

Nevertheless, there was a time when the MacArthurs did sample the high life. In the years after World War II, with his fortune mushrooming, MacArthur even owned, and piloted, his own converted B-25 bomber. But his wife made him give up the plane when he reached 60 for fear he would kill himself. Perhaps she remembered how MacArthur had learned to fly. Eager to fight the Germans when World War I broke out, MacArthur joined the Royal Canadian Flying Corps, got his wings, and was court-martialed after crashing three airplanes. (That's according to his son, Roderick; other versions of the story have it that MacArthur injured his back in a crash, was grounded, and later was kicked out of the military when, persisting in his desire to fight, he tried to smuggle himself aboard a troopship.)

Born March 6, 1897, in Pittston, Pennsylvania, John Donald MacArthur was the youngest of seven children and four remarkable brothers. His father was a farmer and the third in a line of self-ordained ministers. In his career as a wandering evangelist late in life, he failed to store up worldly goods, and John was shipped off to Chicago, where his older brothers had settled and where he attended grade school until he dropped out after the eighth grade.

At age 17 John got his first taste of the business that was to make his fortune. Rather obviously, he was a duck in water. His brother Alfred, having established an insurance agency, signed John on as a door-to-door salesman. Alfred went on to become a multimillionaire as president of the Central Life Insurance Co. of Illinois and left behind him an estate valued at $175 million when he died. Alfred might have become a billionaire if he had been able to keep his younger brother working for him, but that was not the mistake that bothered him. Speaking of John, Alfred once said that the "darkest day in insurance history was when he entered the business."

Within three months of joining Alfred, John was the top salesman in the firm. He sold his product with evangelical fervor, and by his own account he was "probably" the first man in Chicago to sell $1 million in insurance in one year. Even today the sale of $1 million in insurance confers status on a salesman. MacArthur did it when he was 19 years old in 1916. And, "naturally," as he said later, "got the big head." And quit. For a short time before he took off for the Canadian air corps, he was a newspaperman.

Brother Charles, best known to the general public of the four brothers, worked for the old Chicago *Herald and Examiner* and was able to get John a job as a reporter with the paper. Charles, long the husband of actress Helen Hayes, until his early death in 1956, later used his experiences on the Hearst paper in the heyday of mob wars and newspaper wars in Chicago to write the still popular play *The Front Page* with fellow Chicago newspaperman Ben Hecht.

If a genius for getting money was in the MacArthur Scotch genes (John had himself in mind when he once remarked, "Scotsmen are supposed to be tight; cheap is a better word"), the MacArthurs then and now seemed to have a bent toward newspapering. The fourth brother, Telfer, at age 23 founded what became a prosperous chain of suburban Chicago newspapers. After his death his Pioneer Press was sold for a fat sum to Time Inc. (This was the chain, eighteen papers in all, that Time Inc. sold to Marshall Field V in 1985.)

John D.'s son, John Roderick, started out in journalism too. He was for a time a correspondent with the United Press in Paris, and it was a job he remembered for years with fondness and nostalgia. On the occasion of his father's birthday, Rod MacArthur announced to a gala party that his father was the "black sheep" among the four brothers; John had been the last and the slowest to make his fortune. (The party was a gala even though the Chicago society editors could not find many of their people among the 400 guests gathered in the plush Guildhall of the Ambassador West Hotel. The schedule called for a quartet Las Vegas couldn't afford to lead the guests in singing "Happy Birthday." The four were

H. L. Hunt, the Texas oilman and an authentic billionaire; W. Clement Stone, another rags-to-riches Chicago insurance tycoon; Arthur Wirtz, a Chicago real estate investor and sportsman; and Arthur Rubloff, another wealthy, wealthy Chicago real estate owner, developer, and broker. Unfortunately the quartet didn't perform. Hunt, aged 85, trundled himself off to bed before the birthday cake and candles appeared. MacArthur enjoyed the evening immensely. Always an admirer of the opposite sex, he danced with the prettiest ladies, and radio commentator Paul Harvey, sponsored on the air by MacArthur's insurance company for a quarter of a century, picked up the tab for the orchestra, the caviar, and the two-wine dinner.) It is true that John came late to big money. By 1927 and his 30th birthday he was the vice-president of an Illinois insurance company. But he was an employee, on salary, making less than $10,000.

It was not until the early 1940s that MacArthur began to hit the big time. The Great Depression, of course, had something to do with that long, sterile gap. That, for MacArthur, was a piece of bad luck. Hard-nosed, crusty, a supreme realist, MacArthur always said good luck, "the breaks," was a dominant factor in his success. As he once put it, "I'm not saying an absolute dummy can make it. You have to get the breaks, but you have to have enough intelligence to recognize the breaks when they come and work like hell to capitalize on them."

The first of the breaks came for MacArthur when he quit his insurance company vice-presidency after, typically, a squabble with his associates. In old age MacArthur was fond of sermonizing on the theme that no one man can make it on his own; only the combined efforts of a lot of people had made his billions possible. But over the years numbers of good people left MacArthur voluntarily and otherwise. As a boss, he held the benign belief that a man learned best by making his own mistakes, and he gave his people plenty of rope. But MacArthur always held the end of the rope even when he was absent in Florida for months, and sometimes he jerked it for capricious reasons. But parsimony lost him more people.

Headquarters for his giant and rich Bankers Life and Casualty Co. was a rabbit warren of small, run-down buildings in a secondary commercial neighborhood far from the marble-and-glass skyscrapers of Chicago's Loop. In sweltering summertime Chicago, the buildings were not air-conditioned. Ofttimes MacArthur conducted business wearing nothing but his underwear. Further, as his son Roderick testified bitterly, MacArthur did not believe in complicating the lives of his executives by paying them magnificent salaries. Worse, MacArthur was not about to cut anyone in for a piece of the action. More than one executive deserted when it became apparent that he would always be a salaried employee, never a stockholder.

MacArthur was a man tailor-made to run his own shop, no questions asked, and as he once said, his genius was that he didn't lay too many eggs when it came to making important business decisions. Therein was the big break that came MacArthur's way, or rather the big break that MacArthur created when he gave up the vice-presidency of the insurance company in 1927. Negotiating a cash settlement with the firm, he bought his own company, tiny and struggling Marquette Life. For $7,500 MacArthur picked up a few dollars' worth of existing business, some business contacts, and an important asset, a license to write insurance in Illinois. MacArthur loaded the records of the downstate Illinois company into the trunk of his car, all that was necessary to move the company to Chicago, hired some proven salesmen away from other companies, and began his march toward millions. But the Great Depression was something of a detour. Going into 1930, MacArthur always said, the assets of his company amounted to exactly $15.31. But if MacArthur liked running his own show, he had no problem.

Through the early years of the Depression, MacArthur was a one-man gang. Forced to let his salesmen go, he was chairman, president, and sole employee of Marquette Life. He worked, selling insurance wherever and whenever he could. He'd hit a factory yard during the noon lunch break, he'd sell a man a $1,000 policy, he'd tailor a policy so that the first premium, cash on the spot, would fit "whatever the fellow had in his pocket." On a good day, MacArthur himself would pocket five dollars in cash from new policies. In addition, there was an uncertain trickle of dollars that came in through the mails from those policyholders who were able to pay the premiums on their policies.

MacArthur's big break in those days, when few people could spare a dime much less buy an insurance policy, came in 1935. Through the grapevine he heard that the state insurance commission was declaring another insurance company technically insolvent. The owners apparently did not have MacArthur's courage or cash. A MacArthur check for just $2,500 repaired the insolvency and gave MacArthur full ownership of the company—Bankers Life and Casualty. Along with ownership MacArthur acquired a small but welcome number of policyholders who were paying their premiums and more than $20,000 in assets.

It was those dollars that came in through the mail from Marquette and Bankers people that impressed MacArthur. By 1938 MacArthur was not only receiving through the mails; he was also selling.

At age 41, the slow starter was finally into his thing. The money giants of an earlier age—the Fords, Rockefellers, Carnegies, and Vanderbilts—made their hoards by creating whole industries; MacArthur did it by providing a service. He figured that if the sales pitch he used in his weary round of face-to-face encounters would sell five or so policies a day, he might sell dozens, even hundreds, by putting the same message on paper and mailing it out by the thousands together with a coupon or an application blank and a return envelope. Anyone who responded was at the least a target for a MacArthur agent. The idea worked, much to the envy and often to the ethical horror of the insurance industry and the state regulators. But to MacArthur's great satisfaction. "To my amazement," he said, "I suddenly had $70,000 in the bank."

From then on MacArthur gobbled up small insurance companies as fast as he could find them, mainly as a means of quickly getting a license to do business in other states and broaden his mailing list. Eventually there were nineteen MacArthur insurance companies, led by Bankers Life and Casualty. At the time of MacArthur's death the book value of Bankers Life was set at $242 million. That's just the value of the company's assets as carried on the books by MacArthur and his accountants; it doesn't take into account the value of a stream of profits running into the indefinite future and other factors the marketplace might have put on the company if the sole owner had ever decided to sell out. Similarly, the book value of MacArthur's other well-known property, the Citizens Bank and Trust Co., located in suburban Park Ridge, was placed at a meager $36 million.

MacArthur always bridled at putting a figure on his wealth, always a first question when he was interviewed by a reporter. He'd quote his old friend H. L. Hunt, who may have gotten it from another oil millionaire, J. Paul Getty. Hunt was fond of saying that anyone who knew how much he was worth wasn't worth much. MacArthur, in his best humble manner, would say he wasn't very good at numbers anyway, he didn't know how many rooms there were in his Colonnades Beach Hotel. But he would admit that he owned about 200,000 acres of Florida real estate, a number that rightly earned him the reputation of being the largest individual landowner in the state. But then he would say he didn't really think of himself as rich. It was just that the company he worked for, Bankers Life, was "stinking" rich.

MacArthur always had a difficult time letting go of money, no matter what his circumstances, unless he wanted to possess something. In the 1930s he divorced his first wife, Louise, the mother of his two children. Those were anything but palmy days for MacArthur, and he felt poor enough to allow his former mother-in-law to support her daughter and the two children. No one knows what his excuse was in 1974— that was the year he sold his AM and FM radio stations in Palm Beach, Florida, to NBC sportscaster Curt Gowdy for $15 million. MacArthur's daughter, Mrs. Virginia Cordova, lived in Mexico, supporting herself in part by giving English lessons. Her son and MacArthur's grandson, Greg Cordova, disappeared in 1974, never to be found, during a hitchhiking trip within Mexico. MacArthur refused to put up a dime to finance a search for Greg. But when there was something MacArthur wanted, he could act differently. In 1968 sentiment and an eye for what was a relic of a bygone era led MacArthur to buy the garden snack bar of the old Roney Plaza Hotel, Miami Beach's first grand hotel, when the hotel's equipment was being auctioned off, and to spend $5,000 to float the bar up the coast from Miami Beach to Palm Beach.

MacArthur's other child, John Roderick MacArthur, once said his father did give him financial help. Twice, but only twice.

Once when they were together in Las Vegas, MacArthur gave his son $100 for betting money. (Rod lost it at the crap tables.) Then, the second time, when Rod was living in Paris in the late 1940s and decided to try his hand at writing a novel. Married to a French woman, he was earning $60 a week working for the United Press. His father agreed to support his dream of writing a best-selling novel and came through with a stipend of $500 a month. At the end of one year Rod had not finished the novel and the checks stopped.

Roderick's claim that his father helped him out only twice is not strictly accurate. When Rod decided it was time to return to the United States with his wife and their three children, his father at least agreed to get a job for him. Rod was installed as editor, at $125 a week, of *Theatre Arts,* a magazine that playwright Charles MacArthur had talked his brother into financing. Eight months later Rod was summarily fired. After a year's stint as a public relations man in

Manhattan, Rod came home to Chicago. Father gave Rod a job with his thriving Citizens Bank and Trust Co., then the largest bank in Illinois outside of the city of Chicago. Sole owner MacArthur paid his 40-year-old son $190 a week.

In 1962 MacArthur summoned Rod to Florida to work as his general assistant, and Rod put in two years hanging around in what he calls a "phony" job, the superfluous assistant to a one-man band. Rod fled back to Chicago with his family but signed on as a consultant to Bankers Life and to Citizens Bank.

Always, it seemed, father kept son on the string and on short rations. Or son allowed himself to be kept in that strained position. On this score, the son was ambivalent. Father was selfish, narrow-minded, ill-tempered, according to Rod, but sometimes charming, good-humored, even kind-hearted. And more right than wrong in not showering easy millions on his children. With a characteristic grin, Rod said on occasion that it was probably good for him to learn the hard way.

In any event, Rod was allowed to step out on his own to a degree during the six years he served as a consultant to the bank and the insurance company.

"I developed two new businesses for Father," Rod said years later. "There was a new kind of savings account, a bank-by-mail account, for the Citizens Bank, and a new mail-order insurance policy for Bankers Life. The bank account remained for years the only bank savings account that paid interest but allowed the depositor to write checks on it. I spent years fighting the Federal Reserve Board on that one, and once they rewrote the regulations just to try to put me out of business. In theory it was as illegal as hell, but I kept working it out. The last I heard the bank had $160 million in the system with depositors from all over the world, Paris to Hong Kong.

"The mail-order insurance policy was a supplement to Medicare. Within the first ten months we had half a million persons enrolled. That meant the health policy was producing $1.5 million in premiums each month.

"I was being paid $25,000 a year and all that time I never got a raise. I kept going to the old man and saying, 'Gee, Dad, look at all these wonderful things; how about a raise?' And he would say, 'No, you don't need a raise; you would only have to pay more taxes.' I decided then that the next time I had an idea for a business I would own it myself instead of developing it for Dad.

"In 1971 and 1972 [by then Rod had passed his 50th birthday], I started working with a little direct-order mail outfit Dad had called Macmart. It sold things by direct mail and it hadn't been doing very well. The theory was that if you had a list of good names from the life insurance policyholders you should be able to sell them something. Between the insurance company and the bank we thought we knew all about direct-mail selling. But it turned out we didn't know much of anything about product selection or the difficulties of collecting from people on the sale of consumer products. I came up with a couple of ideas that were less than successful; for instance, a stereo system tied in with a cheap psychedelic light.

"Then I got the idea of trying to sell collector's plates by mail.

"I made a deal with Dad. If he'd back me, I'd guarantee to pay him the $500,000 we had lost so far on the direct-mail scheme and also give him half the profits on our sales of the first series of collector's plates.

"But then I'd walk away with all the marbles and keep the company for my own. He agreed to that, and I made a deal with the Limoges people I had known in France to make a series of Lafayette plates for me.

"The series went very well and eventually it became the most sought after memento of the U.S. Bicentennial celebration. We went a certain distance and I decided to raise my salary from $25,000 to $50,000. Apparently, that was the wrong thing to do. Father decided the whole company was his. [At the time, MacArthur's salary as chairman of Bankers Life alone was $300,000 a year.]

"But I had done some planning this time. I had found a life insurance company that Father had bought years before. There was nothing left there, just a shell corporation. I bought the shell for a couple of hundred bucks. I owned it. Then I changed the name to the Bradford Exchange and put the collector's plate business in it.

"When the showdown with Father came we had a surplus account of $500,000, plus our regular operating account, in the Citizens Bank, which he owned, of course. Father closed both the accounts, so we had no money to operate the business. Then came the day of the Great Crockery Raid when we stole the business back from my father. Father had us locked out of our warehouse. But we showed the police our papers and convinced them that the plates were ours, and we took seven truckloads of plates worth $750,000 out of there. But that was all back there in 1975. Father was a tough one, but not too tough. Afterwards he claimed he didn't have a thing to do with it, it was all his accountants and lawyers trying to protect his interests.

"We had some other problems in the beginning. When I started to sell the Lafayette plates I guaranteed they would double in value. The United States Securities and Exchange Commission said the guarantee made the plates an unregistered security and I was doing the same thing as offering stock to the public with a guarantee that it would double in value. They said if I kept it up they'd simply put me in jail. That took a little doing to get around. I had to write all the customers and tell them I could no longer make the guarantee, but I said I'd give them their money back if they wanted it. More than 95 percent of the people hung in there. Finally, the market price of the Lafayette plates did double, so I was happy. The beauty is that these darn things do go up in price. So we made a flat guarantee that if you return the plate in one year we will pay you at least the original price.

"Originally, I was so ignorant of the collector's plate mar-

ket that I went into it just as it was on the brink of collapsing.
It was in the late 1960s that the market for plates and other
art objects really took off. It seemed that everybody had
established a mint to produce commemorative medals and
plates and everybody got to overproducing. Then you had
the general economic recession in 1974 and 1975 and everything was crashing. Dealers were going broke right and left
and companies that produced the plates were going out of
business. The Lafayette series was strong, however, and we
were blissfully unaware of what was really going on. Manufacturers would come to us and say how would you like to
buy our plates at 10 cents on the dollar and we'd do it. There
were even silver plates on the market that couldn't be sold
for the value of the silver in them. We began to do business
on a bigger and bigger scale. We'd buy a thousand plates that
originally listed at $25 for $5 and we sell them for $15.
Eventually, we were instrumental in cleaning out the entire
overhang, all the surplus plates, and the market recovered.
All of a sudden those plates we sold for $15 were back up to
$25 and beyond. It helped that the manufacturers who re-
mained in the business sobered up and cut way back on new
production.

"And we started the Exchange. That created a secondary
market and a more reliable market. In our tiny world, the
world of plate collecting, we are the New York Stock Exchange. Of course, you can't just pick up a telephone and tell
a broker to buy or sell a plate the way you can a stock. We
maintain a list of buyers and sellers. When a customer sends
the Bradford Exchange an offer to sell a plate, for instance,
we will do our best to match the offer with a buy order. For
our services, we get 3 percent of the price from the buyer
and 20 percent from the seller. That's not bad when you
consider what prices for some plates have done. For instance, a Haviland china Christmas-scene plate issued in
1925 at $25 sold in 1978 at $240. We constantly monitor
prices all over the country and we publish a directory that
carries a price list of some 950 different plates.

"It is a broad market. About 80 percent of our revenues comes from the sale of plates—we don't manufacture ourselves now except in rare instances; what we do is sponsor an issue made by one of the major houses and we'll take on an allotment to sell. The other 20 percent of our revenues comes from the Exchange. In 1977 Limoges sold its one millionth plate through us. There must be two or three million collectors in the United States alone. Hell, our own mailing list covers one million names, not all of them customers. In 1977 the gross value of the plates we handle came to about $25 million. That went up to roughly $45 million in 1978 and we could go to $50 or $55 million if we wanted to go for volume only."

Plate, barrel, and building, Rod MacArthur owned his own company and it made him a multimillionaire in his own right. "I disagreed with my father on a lot of things, but that's the way he always ran his business and I do agree with it," Rod said some years before his death. "If my company should get into trouble, I can hold a meeting of the board of directors in a telephone booth, discuss things with myself for ten minutes, and adjourn the meeting with a decision."

Roderick MacArthur was 57 years old when his father died in 1978. Finally, finally, the old man told his son that he was proud of him. He left him money he did not need. A neat, smallish man with wavy white hair, a pleasant, strong face, and eyes that sparkled when he laughed, as he did frequently, Rod enjoyed his world. When he took his French wife to Paris, he would fly on the all-first-class, extra-fare Concorde and live in the apartment he kept in Paris.

John D. MacArthur stayed in pragmatic character to the end. His will stated that his body should be handed over for medical research and that there should be no funeral. He wanted, the will said, "to spare my friends and relatives the inconveniences involved in attending a funeral."

But he did decide to let go of a large chunk of his money—slowly and carefully over the years. The golden egg, the Bankers Life and Casualty Co., was left to the John D. and

Catherine MacArthur Foundation, and the stock in the Citizens Bank and Trust Co. went into another charitable foundation, the Retirement Research Foundation.

Beyond a few minor bequests ($5,000 went to his former wife, Louise), the rest of the estate was divided one-half to his widow, one-fourth to Roderick, and one-fourth to his daughter, Virginia Cordova. Once Rod went for a ride around Manhattan with his father and found himself amazed as John pointed out building after building (e.g., the Gulf & Western Building, 410 Park Avenue) that MacArthur owned. The family's share of the estate included, Rod said, "more real estate than I ever heard of in my life, but it is still peanuts compared with the whole." (Actually, many of MacArthur's real estate investments, from Michigan to Colorado to Texas, were made through Bankers Life, rather than personally.)

Whatever the value of the real estate, it has to have gone up tremendously over the years. MacArthur always said he had a Braille-like feel for sick properties that could be turned into something. That's the way he first got into Florida real estate. In the early 1950s he had made a personal loan to Carl Byoir, the public relations man he later sued for libel. When Byoir's development plans turned turtle, MacArthur foreclosed on the loan, acquiring the collateral, the land on the unfashionable north side of Palm Beach that he later expanded into a 15,000-acre, 3,400 unit development, Palm Beach Gardens.

Certainly the estate was big. In 1985 the MacArthur Foundation sold off ten of those Manhattan buildings that had so impressed Rod MacArthur. The selling price was indeed impressive. The foundation picked up $480 million. In the years since the death of MacArthur, the foundation accumulated $1.3 billion from the sale of MacArthur's real estate and other assets. Even if it invested only at bank rates, the foundation would have money to burn for years. In 1983 alone it authorized $57,185,854 in grants.

This included nearly $10 million for Rod MacArthur's favorite project. A hardheaded businessman, an entrepreneur with a wide-ranging imagination, and a romantic who always wished he could have had the money to stay on in Paris to write his novel, Rod pushed the formation of the MacArthur Fellowship program and the MacArthur Laureate Awards. Winners, picked on the recommendation of anonymous judges, are given bountiful awards to do with as they will. For instance, the happy recipient of a laureate might get $60,000 a year for life.

In just a few years fellowships were awarded to people doing work in such diverse fields as Mayan hieroglyphics and astrophysics. Still, Rod felt the foundation board had a limited view of the world and he sued to have the board thrown out.

On December 6, 1984, MacArthur withdrew his lawsuit. "I believe the foundation would be best served if I wipe the slate clean while I am still able to do so," he said in a letter to the foundation.

He was suffering from cancer of the pancreas, the same affliction that had killed his father, and he knew he had only a few days to live. Nine days later MacArthur was dead at age 63.

On his own, without his father's help or in spite of his father, he had built a noteworthy empire. He had turned the mail-order selling of decorative and commemorative plates into a $100 million business. One of his innovations was the creation of the Bradford Exchange, an organization that aped a stock exchange as nearly as practical, offering amateur and professional collectors a best-effort way to buy or sell plates at a public price.

At MacArthur's death, the Exchange was handling upwards of 9,000 transactions a day in plates created by such as the Norman Rockwell Society and Limoges of France and it had established itself in Great Britain and on the Continent.

MacArthur, amused by and attracted to the store's displays of far-out and luxurious products, also bought Manhattan's famous Hammacher Schlemmer retail store, paying

$4.8 million to extract it from the Gulf & Western conglomerate.

He promptly opened a version of the gadget lovers' shop on Michigan Avenue in Chicago and christened it MacArthur's Hammacher Schlemmer. To outsiders the purchase looked like something a playboy millionaire might do. MacArthur, an expert in the direct-mail or catalogue business, knew that the greater part of Hammacher Schlemmer's promising business was done by mail order.

MacArthur, a perhaps unwelcome member of the board of directors of the MacArthur Foundation, persuaded the foundation along with the Arco Foundation to rescue *Harper's Magazine,* then (1980) in danger of folding.

The MacArthur Foundation is, of course, a force to be reckoned with for years. On a slighter scale, so is the family. Rod MacArthur's French wife, Christiane, known to friends as Cri-cri, divides her time between Chicago and Paris. The MacArthur children are in their early thirties. Daughter Solange is a physician. Son Grégoire, or Greg, in his father's footsteps, is with the Associated Press in Paris. Son John Roderick is the hard-working publisher of *Harper's.*

The four of them gather from time to time in Chicago to see how the family fortune is prospering at the Bradford Exchange and how it is being spent at the foundation.

V

THE GANG

The cliché is that no one can afford to live today the way the rich did in a bygone era. True enough, depending on who, what, and where the comparison is made. Sure, the heirs of Lolita Armour Higgason were glad to get the million dollars an auction of her household possessions raised in 1976 after her death. J. Ogden Armour's daughter was almost 80 when she died and ready cash was needed to pay the taxes on her estate. There was no way her son and daughter could live as she did or had once done: in years past, twenty-five full-time gardeners had tended the fifty-five acres of El Mirador, her estate overlooking the Pacific near Santa Barbara.

Still, there are people, an ever-increasing number of people in the late 1980s, who can live any way they wish to. If you are wealthy and also pushing 80, maybe you try to live on the interest on the interest and shun any unnecessary expense. As one Chicago widow of advanced age remarked when a young stockbroker sought to interest her in an investment that promised generous returns in future years, "Son, I don't even buy green bananas."

Certainly Gaylord Donnelley and others with a share of

the hundreds of millions of dollars represented by R. R. Donnelley & Sons, the nation's largest printer, could live as they might want. The same could be said of W. Clement Stone, who made use of the power of positive thinking to build Combined International into a fortune that allowed him to be the largest single contributor to Richard Nixon's campaign chests. Even after those millions disappeared with no thanks from the Nixons and after Stone had contributed more millions to various other public causes, he still had, at age 81, a fortune worth on paper more than $40 million in the stock of his company when it was merged with Patrick G. Ryan's insurance group in 1984. Pat Ryan and his wife were a popular couple on the social circuit. At the time of the merger Ryan was only 46 years old, but for openers he had close to $20 million in Combined International common stock and his position in the business world was denominated by his membership on the boards of the First Chicago Corp., the Gould Corp., and Commonwealth Edison along with his serving as a trustee of Rush-Presbyterian-St. Luke's Medical Center.

Michael P. Richer lives up to his name. Three years after he helped to form Allnet Communication Services in 1981 he bought the top floor of the Outer Drive East condo building, once the home of a luxury French restaurant overlooking Lake Michigan, as just the place to remodel for a residence for his young family (he was 39 years old then). Richer and his colleague, Melvyn Goodman, have had their financial ups and downs. When Allnet went public Richer owned 15 million shares of stock and Goodman and his father a like amount. At $10 a share, they were well off. But the stock dropped to $4 a share; there's no telling how they felt about seeing a fortune of $150 million shrink to a paltry $60 million. Very probably Richer's $300,000 salary helped to sustain him.

Richer and Goodman came out of nowhere, saw an opportunity, seized it, and made a phenomenal success on their own almost overnight. Going back at least to the first Marshall Field, Chicago has had its groups of men who worked together, lending each other money when needed, investing in the companies and schemes each might promote. Colonel Henry Crown and the Pritzkers, for instance, have been very close over the years, particularly in joint investments in real estate.

In the years, the 1950s and 1960s, when the late J. Patrick Lannan was a feared corporate raider—"raider" was the word then and covered the tactics that became known in the 1980s as "greenmail," the "leveraged buy-out," and the "unfriendly tender offer"—and was establishing the fortune that among other things made him at one point the owner of the old *Collier's* magazine and at another the largest single shareholder in the multibillion-dollar ITT Corp., he always had a group that followed him or went with him, putting up the money to seal a deal or simply profiting from Lannan's eye for a dollar. (Much to the chagrin of his children, Lannan left the bulk of a $70 million fortune to a foundation to support his Palm Beach art museum, his suspect theory being that he had been generous to his offspring during his life.)

Ralph Bogan, Jr., or earlier, his father (Greyhound), was a Lannan investor. Bogan Jr., a marathon runner and a fan of helicopter skiing, was more properly a member of another informal investment group operating in the 1970s and 1980s.

When Bogan moved in and revitalized the National Security Bank of Chicago, a neighborhood institution that was going nowhere, he had power with him. There was, for instance, William Bartholomay, millionaire director of the Chicago operations of the Frank B. Hall insurance firm, and Thomas A. Reynolds, Jr., 56 years old in 1985, managing partner of the top-drawer law firm Winston & Strawn and a director of a number of corporations, including Butler International, Atlanta–La Salle Corp., the Jefferson Smurfit Corp. and the Reading Co. There are some interesting connections there. Atlanta–La Salle is the holding company Reynolds, Bogan, and the group set up to acquire the Milwaukee Braves baseball team before they moved it to Atlanta, where the television potential was greater. Reynolds is still chairman of Ted Turner's baseball team. That Jefferson Smurfit name belongs to a Dublin family, and the company is a $750 million paperboard and packaging corporation operating in the United States. A company acquired some years back by Smurfit was Time Industries, a $30 million packing company started and built by Don Hindman with a little help from his friends. Hindman is also a director with Reynolds on the Smurfit board.

The Reading Co. is the old Pennsylvania Railroad, long since bankrupt. Reynolds and others bought control of the company years ago, and one prominent member of the group, John W. Sullivan, former president of the Skil (tools) Corp., moved to Philadelphia to direct a multimillion-dollar downtown real estate development on property that the Reading Co. just happened to own by way of track and terminal rights.

Another investor with the group from time to time, and once a part owner of the Bogan bank and the Braves baseball team, was Potter Palmer, great-grandson of *the* Potter Palmer. In contrast to his flamboyant great-grandfather and his society queen great-grandmother, this Palmer manages to stay pretty well out of the limelight in spite of his sometimes odd and public investments. However, if he is more reserved than his forebears, he does carry at least one or two of their genes, the ones that have to do with making money.

(Mrs. Bertha Honore Palmer, the Kentucky beauty Palmer married when she was 21 and he was 44, may have made more money after Potter's death than he did in his lifetime. Even as she kept up her position in Chicago and international society and also campaigned effectively for women's suffrage and what would now be known as women's rights, Bertha did well for her children. When she died in 1918 the press gave the value of her estate in probate at $20 million. Supposedly she had inherited $8 million when her husband died sixteen years earlier. The $20 million didn't put a price on her collection of Monets, Manets, Degases, and Renoirs, among other paintings. Nor could it possibly have estimated the value of the land she had bought in Florida. At her death she owned 70,000 acres in and around Sarasota and Tampa. Among those who inherited some of the land: her sister Ida, the widow of General Grant's son, Frederick Dent Grant.)

At one time or another the current Potter Palmer was part owner of the Harlem Globetrotters, a couple of radio stations, a toy store, a computer software firm, and Le Perroquet, frequently called the city's best restaurant.

A founder of the restaurant and a couple more was Jovan, a Yugoslav who escaped from the Germans and the Tito forces during World War II by stealing the Yugoslav Navy's ancient submarine and with a green crew piloting it to British hands in Egypt. A silent partner in Jovan's enterprises was socialite and investment banker Gordon Bent. Bent is a voluble and humorous man suspected of wishing he could have gone on from Hasty Pudding to a stage career. Breaking out of the conservative North Shore mold, Bent may have sponsored the best-remembered debuts in recent society history. He flew one of his daughters with a planeful of her friends to the Caribbean for her coming-out party; for another daughter he flew a smaller party to more distant shores in the Mediterranean.

A few eyebrows were raised and any number of jokes were made in 1984 when Potter Palmer completed a major real estate deal. His Yankee great-grandfather had changed the face of Chicago, widening and improving muddy, run-down State Street and making it the premier retail street, and had then dramatically demonstrated his faith in the city and real estate by borrowing a nearly unheard-of sum, close to $2 million, to rebuild the street and replace the thirty-two buildings, including the almost-new Palmer House, that he lost in the Great Chicago Fire.

The Potter Palmer jokes in 1984 concerned his heir's belief in real estate and future growth. What he bought was the Rosehill Cemetery and Mausoleum. Although Rosehill was established in 1860, it is not quite the rival of Graceland Cemetery, the last resting place of an astonishing number of Chicago's wealthiest Wasps, including McCormicks, Fields, Pullmans, Armours, and Palmer's illustrious forebear. Rosehill does have its claim to prestige; more than a dozen mayors are buried there and so are two giants of national retailing, Montgomery Ward and Richard Sears.

At the time he purchased Rosehill, Palmer told the newspapers that one reason he had bought the cemetery was that he was able to buy it outright and he had never before owned 100 percent of a business. Beyond that, he said, the cemetery had a proven record of earnings and should have an "excellent future" in that there were still 80,000 spaces left for burial although 170,000 persons were already buried on the 375 acres.

John J. Louis, Jr., has joined in the group's usually profitable ventures from time to time. Louis happens to be a director of S. C. Johnson & Son, Inc., better known as Johnson's Wax. By virtue of marriage, Louis and his wife are major shareholders in the company, one of the country's very largest family-owned enterprises. But even without the Johnson millions Louis is a wealthy man, having founded in 1968 Combined Communication Corp., a company with healthy radio and television properties. A cultured and competent man, Louis was a major contributor to the Ronald Reagan campaign and served as Reagan's ambassador to the Court of St. James's. Somehow that didn't work out and Louis quit in late 1983.

Louis has been both a friend and a client (corporate) of Arthur C. Nielsen, Jr. Or he was a client until Nielsen retired in 1984 as chief executive officer of A. C. Nielsen Company, the company that piles up revenues of more than half a billion dollars primarily by snooping on the habits of the public. That same public knows Nielsen for the Nielsen television rating service, which with its ratings supposedly makes or breaks a TV program. That may make the company as powerful from a sociological standpoint as any in the country, but Nielsen earns its big money on other market-research services.

Among a hundred or so specialized services sold to businesses in this country and dozens of other countries, the big one for Nielsen is the inventory-control service that Nielsen runs to tell companies like Procter & Gamble and Colgate-Palmolive how their toothpaste is selling in the drugstores and the supermarkets. That may depend, of course, in good part on what television programs Nielsen tells them have the biggest audiences and therefore the biggest draw for their commercials. It may say something about the fates that a television set once saved the life of the Nielsen family. Nielsen was able to get his family out of the house barely in time when the heat of a fire raging in the home in the middle of the night exploded the tube of a television set with a report loud enough to wake Nielsen.

The Nielsen company was founded in Chicago in 1923 by Arthur Nielsen, Sr., who graduated from the University of Wisconsin with the highest marks in the history of the engineering school. Art Jr. and his father won the U.S. father-and-son tennis championship in 1946 and 1948, but they may have a place in history beyond that and beyond the impact of their rating services on everyday life.

They created the computer. And if anything is more intrusive in society today than television, it is the computer.

The story goes like this: During World War II, Art Jr. served in the Corps of Engineers, eventually becoming a major. He built a lot of buildings, including one at Edgewood Arsenal in Maryland. The weird thing about the building was that it had to have a vast network of wiring. As Nielsen eventually learned, the Army was going to install a fantastic machine put together out of hundreds of vacuum tubes that would allow the Artillery Corps to do dozens of calibrations on thousands of artillery pieces in a flash. Art Jr. came home from the wars to tell his father about the machine. Two University of Pennsylvania professors, Eckert and Mauchly, having built the thirty-ton Eniac, knew how to build one, and it could do in a flash all those calculations about toothpaste and soap that the Nielsen company hired hundreds of clerks to do in those days.

Nielsen Sr. agreed to put up research money. It was, for the times and for the Neilsen company, a large sum of money, all of $250,000.

Hired on, the two professors spent three times that much of Nielsen's money and they were still wiring vacuum tubes. Desperate, Nielsen enlisted others to bankroll the project. One interested outfit was the old American Totalizer company, the firm that flashed the odds on the tote boards at racetracks. Finally Nielsen became convinced that a business machine corporation might see some potential in this very expensive Rube Goldberg contraption.

No one was interested, none of the biggies like IBM, except for the corporation known variously over the years as Remington Rand, Sperry Rand, and most recently the Sperry Corp. The corporation had hired General Douglas MacArthur, and MacArthur had hired General Leslie Groves, who had been head of the Manhattan Project during World War II. As such, Groves knew more than a little about the ability of a collection of vacuum tubes to compute. Sperry (Remington Rand Honeywell) bailed Nielsen out. As the Smithsonian Institution notes, Univac I, 8 feet by 7 1/2 feet by 14 1/2 feet, went to the U.S. Census Bureau, not the Nielsen company.

In return for an agreement to cancel the contract Nielsen had calling for delivery of commercial computer No. 1, clearing the way for its sale to the Census Bureau, Sperry gave Nielsen back all his research money. At the time Art Nielsen was delighted.

Daniel C. Searle was another young (at that time) Chicagoan who, wealthy by inheritance or bootstrap effort, invested in various projects with the Reynolds-Bartholomay-Bogan group. For instance, he was a stockholder and direc-

tor of the Atlanta Braves baseball team. For Searle, the Atlanta investment was a tax proposition and fun. He had all
the money he might want and was to have more later on.

Searle followed the advice of Marshall Field V. He chose
his parents wisely. That made him the great-grandson of one
Gideon D. Searle. Gideon Searle was a Civil War veteran
who apparently thought there might be something of more
medical worth than the Civil War's prime cure: amputation
of the offending part. After his own war wounds healed,
Gideon acquired a drugstore in Fortville, Indiana, in 1868.
By 1888 he had half a dozen or more stores and had made
the not unreasonable assumption that he could make additional money by manufacturing some of the nostrums he
sold. G. D. Searle & Company was the result. His son, Dr. C.
Howard Searle, took over the thriving company in 1917
after his father's death. Howard's son John was president of
Searle by 1936, and his son, Daniel, moved into the president's chair in 1966, with John moving up to chairman. John
served as chairman until 1972 and held the title honorary
chairman of the board when he died at age 76 in 1978.

In the modern era G. D. Searle & Co. concentrated on
cardiovascular pharmacology. Two of its over-the-counter
drugs established Searle with the general public, Dramamine for motion sickness and Metamucil for constipation.
Then in 1960 the Searle company leaped to the front pages
and attention in world markets, financial and otherwise. It
was first to introduce an oral contraceptive, and its Enovid
pill changed the company and played a substantial role in
changing society.

With Daniel Searle leading the way, the company tried
diversification, expanding research activities and moving
into the hospital supply field and eye care at the retail level.
In 1976 the company was in the charge of Daniel Searle, as
chief executive officer, William L. Searle, his brother, as
chairman, and Wesley M. Dixon, Jr., their brother-in-law, as
president. But profits that year dropped an alarming 24
percent to $61.5 million on sales of $761 million. The family,

outside directors, and the financial community concluded that the corporation was in need of treatment for various diseases of the aging process.

The solution came very quickly.

In June 1977, the board, for the first time in company history, turned over active management to an outsider, a non-member of the family, Donald Rumsfeld. Then 45 years old, Rumsfeld had done yeoman service for President Nixon in shaping up some government bureaucracies, had moved on to become U.S. ambassador to NATO, and had then served as Defense Secretary for President Gerald Ford. As president and chief executive officer of Searle, Rumsfeld set about putting the house in order; in his first year he trimmed staffs top to bottom, put twenty Searle "businesses" on the block, and provided for a loss of $59 million to cover the red ink.

If 1977 was the year that Rumsfeld devoted to pruning, he also succeeded in putting a new push behind the drive to gain approval from the Food and Drug Administration for Searle's low-calorie sweetener, aspartame. By 1985 Searle had struck a gold mine called NutraSweet. The food-processing and soft-drink industries had accepted it, and consumer-product sales, led by NutraSweet, produced $585 million of Searle's combined sales of more than $1.2 billion. The only cap on the sale of NutraSweet to a market of almost unlimited, worldwide dimensions was the appearance of a competitive sugar substitute.

Having stepped aside, Dan Searle and his uncles, cousins, and aunts decided they would just as soon have money in the pocket as stock in a safe-deposit box. Along came the Monsanto Co., the big chemical company based in St. Louis. Monsanto was looking for a way to diversify. In tune with the merger madness of the 1980s, Monsanto happily agreed to pay $65 a share for Searle's stock. The offer worked out to a tidy sum for members of the family in that the family owned almost 9 million shares of the stock.

Charles Rudolph Walgreen III certainly didn't have to work for a living. In 1901 his grandfather, the owner of a drugstore on the South Side of Chicago, conceived and held a couple of ideas. He thought he could make a lot of money if he owned several drugstores. Furthermore, he thought the stores could dispense something more than prescription drugs, nostrums, and sodas and ice cream. In 1984 Charles III, born in 1935, presided at modest ceremonies when the Walgreen Co. opened "drugstore" No. 1,000. It was located on the Near North Side of Chicago, but at the time the company had stores in thirty states and Puerto Rico. Sales were certainly on the impressive side.

That year Walgreens rang up sales of more than $2.7 billion. It did a big prescription business, but Grandfather would no doubt have been more thrilled with its shelves crowded with everything from liquor to appliances.

Charles III, having picked up a degree in pharmacy at the University of Michigan, went to work full-time for the company in 1958. Years later he inherited a lethargic company that was well satisfied with itself. What it did best was generate a profit that permitted a solid balance sheet and consistent dividends. As president and chairman, Charles certainly kept a good eye on the bottom line, and at one stretch the dividend to stockholders was raised ten times in seven years. But the heir also stirred things up and set Walgreens on the road to that thousandth store opening. The sales total of $2.7 billion in 1984 wasn't half bad in comparison with $835 million in 1975.

In many families the children want nothing to do with the family business. Horse racing or Tahiti or the Riviera have greater allure. But, like Charles Walgreen, William Wrigley went right into the family business after college (Yale). Born in 1933, Wrigley was elected a member of the board of directors in 1960 and became president and chief executive officer of the corporation the following year.

That put him, at age 28, in charge of the worldwide chewing-gum empire when he was one year younger than his grandfather, William Wrigley, Jr., had been when he arrived in Chicago in 1891 hoping to make his fortune in the country's fastest-growing city.

Grandfather was a soap salesman with, to say the least, an interesting background. He hailed from Philadelphia, where his father was a manufacturer of soap. The eldest of nine children, he must have baffled his father. Described as energetic, mischievous, and strong-minded, he was repeatedly kicked out of elementary school. One year he ran away from home and spent the summer in New York City, sleeping on the streets and doing odd jobs to earn enough for food. Back in Philadelphia he lasted only a short time in school. His father put him to work at manual labor in the soap factory. At age 13 he somehow persuaded his father to let him combine his restless wanderlust with useful work. He toured the nearby countryside selling his father's soap to crossroads stores. Wrigley was for sure a salesman. He did well enough so that he was soon driving a horse and buggy all over Pennsylvania and New York with forays into the New England states. However, there was the one time when he took off and headed for the gold and silver mines of Colorado. He got as far as Kansas City before deciding to give up silver to return to soap.

It took thirteen years all told for Wrigley to make his big break. He had only $32 in his pocket when he landed in Chicago in the spring of 1891. Announcing himself as a wholesaler of soaps, he rented a desk in an office in a building on Kinzie Street almost in the shadow of the Michigan Avenue towers the company later built.

Without a doubt Wrigley was a great personal salesman and his basic approach was sound, even brilliant. He honestly sought to give the customer a good product at a fair price, and he sought out products that he could give away as premiums to his customers. But early in his efforts he was almost wiped out at least five times, two of those being by fires. Once one of his promotional schemes almost ruined him. One of his premiums was an umbrella—fine except that the dye dripped from the umbrella along with the rain.

What's perhaps more interesting than the disaster is the fact that his business was such that he had bought 65,000 of the umbrellas.

In any event, it was the premium idea that set Wrigley's course to fortune. He had given up on soap when he offered baking powder as a premium with his soap products and found that there was a bigger demand for the baking powder than for the soap.

When he tried chewing gum to sell baking powder, he had found his home. In no time at all he was able to buy the chewing-gum firm, the Zeno Company, and just eleven years after he had opened his office on Kinzie Street, he expanded his sales territory to include New York.

The New York invasion says something about Wrigley and about the company, then and now. By 1902 Wrigley had decided that advertising to the gum chewer was the way to build sales of gum. He put together an advertising budget of $100,000, a considerable sum at the time, for the attack on New York. It didn't work. Wrigley retreated, accumulated another $100,000, and returned to the attack. Again he failed. Back Wrigley came, the third time with an ad budget of $250,000. He was going to win and he did.

Two often-quoted comments of Wrigley on his business philosophy wouldn't make the *Harvard Business Review* but do make immediate sense. Talking about a stick of wood, not a stick of gum, Wrigley said, "In no deal did I ever figure our own profit first. I always mapped out a proposition whereby the dealer or jobber would make a mighty good thing. . . . We must give them the thick end of the stick. No matter how thin our end is, remember we have thin ends coming in from everywhere. And many littles make a lot."

Then there was Wrigley on advertising: "Tell them quick and tell them often. You must have a good product in the first place and something that people want, for it is easier to row downstream than up. Explain to folks plainly and sincerely what you have to sell, do it in as few words as possible, and keep everlastingly coming at them."

His son, Philip Knight (P.K.) Wrigley, and P.K.'s son, William, have certainly been everlastingly telling "them" to double their pleasure with Doublemint and the other Wrigley offerings, and few companies have worked as hard to have a "good product in the first place." During World War II the gum that carried the Wrigley name went to the military, 600 million sticks of it, while a gum made with ingredients available to the civilian market carried the substitute name, Orbit. Later on, when the company started experimenting with such as sugarless gum, the work was done by a subsidiary called Amurol Products.

P. K. Wrigley, born in 1894, flunked out of Phillips Academy at Andover, Massachusetts, where he was supposed to prepare for a degree at Yale. Instead he took some courses at the University of Chicago in chemistry and lived with the joke that he sometimes forgot how to spell his name. Nevertheless, P.K. ran the company from the late 1920s until his 67th year—for just as long as he ran the Chicago Cubs National League baseball team. The team had been acquired in stages during the 1920s by William Jr., who died in 1932 at age 71.

P.K. had a personal fortune estimated in the years immediately after World War II at $100 million. The fortune included such niceties as Catalina Island, 400,000 shares of Texaco, the estates at Lake Geneva and Scottsdale, and of course control of the world's largest chewing-gum company.

In 1957 P.K. knocked $1 million off the price Walter O'Malley, intent on moving the Brooklyn Dodgers to Los Angeles and looking for a home for the team, was being asked to pay for Wrigley's Los Angeles Angels, a minor-league team. P.K., who loved baseball and who as a young man had played it when he could, thought Californians deserved a chance to see major-league baseball and a million dollars certainly could be tossed away to assure the Brooklyn deal.

In the Wrigley Restaurant in the Wrigley Building (owned mortgage-free) they still toast special saltine crackers the way P.K. liked them and serve them daily at lunch at the Wrigley table even though P.K. died at age 82 in 1977. Many things are still done the way they always were around the William Wrigley, Jr., empire. P.K.'s death precipitated the most noticeable. The death of his wife, Helen Blanche Atwater Wrigley, at 75, less than two months later, complicated the family's tax problems and forced the sale of a number of assets.

But other reasons no doubt had more to do with the subsequent sale of the Cubs baseball team to the Chicago *Tribune* than taxes and any need for cash. Even though the Cubs had been owned by the Wrigleys longer than any other major sports franchise had been held by one entity, William Wrigley was not sentimental about the team or baseball. And there were problems, including the Cubs' deeply embedded inclination to lose baseball games. More important to the Wrigleys was the certainty of a slam-bang fight over Wrigley Field, the only major-league park without lights for nighttime play. In the 1980s the words Wrigley Field were fighting words in Chicago and elsewhere in the world of baseball: the team would move or lights would be installed over the violent objections of the neighborhood and fans addicted to baseball in the sun.

Bill Wrigley got rid of that problem by selling it. Earlier he had inherited other problems involved with tradition. That would have been in 1961, when he became chief executive officer of the corporation. Blunt, Ellis & Loewi, Inc., a well-established Chicago and Milwaukee investment banking house, once used these words to describe the company: "a rather stodgy, family-run organization, secretive, unaggressive and slow to react."

The truth is that until Bill Wrigley established his reign the company was content to push its traditional products, Juicy Fruit, Spearmint, and Doublemint, and to let its big competitors, American Chicle and Beech-Nut plus a host of smaller companies, chew away at its markets. Where once Wrigley owned 70 percent of the chewing-gum market in this country (and so much of overseas markets that competitors copied Wrigley package designs to steal sales) the Wrigley share had slipped down close to 30 percent in the later 1970s. But newly aggressive marketing and most particularly new products were slowly turning things around and Wrigley's market share in the United States was back up to the 50 percent mark in the mid-1980s.

If the kids and those in need of an "adult pacifier" (P.K.'s phrase) were pleased with Wrigley's new and newly competitive brands like Big Red, Hubba Bubba soft chunk bubble gum, and Extra sugar-free, Bill Wrigley should be happy with the way things were shaping up for the 1990s.

In 1986 the company was earning more than $5 a share and paying a dividend of something like that, and Wrigley owned more than 1.9 million shares of a stock that often traded at $80 a share. In addition, Alison Elizabeth, his daughter by his first wife, was married to California lawyer Geoffrey Rusack in a royal wedding in California, with the groom's father, the Episcopal bishop of Los Angeles, presiding. Furthermore, his lawyers had already succeeded in reaching some kind of financial settlement (sealed) with his second wife, Joan, after she had sued for $55 million. Wrigley had secured an annulment of the seven-year marriage in 1978, when he was 45, claiming that her two previous divorces, both obtained in Alabama, were not legal.

On the surface at least, the only thing Bill Wrigley had to worry about was the possibility that the public might blame him instead of the Chicago Tribune Co. if the new owner ignored sizable and vocal public opinion and installed lights in Wrigley Field for nighttime baseball. Or, failing that, moved the Chicago Cubs, the only major-league team to play all its home games in the sunshine, out of the city in order to increase attendance.

Wrigley married again in 1981. His third wife was Julie Burns, a vivacious Californian, an attorney, a private pilot, and a horsewoman. That last made her at home on the Wrigley Arabian-horse farms near Chicago and Scottsdale,

Arizona. Wrigley's elder son, bright and personable and another William, signed on as a management trainee in 1985, possibly assuring that a fourth generation of the family would command the corporation.

VI

SWIFT

No other city has given the country so many family names that are part of the language and of daily life: Swift, Armour, Wilson, Pullman, Wrigley, Ward, Sears, Morton as in salt, Walgreen as in drugstore, Nielsen as in television ratings, and in an age when gasoline stations charge a dollar or two for road maps, McNally as in atlas.

Too often, however, the names have disappeared from Chicago, either by attrition, by migration, or by marriage. A student of such matters says there are logical reasons why the family corporation ends up being run by in-laws. A son may work at becoming a playboy and spending father's money. Or he may choose to do anything other than work for the old man. For reasons of his own, the man who bore the name Gustavus Franklin Swift III, the grandson of the founder of Swift & Co., chose to take his Harvard degree in the classics and fine arts and go on to do graduate work in anthropology and archaeology. He earned a world reputation in his specialty, the Lydian Empire of ancient Turkey, and on his death in 1976 was curator of the museum of the University of Chicago's world-renowned Oriental Institute.

Often, too, according to the expert, the heirs of the great man turn out to be female, and "ambitious young men, hoping to make it up the ladder in the corporate world, are not averse to marrying the daughters of the rich and the powerful." Again the name disappears.

In 1931 the board of directors of Armour & Co. elected a veteran manager to be president of the company. Philip D. Armour III, grandson of the founder, promptly resigned from the company, leaving no member of the family at the top. Armour, a vice-president, was only 37 years old, and the directors said the big meat-packing firm needed an executive of more experience as president.

Nearly half a century later, Edward F. Swift left the family firm, where with his abilities he had risen to the position of executive vice-president. The situation was somewhat similar in that it was apparent that he was not going to become president, or chairman or chief executive officer. The professional managers were running the corporation without sentiment and according to the bottom line as writ in the handbook for all possessors of master's degrees in business administration. The bottom line reads something like this: chop the company up, sell off the parts for the best price, and let someone else worry about making the business run.

A little belatedly, because the organization was only formed belatedly, the first Philip D. Armour was inducted into the Chicago Business Hall of Fame in 1983. A grandson, Vernon Armour, who maintained a low profile during a La Salle Street career as a banker and stockbroker, accepted the award and remarked that he doubted the original P.D. was "quite the knight in shining armor my father made him out to be or quite the rogue my mother would have us believe."

If Mother had reference to anything other than some of Armour's rough or ruthless business practices, she was keeping the information to herself. Always Armour was a gambler both in the grain futures markets and on his own judgment of the market for meats. The meat packers and sausage makers of Cincinnati and Milwaukee were apparently good, solid, hard-working Germans, not gamblers. For long years Cincinnati nursed the hope that its position on the Ohio River would make it the capital of the "West," but as matters turned out, the fertile farms of the Ohio Valley, the river traffic, and the traditions of its German population only succeeded in earning it the somewhat lesser title of Porkopolis, the leading city of pork.

If Armour made his first big money in Milwaukee as a pork packer and a gambler on a Ulysses S. Grant victory that would knock the price of salt pork down from $60 to $18 a barrel, he also saw that Chicago, with its better waterways and railroads and close proximity to the grass of the plains states, would become the pork and beef center of the country. Armour arrived in Chicago in 1875, already a major factor in the industry. By then he had offices in New York City and Kansas City and was shipping to Europe.

Gustavus Franklin Swift also arrived in Chicago in 1875. He was doing all right for himself, but the main thing he had going for him, then and later, was his very acute judgment of all things concerned with getting meat from farm to table. That, the judgment, and a dogged belief in his judgment.

Basic to much of what Swift accomplished in his early years was a simple matter of judgment: most of the people in the United States lived on the East Coast while the West was the place to grow farm produce and raise cattle and hogs. Originally the West to Gustavus, or Stave as the family called him, was anything farther inland than Boston.

He was born at West Sandwich, later Sagamore, Massachusetts, out a way on Cape Cod. There weren't many people thereabouts even though in 1839, when he was born, people named Swift had been on the Cape for seven generations. The ninth child and the fifth son in a family of twelve children, he apparently realized a few facts of life early on, the most important being that a farm on Cape Cod would not provide riches for a family with a dozen children. A bright child, he translated that into a need to earn money, and the first money he earned came from picking cranberries in the Cape bogs. At age 16, the story goes, he talked his father into lending him $16, used the money to buy a heifer, butchered it himself, and sold the meat door-to-door, realizing a $10 profit. The story may be substantially correct. It helped that he had all those older brothers. One brother ran a butcher shop, and Stave naturally enough worked in the shop as soon as he could be of use.

But in short order he had really set himself up in a continuing business, buying, butchering, and selling dressed beef from a wagon. By the time he was 18 he had broadened the business to include buying live piglets at a market near Boston and selling them off to farmers one or two at a time as he herded them back toward home. Inside of a few more years he had his own butcher shop in Eastham, selling dressed meats to the public and also wheeling and dealing in live cattle and pigs.

After his 1861 marriage to Ann Marie Higgins, the daughter of a Cape Cod fisherman in Eastham, Swift began an odyssey following his own star that eventually took him to Chicago. Over the next decade he moved with his long-suffering wife and an ever-growing brood of children to Barnstable, Clinton, and Lancaster. In Lancaster, forty miles west of Boston, child No. 4 was born. In each town Swift opened a meat market as a base and went on buying and selling cattle. He was getting nearer and nearer to the source of supply. Albany in 1872 was even closer.

Chicago was it, right there on the edge of the Great Plains with herds of iron horses now thundering into the city from the West and running on to the East. A weird distortion brought about by the Civil War was of importance here. During the Civil War years Texas was cut off from the Eastern markets and its herds of longhorns proliferated. In the 1870s they were being driven north both to feed on the prairie grass and to be put aboard trains bound for Chicago, adding huge numbers to the cattle already available on the farms of the territories west of Chicago.

When Swift first set up in business in Chicago he bought cattle at the huge Union Stockyards, already ten years old, and had the cattle shipped East to his old partners.

That was the way it was done. Cattle were jammed into cars and banged around for days before they reached an Eastern slaughterhouse, much the worse for the punishment and too often, without food or water, having lost large amounts of weight.

On every count this was a terrible system, as Swift saw it. The railroads didn't much care about the treatment the animals got or weight loss or damage. They were being paid anyway. But it didn't take a genius to see that the economics of shipping a live animal 900 miles across the country were bad. Swift was hot on the subject. He had moved his cattle buying right to the greatest source, the Chicago yards, and he was an acknowledged expert at buying the best for the least. The next step was dressing the cattle in Chicago and shipping only the carcass East.

Swift was determined to overcome the two or three great obstacles to that. First, and obvious, was spoilage. Swift and others had experimented with shipping dressed beef during winter's cold. But that was a chancy thing. He needed rail cars that were cold.

Technology problems aside, the railroads were aggressively uninterested. Why go to the expense of designing and building refrigerated cars to ship a smaller, less profitable product?

A third problem was the butcher and the customer in the East. Swift was proposing to put a lot of people in places like New York and Boston out of work. That included people he would ask to buy from him. And, as Swift knew from his experimental shipping during cold weather, the market was extremely skeptical about buying beef that had been dressed much earlier in faraway Chicago. In fact, when Swift first started dealing in fresh Chicago beef, his longtime New York partner quit.

Swift beat his head against a few walls but he persisted and finally won. The Grand Trunk Railway had a very small part of the cattle business, so it was receptive. Swift spent his own money to develop a workable refrigerated car, an early version of which simply circulated air blowing over ice. Having worked the Eastern market for years, Swift had many a contact and convinced a number of meat purveyors that the economics made sense. Translation: you can make more money on beef dressed in Chicago in a big-volume operation.

Those staid German pork packers and sausage makers in Porkopolis had more than a little to do with the development of the big Chicago slaughterhouses. Cincinnati early put the dressing of pigs on a mass-production, or mass-disassembly, basis, with various members of a team performing a given part of the operation, and their methods were copied in Chicago.

On a more appetizing level, the Germans of Milwaukee also made a substantial contribution to the development of the industry. If they were interested in bratwurst, they were also interested in brewing and they needed preservation and cooling for the brewing process.

Swift, of course, was not alone in revolutionizing the industry. Initially at least, both Armour and Morris were bigger and stronger than Swift and they were not about to let Swift get a jump on them. (A daughter of Swift's later married a son of the Morris founder, Nelson Morris. Nevertheless, the Morris company still later agreed to a marriage with Armour & Co.) Wilson and Cudahy came in later, and there were any number of smaller "packers" working hard to gain a share of the market.

A couple of sidelights of interest: In those years around 1880, ice was "harvested" from lakes during the winter months and kept under sawdust and other means of insulation in icehouses for later use. One minor facet of Swift's move into shipping dressed beef was a rather frantic campaign to buy up harvesting rights on Wisconsin lakes. Beyond that there was a need to build ice stations along the railroad lines and ice warehouses in Eastern terminal cities. Swift's New York City iced warehouse opened in 1882. It was Nelson Morris who pioneered the shipment of live cattle from the United States to Europe, but Swift was the man who later on went the whole way and succeeded in shipping "chilled" Chicago beef to Europe—and selling it, even to the beef eaters of London.

Very quickly Swift & Co., the Swift family, and the Chicago industry moved into the big time. In 1885 Swift & Co. was incorporated with capital stock valued at $300,000. Two years later the capitalization went to $3 million. By 1896 the valuation was $15 million, and Swift, way ahead of his time, was offering stock to employees and making purchases easy with low-interest loans. Swift's older brother Noble declined an offer to buy more stock in the company, warning Gustavus against the day when all the cattle would be killed and eaten.

Swift expanded from his home base, New England, to the rest of the country and as a packer also moved closer and closer to supplies. Purchasing offices, stockyards, and packing plants were opened in St. Louis, Kansas City, St. Paul, St. Joseph, and Fort Worth.

Swift was also aggressive in making money where money was to be made, that is, by making use of "waste" from the slaughtering operations. That was more or less natural. Going back to the time when he sold meat from a wagon door-to-door on Cape Cod, Swift was something of a fanatic about the product. It had to be good and it had to be healthy. That was only good business. There was no profit in waste or spoilage.

Considering the standards of the times, Swift was also fanatic about conditions in his plant in Chicago. A controlled and disciplined man who retired by nine o'clock every night and always attended church with his wife and family on Sunday and who wrote letters on half-sheets and fought against such unnecessary frills as curtains at the windows of his home, Swift expected his plants to operate the same way.

A man wearing stained clothes was not only unsanitary but also possibly wasting a salable product. The awful and often-told story about Swift in the early days of his Chicago operations was that he frequently inspected the drainage from the plant that led to "Bubbly Creek." At the time Bubbly Creek passed for proper disposal of wastes, and what Swift was interested in particularly was any undue show of fats that might indicate to him economic waste in the plant operation.

Very early Swift & Co. was producing lard and oleomargarine, soap, glue, and fertilizer, and before his time Swift had a research laboratory, even though it was a one-man operation.

Although it would have been fairly hard to miss in a country that was growing and prospering and generating urban populations that had to be fed by farms that had been opened up by McCormick and his reaper, all was not exactly straight up and easy for the meat packers. Industrialization, immigration, revolutionary ideas imported from Europe, and a business class that generally believed it was doing a person a favor in providing any kind of job at any wage made for unrest.

A strike at the McCormick reaper plant in 1886 and the killing of two men when police fired into a group of strikers led to a meeting of workers in Haymarket Square the next day and a bomb explosion that killed seven police officers and wounded perhaps sixty others. An unknown number of workers were also killed or wounded. Eight admitted revolutionaries were quickly put on trial and five executed by hanging. Public opinion was hysterically divided between those who thought the country was in for bomb-throwing anarchy and those who thought the American system of justice had been subverted and men killed by the state for their opinions.

The Pullman strike of 1894 resulted when George Pullman laid off thousands and cut wages drastically in the Panic of 1893—in those days recessions were called panics in the wake of a financial disaster of one kind or another—but refused to reduce rents or other fees charged the workers living in his model town where all was to be peace and uplift without the intrusion of alcohol or other immoralities. The strike grew into a general railroad strike, and federal troops were called in to move trains, including "meat" trains, and quell rioting in the streets of Chicago. Whether Swift knew it or not, powerful unions were in the making.

The government was also moving against the meat packers. The industry was officially and generally cleared in the "embalmed beef" scandal of the Spanish-American War, but, again, change was on the way, with tougher federal meat inspection.

Then there was the era of trust busting and the passage of the Sherman Antitrust Act in 1890. By then the big three Chicago packers were powerful enough to push ranchers, railroads, and retailers around. Several congressional investigations were inconclusive, and a formal antitrust case involving Swift, Armour, and Morris and eight smaller companies ended in a not-guilty verdict. But a second antitrust effort by the Justice Department produced a 1920 consent decree that divorced the packers from owning stockyards, rail terminals, and warehouses and barred the packers from moving into other food lines. The decree held until 1971, when the restrictions were liberalized in recognition of the reality that the packers were struggling to survive rather than threatening the lives of other companies.

The health of Gustavus Franklin Swift began to fail when he was in his early 60s, and he suffered a hemorrhage and died in 1903 at age 64 while recuperating from an operation.

His eldest son, Louis Franklin, took over a company that had grown to what for 1903 was a rather remarkable sales level of $200 million annually. With the help more or less of five brothers, L.F. headed the enterprise until his retirement in 1931. Before the Great Depression of the 1930s eroded the company's best gains, sales were running at $700 million and there were 55,000 people on the payroll.

Sales had already topped the $2.4 billion mark when the company officially celebrated its 100th anniversary with the usual self-congratulatory speeches and predictions of a second century of progress. But little more than a decade later the corporation was off on the track prescribed in the business schools—all that counts is return on assets and return on investment. Translation: get rid of losers, keep or acquire winners.

Swift & Co. had not had a winner in the business school sense since Gustavus borrowed the $16 from his father and generated the return or profit of $10. It was stuck with the fresh-meat business, where making a return of 1 percent was miraculous. It didn't matter that the 1 percent might mean a net profit of $10 million or more.

Among other things, Swift, like the other traditional packers, was stuck with a number of antiquated and inefficient plants and with union labor contracts providing uneconomic wage scales, work rules, and benefits. Meanwhile, a company called Iowa Beef Processors had finally carried Gustavus Swift's basic idea to the logical conclusion. Its big thing was a plant, a factory, out there where the animals practically walked in the door from pasture or feed lot and unskilled labor working at local wages really were on a production line. And what came off the line was so-called boxed meat, the various standard cuts all ready for the supermarket to place on display. Finally the local or store butcher was being eliminated.

In the 1960s the corporation set out to remedy matters. It began buying companies that did churn out high returns—oil companies, for instance. In 1973, to straighten out the organization chart, it formed Esmark, Inc. (S-mark, the S for Swift) as a holding company that could get into just about anything. Just about anything included International Playtex, a maker of brassieres. It took the new Esmark until 1980 to get rid of the annoying fresh-meat business that had built the company. Swift Independent was established as a separate company with public stock to carry on the old-fashioned task of supplying stores, hotels, restaurants, and others with fresh beef and pork. Swift had some problems to solve, but it was a nice $2.5 billion, independent business. During the merger madness and financial maneuverings of the 1980s, Esmark ended up as an appendage of Chicago's Beatrice Foods. And a Texas entrepreneur took control of Swift Independent and moved the headquarters to Dallas. The Chicago stockyards were closed and the big packers gone from the city.

Edward F. Swift, the former executive vice-president, went on to a second career in investment banking on La Salle Street.

VII

SOCIETY

A century or so before the feminist movement broke down the barriers, the Chicago Club—that's *the* Chicago Club—allowed women to penetrate its august portals but only on special occasions. Or as the club bylaws of 1876 had it, the executive committee of the club was authorized in its wisdom to permit the admission from time to time of "strangers and visitors, including ladies."

This shockingly liberal exception to the rules of such men's sanctuaries may have been forced on the club. As the outstanding representative of the city's business and social elite, it often fell to the club to welcome to the city strangers and visitors from the great Eastern capitals and from Europe. It would have been a bit sticky to hold a reception for members of European nobility or royalty, New York or Boston millionaires, or such as Presidents of the United States and to tell them that the hospitality of the capital of the Western Territory did not extend to their wives.

William Graham, a resident of the exclusive North Shore suburb of Kenilworth, the executive who built Baxter Travenol into a billion-dollar corporation, and a 1980s president of the Chicago Club, tells one story that may suggest a flavor of the times in an earlier Chicago.

The club had scheduled one of its grand receptions for a visitor, this one being President Ulysses S. Grant. In that Mrs. Grant was accompanying the President, wives of club members were invited. Shortly before the scheduled day, a member called upon the club president. The gauche fellow had a question: would it be all right if he brought his mistress? Without pause, the club president, one of the educated Eastern transplants sought by the club membership committee, said, why, certainly, as long as she is the wife of a member.

This nice distinction may reflect something of the long struggle in Chicago society to achieve a certain degree of refinement divorced from a rowdy, frontier, and not very distant past. After all, possibly even more than in the older Eastern seaboard cities, money is society in Chicago. Money and current position in the business hierarchy.

The most respectable "old" wealth dates only from Chicago's contributions to the robber baron category and the great builders of the last years of the 19th century. Right up until his death in 1901, Philip D. Armour told almost anyone who would listen that he had started out on the career that led to his meat-packing empire by pushing a wheelbarrow.

Still, today the most often repeated "society" story, at least among those with a jaundiced view of the rich and powerful, tells of the time during the Chicago world's fair of 1893 when Mrs. Bertha Palmer, the acknowledged queen of Chicago society and the wife of Potter Palmer, invited the visiting Princess Eulalie of Spain to a reception. The royal princess declined the invitation of an "innkeeper's wife." (Later on when Mrs. Palmer invaded aristocratic Paris and London society and was taken up by Queen Victoria, the Princess was publicly sorry.)

It wasn't until 1911 that a reform mayor closed down what may have been the city's most prestigious club after the Chicago Club. This would be the Everleigh Club, operated

by two ambitious and tasteful sisters from Nebraska on the
South Side of Chicago not far from millionaires' row on
Prairie Avenue. In a fifty-room mansion the sisters provided
beautiful and compliant women, fine champagne, antique
furniture, gold spittoons, and charge accounts for the
wealthy. (Bills were sent to offices on a letterhead that indicated a conventional service.) The only readily believable
part of the gossip that the second Marshall Field was shot in
the Everleigh Club by an angry prostitute was the locale. If
young Field was not a patron, many of his friends and his
elders in the business world were.

The city cannot escape its heritage from the Capone era.
"Gangland-style slaying" is a cliché of the frequent newspaper story reporting the death of a "business executive" or a
person not easily identified. The phrase is code meaning the
newspaper knows the mob has concluded the settlement of
another dispute but the facts are difficult to come by. In
recent years the weapon of choice has been a .22 pistol or
rifle rather than the submachine gun of the Prohibition mob
wars and the preferred place for disposing of the end result
is the trunk of a car, usually a Cadillac. Unfortunately for
Chicago, someplace in the U.S.A. late-night television is still
showing reruns of the 1960s series *The Untouchables,* Hollywood's version of the battles among the mob factions during
Prohibition for control of the beer and whiskey trade and
between the mobs and the government agents. And someplace in the wide world, reruns of the series with a dubbed
sound track add luster to Chicago's image. A travel writer
reports sitting in a restored Roman arena at Nîmes, France,
and watching a circus that featured a team of acrobats wearing double-breasted blue suits and white ties. The acrobats
dashed and tumbled about, firing revolvers equipped with
blanks. The action was billed as Le Chicago.

If society in any city is suspicious of the credentials of any
outsider, Chicago society also looks over its shoulder at the
mob.

Let a "new" millionaire, propelled perhaps by an ambitious wife, pop up by the usual means—that is, by purchasing a table for ten at a charity ball at $125 a person—there will be questions about the man and his money. The money is readily accepted but not the man. Unknown, it is assumed that he and the source of his money must be, just must be, the mob.

Chicago has always suffered from what writer and critic A. J. Leibling codified as the Second City syndrome. Californians pity the rest of the country, Texans brag of their superiority, Southerners in general will tell you they were born as Americans but they thank God for placing them in the South, and New Yorkers think the country ends at the Hudson River. Chicago is simply somewhere in between. No one ever heard a resident of Chicago boast of being a Midwesterner, and Chicagoans tend to sound a bit defensive when they extol the Second City, in 1984 moved by the population statistics and narrow city boundaries down to third rank behind Los Angeles, that sprawling collection of villages.

First-time visitors to the city are astonished at Chicago's size, wealth, and lakeshore beauty, and rightly so. But with few exceptions, when you hear a native tell the visitor that he or she loves Chicago, you can also almost hear the unspoken phrase: believe it or not. What you do hear loud and clear is the assertion that Chicago is a great place to work and make money.

Therein the origin of one of the city's embarrassing nicknames, the Windy City. Chicago does have its prairie winds, especially fierce on occasion in the canyons of the central city and often dangerous in the suburbs, where they may hit full blast. But the winds are not necessarily worse than those of other cities, Dallas, for instance, where there is little between the city and the Arctic Circle and the Great Plains except barbed wire. (The Chicago Association of Commerce and Industry insists that fourteen major cities in the country have worse winds than Chicago. That may be a bit like the average temperatures claimed by cities and resorts: the average is pleasant in that the weeks of 105 degree summer temperatures balance out the weeks of zero temperatures.)

Windy City was a term originally hung on Chicago at the turn of the century by Charles A. Dana, editor of the New York *Sun,* to put down the Chicago businessmen and promoters who streamed into Manhattan looking for capital and telling everyone that nothing in the world could beat the great city of Chicago.

In truth, in the years after the Civil War and on through the first decades of the 20th century Chicago was a city of explosive growth, noteworthy innovation, and progress. Meanwhile, Boston, New York, Philadelphia, were increasingly more interested in conserving wealth and power. In 1893, when Dana first wrote about the brash citizens of the Windy City, Chicago had achieved stature sufficient that the breezy boasting of its citizens could very well arouse antagonism. Maybe, just maybe, Chicago would threaten New York's leading position.

Going way back, Chicago society sought greener fields elsewhere. One could always seek the broadening experience of the Grand Tour in Europe, and the wealthy families of Chicago were as eager as those of New York to marry a daughter to a European title. But solid position demanded, and still demands, staking down some kind of Eastern seaboard position. The first Mrs. Marshall Field spent the last years of her life in France; a later generation maintained a mansion in Manhattan and estates on Long Island and in South Carolina and Florida, while the current Marshall Field, number five, has his Lake Forest estate and anchors his yacht, actually a boat designed strictly for fishing, off the family's longtime Florida home at Hobe Sound, where some quiet souls look down on the Palm Beach swirl. The William McCormick Blairs, with a fortune as old as if not as large as the Fields', had their town house on fashionable Astor Street on Chicago's Near North Side, a summer home on Lake Michigan in the North Shore suburb of Lake Bluff, and a second summer home in Maine.

Today William Farley, a self-made multimillionaire at age 41 in 1984 and in full possession of an industrial empire valued at something close to $1 billion, has a luxury condominium on Astor Street on the Near North Side and homes in California and Maine. The Wrigleys were the first of the Chicago millionaires to prefer the West. The Wrigley mansion and the Biltmore in Scottsdale, Arizona, are on the bus tour, and the Wrigleys succeeded in buying up most of Catalina Island off the California coast.

From its earliest days the Chicago Club pursued decorum, dignity, the best of manners. Eastern transplants from the better families and anyone who happened to have a college degree or a membership in a New York or Boston men's club was sought after by the membership committee. Upgrading was the order of the day. From time to time over the years the club found it necessary to take stern measures to achieve a proper tone. In 1881 poker was banned from the card rooms and even the private rooms and the following year two members were censured by letter for telling "indecent stories" in the bar. However, a fuller explanation is not forthcoming of a change in the bylaws adopted during this same wave of puritanism: ladies were to be permitted to be invited by a member to an "entertainment" in a private room if the house committee approved twenty-four hours in advance.

For decades before and after the turn of the century, the dining room of the Chicago Club had its millionaires' table featuring such as Marshall Field, N. K. Fairbank (weighing scales), George M. Pullman (the car, the Pullman strike, and the Pullman village, the company town to end company towns), and Robert Todd Lincoln (Lincoln was not a millionaire, but he was the son of the President and an obviously prominent lawyer).

There was also a railroad table in the club dining room. Long before the turn of the century the railroads had made Chicago the Queen City of the Western Territory, and the table for the railroad tycoons recognized the place of railroading in the hierarchy of the club and the city. The railroad table survives today as the Railroad Room, one of many clubs within the club, most founded in the 1920s as one of the necessities of the Prohibition years.

Of special note is room 1871. The number identifies the disaster of the Great Chicago Fire of 1871. In the room there is a plaque referring to another disaster. It reads: "The Chicago Club, R.I.P., November 1, 1978, Farewell to a Golden Era, 1869–1978." The first year was the year the club was founded, the second was the year the club relaxed its rules against women. In the closet of the room there is a sign to be put to use when needed. "No girls allowed," it says, and the use of the word "girls" no doubt pegs the era of the writer.

Very probably he belongs back a half century and more with Aunt Clara. For a decade or two Aunt Clara was the feature of the annual Chicago Club lunch on New Year's Day. A convivial occasion, once attended by men in full morning dress, the lunch ended with a round of song, and the song of the day concerned Aunt Clara, supposedly a choir singer shamed into fleeing her small Midwestern town. Instead of mending her ways, she is next found, according to the ballad, living with the help of her admirers in a villa on the Riviera. Aunt Clara's portrait, always displayed at the New Year's lunch, still hangs in the club. Visitors see a proper and attractive woman in evening dress, but the framed portrait hangs on concealed hinges. Swing it around and there, horrors, is Aunt Clara in scanty undergarments. Raucous elements did prevail at times over the pursuit of decorum.

By the 1960s the times were catching up with the club. Very quietly in 1964 the club admitted its first Jewish members, top, top-drawer businessmen—Joseph Block, at the time chairman of the multibillion-dollar Inland Steel Co. and a member of the family that had founded Inland in 1893, and Gardner Stern, head of a chain of specialty food shops and the city's top catering firm.

The Standard Club is to the Jews what the Chicago Club is

to the Gentile business community. The building at the
south end of the Loop is not quite so 19th century, men's
club grand as the Chicago's. It is a warmer, more family-
oriented club with women much in evidence. The handful
of women at lunch in the Chicago Club dining rooms most
often appear to be junior executives in the company of the
boss, there for a business lunch amid the dark wood and
polished brass.

The main dining room at the Standard, lately redone with
red wallpaper and looking like a giant-sized version of the
dining room in a millionaire's home, is regularly crowded
with women who are rather obviously wives and daughters,
dining usually without the male member of the family. As
far back as you go and straight through the years, the Standard held an annual "gala" or two, balls, and "shows," the
last being amateur musicals with women in the audience
and on the stage. In that widows could retain a membership,
the club roster in 1968 included nearly 250 woman members.

The menu at the Standard is more extensive than the
Chicago's and the quality of the food is higher. Something
else: the "bar" resembles a cocktail lounge in an expensive,
small hotel and it is nearly deserted most of the time. The
club, following the Chicago Club lead, now has a scattering
of Gentile members but most members are unaware of it.

The club does not pretend as strenuously as the Chicago
Club that it is solely devoted to good fellowship and good
works. While the Chicago Club's earliest bylaws declare that
the club should not be used as an "exchange or salesroom of
any kind" and while in modern times the president of the
Pennsylvania Railroad was once escorted to the door because he was being interviewed by a newspaper reporter,
legend has it that A. N. Pritzker cut many of his famous
"handshake" deals at a corner table in the Standard Club
dining room.

The Chicago Club traces its history to a meeting in January of 1869. Not claiming anything, the Standard Club says

its first organizational meeting was held on April 5 that same year. (Chicago was a substantial city of nearly half a million people in 1869, which also happened to be the year that Chicago and the East were linked to populous California with the driving of the "golden spike" at Promontory, Utah, joining the Union Pacific and the Central Pacific railroads.)

Like downtown clubs in every city, the clubs in Chicago have had their financial troubles in the age of the flight to the suburbs, and a cynic might suggest that a lack of membership dues and empty dinnertime tables had as much to do with the decision of almost all private clubs to admit women and blacks as the civil rights and feminist movements. A couple of the major clubs have closed their doors over the years, including the family-oriented Lake Shore Club and more recently the Illinois Athletic Club. The flourishing indoor tennis clubs and then the all-things physical-fitness clubs, keyed to younger enthusiasts and to joggers and marathon runners of all ages, have become social centers and have taken away some of the panache of the traditional clubs.

Huge, luxurious, and very expensive, the East Bank Club was tabbed as a white elephant even as it was being built on a site just across the Chicago River from the Loop. But immediately it had a waiting list of racquetball players, swimmers, runners, and others determined to be trim and fit. (In spite of their dedication to flat stomachs, the members managed to support a large and attractive restaurant and bar.)

Even as some of the older clubs were struggling with changing living patterns, Chicago's usually thriving business community made new or expanded clubs possible. John Swearingen, for two decades the head of Standard Oil of Indiana, succeeded in moving the Mid-America Club, founded in 1958, from a top floor of the Prudential Building to larger and more lavish quarters on the eightieth floor of his monumental, marble-clad new Standard Oil Building (now the Amoco Oil Building). With an initiation fee of

$1,000, the new Mid-America retained or attracted a membership nearly but not quite paralleling the Chicago Club's. Its impressive if somewhat coldly modern decor and its striking views of the lakefront and the city make the Mid-America a fitting place to entertain business contacts, particularly people from out of town, and its annual Christmas banquet and dance is as lavish as any party given in Chicago. Only slightly less expensive, the Metropolitan Club on the sixty-sixth and sixty-seventh floors of the Sears Tower was also a success with the help of Sears, Roebuck clout when it opened in 1974 as primarily a lunch and dinner club. Like the Mid-America, it offers numerous private rooms for business lunches and meetings.

The La Salle Street crowd, brokers and bankers and their allies, gather primarily for lunch or business meetings at the Attic Club (founded in 1923) atop the 135 S. La Salle Building and at the Mid-Day Club (founded in 1903) on the fifty-sixth floor of the first National Bank Building. Among the Mid-Day's distinctions is its martini. Decades ago the chairman of the house committee, wishing to avoid embarrassment at a procession of martinis at his table, decreed that a first order would be a generous double. In an age of Chablis and Perrier water with a lime kicker, the tradition survives. The Monroe Club, opened as late as 1976, also gets its share of patronage from the Loop financial community, with the members tending to be somewhat younger.

South on Michigan Avenue in Orchestra Hall there's the Cliff Dwellers Club, another product of the affluent 1920s, dedicated to music and the arts. If the members are not artists of one sort or another, they have a claim as patrons of the concert halls and galleries. Strangely enough, the Cliff Dwellers was the only club of substance to maintain a men-only status into the 1980s, finally giving up in 1984 and admitting women to full membership.

North on Michigan Avenue on the twenty-fifth and twenty-sixth floors of a building overlooking the Chicago River is the Tavern Club. The Tavern also has a cultural orientation; many members are authors, photographers, and professional or amateur artists. But the Tavern does not take itself too seriously. The club bylaws put qualifications for membership this way: "Any man who has ever done anything, or thought anything, and is of clubbable nature will find himself at home in the Tavern Club whether his work or his hobby be in the arts or sciences, in the world of romance and adventure, or in the practical affairs of men."

The Tavern, which confines women to a twenty-sixth-floor dining room at lunchtime, puts on some interesting dinners, dances, and special events, including a well-attended annual affair for artists featuring nude models. Over the years the artists and models night has gone well, but the club did feel it had to expel the member who undressed and asked one of the models to dance.

Altogether the city, not counting the suburbs, has at least twenty-six "businessmen's" clubs that convey a degree of rank on members. That's not counting the Racquet Club, the Saddle and Cycle, and the Casino Club, where social standing and old money are still more important than position in the business world. No one need be told the status of the Casino Club, dominated by society women and the place where one must have at least one party if one is to properly celebrate a wedding or anoint a debutante. Among the young ladies of 1939 who appeared at the Casino was Nancy "Pinky" Davis, the daughter of fabulously successful Dr. Loyal Davis and later known as Nancy Reagan. The club's squat black building proclaims its standing. It sits on some of the most valuable real estate in Chicago, just off North Michigan Avenue in the Gold Coast district right next to the 1,105-foot height of the John Hancock Building, refusing to move for anyone or any amount of common money. For decades a guiding spirit of the Casino was Lucy McCormick Blair, the Blair family being one of the relatively few constants in Chicago with wealth going back to pre-Civil War retailing and real estate and still most visible in the form of William Blair & Co.

The two top Jewish country clubs, Bryn Mawr and Lake Shore, are within easy driving distance of heavily Jewish Glencoe and Highland Park. Bryn Mawr is also close enough to the city to appeal to people who live in town and convenient enough for the standard lunch and afternoon foursome for business contacts. Louis Goldblatt, former chairman of the store chain, did not take up golf until after his second retirement, but he breaks 100 nicely on the tough Bryn Mawr course. J. Ira Harris, the slightly aging boy wonder of Salomon Bros. who picked up $30 million when Philbro bought Salomon in the early 1980s, is another Bryn Mawr player. Would-be members understand that a requirement for membership is very generous support of Jewish charities.

In the past two decades the Oak Brook area southwest of Chicago has seen remarkable growth as a home for both corporations (e.g., McDonald's) and corporate executives.

In good part this has been the doing of the late Paul Butler, a man of many parts who added acres to the old family farm, founded and for twenty years was chairman of Butler Aviation, built and owned the Butler Paper Co. until he sold it to Nekoosa Edwards Paper, sponsored one of the first straw-hat theaters (Salt Creek), and, once a four-goal polo player, made Oak Brook a polo capital. One of his sons, Michael, who horrified the establishment with his production of the 1960s rock musical *Hair*, confounded the same people by making millions on the show. Michael took over the administration of the Oak Brook Polo Club after his father's death. Such as the Viscount Cowdray, the Maharaja of Jaipur, George H. Swift, and William T. Ylvisaker, who came west to Chicago as a young man to play polo and stayed to become chairman of Gould, Inc., have been members of the club's board of governors.

Michael does things up at the club with the flair that took him and productions of *Hair* to Broadway—and Los Angeles and London. On a typical summer weekend at the club he transformed the Butler tennis house—the club includes a tennis and bath complex—into what was described as a tented Moroccan oasis for a Saturday-night benefit dinner-dance sponsored by the Women's Board of the Goodman Theater. A twenty-one piece orchestra played for dancing. A Carson Pirie Scott & Co. fashion show was the halftime feature of the Sunday-afternoon polo match.

Sister Marjorie (Jorie) Butler Kent and her husband ran their own successful business, an African safari service, but now concentrate on managing vast and varied Butler interests with the advice and the votes of Michael and brother Frank. Michael, seeking a new respectability as he moved into his mid-50s in the Ronald Reagan era, was busy with a new multimillion-dollar residential development within the older Butler development, which once took in a rather incredible sixteen square miles.

"One of the truly remarkable things about Oak Brook is that it is hard to find a house in the entire community that is older than twenty years," says an old resident, the owner of a nine-year-old home. It is easier to find homes that sell in the $1 million to $5 million range. (A 1985 estimate was that the average single-family home in Oak Brook carried a price tag of $300,000.)

The Butler enterprises are many and the money big. The family goes back to colonial times when some of that not-worth-a-continental money was printed by the Continental Congress on Butler paper. Paul Butler's grandfather, Julius, arrived in Illinois in 1841 to establish the paper company. That date, says Michael, makes the family enterprise the oldest family-owned business in the state.

Paul Butler was killed on the road in front of his Oak Brook home the day after his 89th birthday. As was his habit, he was out for a stroll on a fair evening in June 1981 when a car hit him. A man of multiple marriages and affairs of the heart, Butler in late years divided his time between Oak Brook, his Palm Beach home, and a ranch in Montana. He always enjoyed his reputation as a ladies' man and bon vivant. It was an inelegant and ironic way to die for the multimillionaire builder, a man who had turned 3,000 acres of farmland into a thriving village of impressive office buildings, splendid homes, and, of course, automobiles.

Oak Brook is next door to two older communities of substance, Naperville and Hinsdale. Strangely enough, Naperville and Hinsdale grew up much earlier than Oak Brook, even though they are more distant from the city than Oak Brook. But that may have been because in the early 1920s it was the polo club that Paul Butler wanted to develop on his lands; until after World War II he seemed to think land was something you held, not something you sold.

The Chicago Golf Club and the Butterfield Country Club may have had something to do with stimulating early real estate development in Hinsdale and Naperville. Any number of the Chicago suburbs got their starts as summer vacation sites or as enclaves where the members of one religion or another could escape from the evils of roistering Chicago with its thieves, murderers, anarchists, and waves of European and even Chinese immigrants with their strange languages and strange ways. For instance, the founders of Lake Forest and of what became Lake Forest College were concerned with the health of the Presbyterian Church, while Billy Graham is the most famous graduate of fundamentalist Wheaton College, the institution that built the town of the same name.

A major reason John D. Rockefeller started contributing in the 1880s to the Baptist theological seminary that became the University of Chicago was John D.'s conviction that the Church had to do more toward the education of the young if the Baptists hoped to match other churches. After all, the Methodists were still working hard to build Northwestern University in nearby Evanston and that town was growing with the university.

A certain idealism and belief in the future of the United States of America and in the hereafter was certainly evident in the raw, burgeoning West in the second half of the 19th

century even though devotion to material matters decorated with dollar signs may have dominated.

Butterfield Country Club was founded in the Roaring
Twenties simply because the better country clubs of Chicago did not admit such strangers as Catholics, Irish or otherwise.

Today Butterfield sports three dovetailed nine-hole lay-
outs, a handsome clubhouse, and a membership that is troubled only by the clamor of those seeking to get in. Prospering, corporate Oak Brook has too many young, ambitious
executives willing and eager to pay the $22,000 initiation
fee.

The story at the Chicago Golf Club is different. It goes
back to a time when Americans knew there was such a thing
as golf, but it was something those kilted Scots played. The
new millionaires on the North Shore rode to the hounds, and
played tennis and croquet, but couldn't play golf without a
golf course.

One place you could play at golf was on the lawn of your
Lake Forest estate. John V. Farwell, who made his fortune in
a wholesale dry-goods firm, became a Marshall Field partner, and invested wisely in real estate, turned his front lawn
over to a close friend, a confident Scot named Charles B.
MacDonald. MacDonald oversaw the construction of a
seven-hole course. Seven holes of improvised golf was
enough to whet the appetites of Farwell, his family, and
wealthy friends. (The family was considerable; brother
Charles B. Farwell, at one point a U.S. senator from Illinois,
had an eighteen-acre spread nearby and, if not a golf course,
a garden with pond laid out by Frederick Law Olmsted, the
designer of, among other landmarks, Manhattan's Central
Park. Most recently, Francis C. Farwell, a partner in the
William Blair firm, served as the part-time mayor of Lake
Forest.)

It was MacDonald who organized the group responsible
for the Chicago Golf Club. The club's charter is dated 1892
and states that Chicago Golf has been formed for "pleasure

and playing the game called golf." By 1894 MacDonald had found suitable land, although the 200 acres he bought for the group did have some hills and valleys not quite in keeping with the flatlands and dunes where the ancient game was played.

What was very strange then, and still a puzzle, was the location. The farm was out at the end of nowhere, near the village of Naperville, since grown to 40,000, and thirty miles from the Loop but more than that from the Farwell front lawn. The trip from the city is not an easy one today, and it is difficult to understand the success of the club in the 1890s, when railroad, horse and buggy, or unreliable car made the trip a very long one. But if you hankered after hitting a small ball around a pleasant landscape, Chicago Golf was the only place to be. So there was Marshall Field the first, catching his death at the club in midwinter.

Charles MacDonald did his best to turn Illinois farmland into Scottish links land. He stretched huge bunkers towering twenty feet and more across the greater part of the fairway. He dotted the course with acres of sand, and he lined the fairways with tough grass that can completely hide a golf ball.

The bunkers, the sand, and the deep rough make it only too easy for a golfer to get into unexpected trouble, a fact that may help to explain why golf histories note a record that has stood for three-quarters of a century. No golfer has ever run up a score of 80 or more on the opening day of a major golf tournament and then come charging back to win the tournament. No one, that is, except John J. McDermott, who shot an 81 for the opening round of the U.S. Open at Chicago Golf and came back to win.

From the earliest days, Chicago Golf welcomed wives and women players. One of the female players was Mrs. Hobart Chatfield-Taylor, a daughter of John Farwell. Rich and social, Mrs. Chatfield-Taylor is said to be the person who established golf as a game that a respectable woman could play even if she appeared on the course wearing a skirt short enough to permit a healthy golf swing. Another very early player at Chicago Golf was Mary Abbott, an accomplished golfer, a Chicago novelist, the widow of a successful importer, and the mother of Margaret Abbott. Margaret married the humorist and newspaper columnist Finley Peter Dunne, still remembered for the Irish character he created, Mr. Dooley.

More or less by accident, Margaret Abbott, schooled by her mother, became the first American woman to win an Olympic gold medal, or something that should have been struck in gold by the Olympic committee. The family was living in Paris in 1900 when the Olympic Games were held there in the second renewal of the Games since the Greeks. The French, not missing a chance to promote an extra franc, made the Games a part of the 1900 Paris Exposition and also mixed in a women's golf match billed as the Paris championship. With a score of 47 on the nine-hole course, the 22-year-old Margaret won the tournament and collected an Olympic title for winning an event not now a part of the Olympic Games.

Almost certainly the members of society and the business community in an earlier day were possessed of more energy than today's breed. Or, perhaps, opportunity for entertainment was more limited in the era of the horse and buggy and even in the days of the first horseless carriages. In any case, Chicago Golf once held a dinner-dance every Saturday night. (The club still has cottage apartments that can be reserved for nights, weekends, or the season.) It also once had a polo field and "Poker Flats," a cabin with fireplace and a bar near the ninth green where members might play cards.

The financial standing of the club members could be gauged by an incident of 1912. That year the main clubhouse building burned. While the structure was still burning, members had pledged $55,000 toward the construction of a new clubhouse.

The Great Chicago Fire of 1871, or the series of fires in the

second week of October 1871, killed almost 300 people,
destroyed 17,000 homes, rendered 90,000 homeless, and did
property damage estimated at $200 million. Depending on
what versions of history you read, the horrendous claims
after the fire bankrupted a flock of insurance companies. Or
perhaps many escaped whole by fraudulently denying liabilities. Or perhaps the companies established such a record for
integrity that the casualty industry henceforth blossomed
nationwide.

The 2,000 acres of the central city that were turned to
ashes had hardly cooled before Chicago started rebuilding.
(Potter Palmer's Palmer House hotel had been completed
less than half a year before it burned to the ground. As soon
as he could raise the money—borrowed on his signature
from an insurance company—Palmer started work on a bigger and better Palmer House, which was fireproof. At least
he claimed it was, and used the claim effectively to attract
guests. As late as 1885 Palmer House dining-room menus
carried the somewhat unsettling boast: "Thoroughly Fire
Proof.")

Obviously, changing patterns went along with the rebuilding. Many of the rich continued to build their mansions
on Prairie Avenue, although why they did is in the mystery
category. The area of choice was only eighteen or twenty
blocks south of the center of the city but that also made it
that much closer to the stench of the stockyards. It was also
an area increasingly threatened by the noise and pollution of
the railroads. But John J. Glessner of International Harvester
built his thirty-five-room mansion on Prairie Avenue (designed by the great American architect H. H. Richardson,
restored by the Chicago School of Architecture Foundation)
in 1885, and at its best some seventy mansions lined Prairie
Avenue.

However, the International Harvester McCormicks went
north of the Chicago River even though the river had not
stopped the Great Fire. Three McCormicks had their magnificent homes on or just off Rush Street only half a dozen

blocks north of the river. Most recently restaurants occupy the three buildings. Cyrus McCormick built his forty-five-room palace fifteen blocks north of the Rush Street compound.

Though Potter Palmer had faith in fireproofing and in the central-city blocks of State Street, the awesome fire had the effect of boosting the suburbs. The wealthy and the middle class who had managed to acquire "summer" homes outside the city reached an easy decision: they would live in the summer house. Occasionally today, a cottage with porch for rocking chairs can still be seen in north and northwest suburbs.

It was in the summer of 1870 that Shelton Sturges, a man of considerable wealth, the co-owner of the Northwestern National Bank and a part owner of the city's largest grain-storage company, took a look at Lake Geneva just across the Wisconsin line, liked what he saw, and bought a ninety-acre farm on the lakeshore.

The next summer he moved his large family (five children) into the remodeled and expanded farmhouse. Over the years, with Sturges remaking the landscape to suit his tastes, the house evolved into a three-story "cottage" with a five-story tower. Even before the place, ranked as the very first summer home on Lake Geneva, was enlarged it was sufficient to house the Sturges family year round while the family home (and bank) in Chicago was replaced after the fire.

It was a help to Sturges that direct railroad service had been established between Chicago and Lake Geneva that same summer of 1871. And, of course, the railroad created a real estate boom for Lake Geneva, a 5,000-acre lake with twenty-six miles of shoreline less than seventy-five miles from central Chicago and only a few short miles into Wisconsin. The railroad made possible and easy that classic summer of a bygone era: wife and children, servants, and trunks off to the cool lake or mountain cottage in June, the husband

arriving from the hot city for the weekend or a week or
more between June and September.

In the fifty years after the Chicago fire more than a hundred cottages, those of the three- and four-story variety,
were built along the shores of Lake Geneva. One of the
earlier houses was owned by N. K. Fairbank, who had
amassed a fortune in a number of activities (weighing scales,
railroad equipment, lumbering), not the least of which was a
company that refined products (e.g., soap) from animal fats.
Fairbank's stature in the city of the Armours, Swifts, Mor-
rises, Rothschilds, and Cudahys was such that he was able to
pledge $50,000 in 1869 toward a building for the Chicago
Club if others would get up an $80,000 pool. His first experi-
ence with Lake Geneva had its painful and ironic side. Car-
penters finished building the eighteen-room Fairbank home
in time for the 1875 summer season. Fairbank was just then
winding up the years he spent full-time with the Chicago
Relief and Aid Society organizing help for the city's homeless and unemployed. In the fall of 1875 the Lake Geneva
mansion burned to the ground. Fairbank immediately ordered the house rebuilt as was. Eventually the estate included stables, greenhouse, tennis court, and a five-hole golf
course, the golf course leading to the establishment of the
now venerable, old-shoe Lake Geneva Country Club.

A continuing problem at the lake in the years before the
growth of the towns of Lake Geneva, Fontana, and Williams
Bay was fire—and a lack of water under pressure to fight fire.
The first clubhouse at the Country Club, built in 1896,
burned in 1915, just one of many lake structures totally lost
by fire over the years. Understandably, many an estate in-
congruously sported a windmill, geared to pump water and
furnish power for other tasks. Some, like the one on the Levi
Leiter estate, were six stories tall with forty-foot blades. This
was the Leiter who was a financial genius, real estate investor, and one time partner of Marshall Field. Much later in
life he and his socially ambitious wife decamped to Washington, D.C., and his three daughters married into British aris-

tocracy, Nancy marrying a cousin of the Duke of Argyll, Marguerite marrying the 9th Earl of Suffolk, and Mary capping things off by marrying Lord Curzon, later viceroy of India.

The main house that Leiter built on Lake Geneva in 1879 cost $100,000. That seems to be the price, plus or minus $10,000 or so, that lawyers, doctors, and executives are paying in the 1980s for much smaller houses, usually town houses and usually built around a newly constructed golf course and providing "access" to the lake's crowded beaches and harbors.

The homes were once, and in some cases still are, owned by people with names like Lawler, Selfridge, Uihlein, Wacker, Billings, Wrigley, Harris, Crane, Ryerson, Mitchell, and Swift. The list was representative of Chicago's social and business leadership, although it was lacking the Fields, the Palmers, and the Pullmans. However, Selfridge was another man made rich by Field, and Uihlein was a member of Milwaukee's great brewery family, the owner of the Joseph Schlitz Co. Years later, after World War II, a descendant made additional millions backing his buddy from college and the U.S. Navy in business. The business became the very prosperous General Binding Corp., with the stock dramatically increasing in value even as Schlitz Brewing went flat. The buddy was William Lane. His son, also William, is now chairman of General Binding and of the Lane group of Chicago banks. The senior Lane was killed in a freak accident—his vehicle plunged down an embankment—on his 300,000-acre ranch in New Mexico. Lane was an enthusiastic buyer of real estate, and he also owned one of the largest farms in the Virginia horse country near Warrenton. Years ago, in part to help out a friend, he bought six lots in Naples, Florida, where fellow Chicagoan Glen Sample, a former advertising man, was developing Port Royal as an exclusive residential resort area. At his death his estate started selling off the still vacant land at prices in the $750,000 range per lot.

Port Royal and Naples, on the southern Gulf coast of Florida, have grown into one of the great resort and retirement areas for Chicagoans and Midwesterners—that is, for those who do or did carry dollar signs or corporate titles of weight behind their names. Sarasota, also on Florida's west coast, is another haven for those escaping Chicago, thanks to the original developer, Mrs. Potter Palmer. If Palm Beach and Hobe Sound have their share of Chicagoans, so too does Palm Springs. Until his death James Kemper, Sr., who built a local insurance agency into the multibillion-dollar Kemper Financial Service empire (insurance, stocks, bonds, and money market funds), was the patriarch of Palm Springs' Racquet Club. Charles H. Wacker came from a wealthy Chicago family involved in the malt and brewing business. He went on to get into banking, stocks, and grain futures. As the longtime chairman of the Chicago Plan Commission, Wacker played a key role in designing the layout of the modern central city and creating the Outer Drive along the lakefront and the boulevard named after him, both noteworthy contributions to permitting traffic to move and the city to breathe and grow.

The newspapers of the time often pointed out that N. W. Harris was a thirty-ninth-generation direct descendant of Charlemagne, and he had the family coat of arms carved into the fireplace in the fifty-foot-long living room of the house he built at Lake Geneva in 1905. Harris was the founder of a bond firm that evolved into the Harris Trust & Savings Bank, in modern times the fourth-largest bank in Chicago. The last of the family to direct the bank, Stanley Harris, a banker of perception and a man with an intellectual bent, retired in 1984. A neighbor at Lake Geneva, with a magnificent home called Villa Hortense after his wife, was Edward F. Swift, son of the patriarch, Gustavus, and one of his eleven children. C. K. G. Billings was something else. Billings became president of Peoples Gas at age 25 when his father decided to give up that post. Father also passed along a $20 million fortune a little later, and Billings became known nationally for his championship trotting horses, his collection of automobiles, his yachts and parties. His wife was the daughter of Andrew MacLeish, the very wealthy Scot who was the silent partner among the Scots in Chicago's second most successful department store, Carson Pirie Scott & Co. And she was the sister of the poet and playwright Archibald MacLeish.

Billings was also known for the building he bought from the grounds of the Chicago World's Columbian Exposition of 1893 and moved to his Lake Geneva estate. It was the fair's Norwegian building, an authentic Norse church, complete with dragon heads flying from the roof peaks. Unlike far too many families and companies, MacLeish and Pirie descendants and their enterprise have persisted into the current era. John T. Pirie was a recent chairman of the corporation, and the corporation, now ringing up sales of more than $1 billion, has diversified into such things as airline catering, restaurants, and specialty shops across the country.

In 1985 the Chicago *Sun-Times* came up with the most titillating piece of gossip since a three-foot-high statue of Mrs. Edith Rockefeller McCormick, the wife of Cyrus McCormick's son Harold, made its appearance in the city more than half a century earlier. (Harold had served for all of four years as president of International Harvester and then in 1922 assumed the chairman's title and allowed non-family corporate men to run the company day-to-day.) Supposedly, the statue, adorned only with hat, necklace, gloves, and shoes, was a sarcastic reference to Mrs. McCormick's penchant for younger men. After helping to plan and furnish a forty-room Lake Forest mansion, Edith, John D.'s daughter, took off for Europe in 1913, not to return for eight years. When she did come back to Chicago her head was full of psychology she had absorbed in Switzerland from Dr. Carl Jung, Freud's dissident student. She also put much faith in what the stars might tell her and in the opinions of her companion, one Edwin Kreen, a young architect who was installed at the Drake Hotel across the street from the McCormicks' intown mansion. Meanwhile, her abandoned husband, Harold, fell madly in love with Ganna Walska, a dark-haired beauty who aspired to be an opera singer but who, the record proved, had a far greater talent for meeting and marrying rich men. Supposedly, she had married a baron, a New York doctor, and Alexander Smith Cochran, called by the newspapers the country's richest bachelor.

Harold pursued Ganna to Paris, where Ganna received him and his pleas one day after her marriage to Cochran. Somehow the Cochran marriage did not go smoothly, especially in that Cochran insisted on upsetting Ganna's sensitive soul by pressing upon her vulgar things like diamonds. There was a divorce. Meanwhile, Harold was busy. Edith agreed to give him a divorce, and having passed his 51st birthday, he girded himself for life with Ganna. Putting himself on a diet and exercising daily, he entered a hospital in Chicago for an operation he sought to keep secret.

In that this was the 1920s and a time when newspapers often carried stories about monkey glands and Swiss surgeons who performed miracles, there was much chatter about Harold's operation.

Something apparently accomplished Harold's purposes. In any event, Ganna later complained of Harold's preoccupation with the physical aspects of love when she had so much to offer in the way of the spiritual. Even so, the marriage lasted for nearly a decade and cost Harold only $6 million in Great Depression dollars.

Edith Rockefeller McCormick always kept a room ready for Harold in the Lake Shore Drive mansion in case he should decide to return, and he always sent her a single red rose on her birthday no matter how far away he was.

Often considered the world's richest woman when she was a McCormick as well as a Rockefeller, Edith squandered a few millions on this and that, most notably her idea to let Edwin Kreen build a utopian village on the shores of Lake Michigan. For starters she paid a thousand dollars an acre for 1,500 acres of land on the lake south of Kenosha, Wisconsin, sixty miles north of Chicago. Millions more went into preliminary work (e.g., dredging a harbor) before the great stock market crash of 1929 halted the easy flow of funds. The Rockefeller family moved in and straightened out her affairs, eventually moving her to a suite in the Drake Hotel and putting her on a budget of $300,000 a year. But she suffered an early death in 1932 and was buried in Graceland Cemetery ("Amazing Graceland," the boneyard of the wealthiest Wasps in the Midwest, writer Hoke Norris once called it) next to the two children she lost, Edith at age six months and John at four years. About that piece of gossip reported by the *Sun-Times*. It went this way:

In 1974 Hollywood was shooting a movie version of F. Scott Fitzgerald's novel *The Great Gatsby* in Chicago with actor Bruce Dern in a leading role, the husband of heroine Daisy Buchanan. Bruce Dern happens to be the grandson of Bruce MacLeish, once the chairman of Carson Pirie Scott & Co. One day during the shooting Dern got a note saying, "Could you come see me for a half hour?" It was signed "Mrs. Pirie." Dern could and did.

Mrs. Pirie, Ginevra, was 90 years old. She handed Dern a shoebox full of what turned out to be "passionate" love letters written to Ginevra by none other than F. Scott. "I wanted you to know that Scott Fitzgerald and I were lovers," Dern quoted Mrs. Pirie as saying. The *Sun-Times* account went on to quote Dern thusly: "She was the prototype for Daisy. Ginevra's father kept her at home in Lake Forest, telling Fitzgerald, 'Leave my daughter alone. She's not going to Hollywood. She's not going to Paris. She's going to live on the North Shore and marry a banker.'" Not quite but near enough. She stayed home and married John T. Pirie.

Lake Geneva is still pretty much a microcosm of Chicago and Chicago society except that developers, as they have for decades, keep on buying up the old estates, razing the big houses, and subdividing the property. Often a most attractive summer residence today was once the boathouse, barn, laundry, or garage on an estate.

Among the aristocrats of Chicago, William Wrigley, Jr.,

was a latecomer. He didn't arrive in Chicago from Philadelphia until 1891, but before the turn of the century the profits from his bubbling chewing-gum company had made it possible for him to send the family to Lake Geneva for the summers even if they only stayed in rented cottages.

But by 1911 he was able to buy the major estate once owned by C. K. G. Billings and to add to the buildings and the grounds. In 1955 his son Philip K. had the old (1892) rambling cottage torn down and replaced with a modern brick house. For one reason and another, the Lake Geneva estate no longer fits the third generation of Wrigleys. William Wrigley III, among other things faced with a disastrous tax bill when his father and mother died one after the other, put the seventeen-room mansion and nineteen acres with 440 front feet on the lake up for sale in 1983 at an asking price of $2.3 million. Two years later no one had met the price, but Wrigley did succeed in unloading the family's thirty-eight-room Chicago mansion on Lakeview in 1984 for $1.2 million. The house had stood empty since 1931, when Philip Wrigley, fearing kidnapping or worse in that Depression era, moved the family to the comparative safety of a high-rise apartment on Lake Shore Drive.

Cynics express the fear that one day Chicago is going to run out of diseases. "Even now," says one young socialite, always on the go, "Monday night is no longer sacred." On the one hand, there are so many charity balls and fundraising events that sometimes there are not enough nights in the week. On the other, if Chicago does run out of diseases, how is an ambitious family to find a cause to sponsor or an exciting event to attend?

"What you always have is what you can see most plainly at the Lyric Opera and the Chicago Symphony," one observer of the social scene says. "You have people like Alfred Stepan who would walk ten miles on a rainy night and pay his last dime to hear great opera. And then you have those whose real interest stops at the opening-night festivities, the social clout that may go with a listing among the sponsors, and the income-tax deduction for their contributions."

(The reference is to Alfred C. Stepan, Jr., who died at age 75 in 1984. A great-great-grandson of a noted German baritone, Stepan was the founder of Stepan Chemical Co., a $100 million producer of basic chemicals. An interesting facet of the company's business goes way back to the time when Congress was getting ready to pass the Pure Food and Drug Act, one aim being to stop the everyday sale of various patent medicines, prepared primarily for the supposed nervous disorders of women, that were laced with opium or cocaine. The Coca-Cola Company, with a product commonly known for years in the South as a "Dope," decided to get rid of the cocaine in the Coke formula. Stepan's predecessor firm was secretly hired to extract the drug from the ingredients for the Coca-Cola formula. Today Stepan is still doing that job and is a principal supplier of cocaine to the dental and medical professions.)

For social status, the place to be is on the board of one of the long-established, good, and best "causes"—the Chicago Symphony, the Lyric Opera, the Art Institute, and the Field Museum of Natural History. Hope McCormick, wife of Brooks McCormick, the last of the name to head International Harvester, for instance, "does" the zoo, the hospitals, the Art Institute, the Field Museum, and the Chicago Historical Society, among other things, says a friend, who adds: "Brooks and Hope have been the real leaders of society in Chicago. She is a fabulous lady with a great sense of humor and unbelievable energy. She will do things like completing the work for a charity ball for a thousand and then take off only hours after the ball with her grandchildren on an African safari. The McCormicks keep an apartment in town on North State Parkway and their estate in the horse country, where, I suspect, Brooks would just as soon these days ride and show horses as attend a banquet for any cause."

As a generalization, the boards of the major institutions are made up of men. And the men are usually officers of corporations, some self-made, some also representative of older, Wasp money. The corporate connection is critical. A man who has succeeded in piling up millions during his lifetime may leave a million or two to his favorite institution or charity. Meanwhile, however, if he is chairman and chief executive officer of a large corporation, he influences the corporation and the corporation's foundation to make or increase its annual contribution.

Furthermore, he can hold little breakfasts at the Chicago Club, where the conversation in polite terms works around to something like this: Okay, Frank, you support my drive (or my wife's drive) and I'll support yours.

Interested or ambitious wives usually end up in, or strive for, a position on the essential women's auxiliary, working up to the chairmanship of the annual fund-raiser and then to head of the auxiliary. As noted, a well-placed husband can help, but not only with a foundation grant. Corporate contributions by the husband's company can also come by way of lending everything from a smart young man to a company truck.

The list of the trustees for the Chicago Historical Society offers a representative look at the power structure in the city as it exists in the latter half of the 1980s, even if membership on the board of one of the larger institutions like the Art Institute carries somewhat more weight. Recently the society's trustees included Bowen Blair (the McCormick Blair family), Mrs. Brooks McCormick, Bryan S. Reid, Jr. (old money, new ventures), Edward Byron Smith, Jr. (the Northern Trust and Illinois Tool Works), Philip W. Hummer (commercial and investment banking), Philip D. Block III (great-grandson of the founder of Inland Steel), and Mrs. Newton N. Minow (wife of the prominent lawyer and former Federal Communications Commission chairman). Incidentally, Mrs. Minow still likes to tell the story of the dressing-down she got years ago when during a driving rain she drove up to the entrance to the old Mike Fish restaurant and asked the doorman if he would see whether or not Mr. Minow was inside.

One of the motivations for the founding of the Chicago Museum of Contemporary Art was a feeling that the Art Institute had a stuffy view of the art world and had also restricted Jewish participation even though the Leigh Blocks, of the Inland Steel family, were fixtures at the Art Institute as important collectors and contributors.

In 1984, Arthur Rubloff donated $6 million and a collection of bronze sculptures to the Chicago Art Institute. It was the largest single money gift to the institute in its existence of more than a century, according to Marshall Field V, chairman of the $40 million fund-raising drive then in progress. A grateful board promptly named a wing of the museum after Rubloff, then 82 years old, always impressive at six feet two, dressed by Savile Row, complete with cane, spats, and black derby, doubly impressive after his 1980 second marriage as a widower to Mary Taylor, blonde, striking, half his age, the former wife of an actor, whom he met at a Manhattan party.

Rubloff came out of a Minnesota iron-range town, Chisholm, where his Russian Jewish father ran a dry-goods store before he moved the family to Chicago. Arthur broke into Chicago real estate as a salesman in the 1920s and with typical Rubloff self-confidence set up his own firm after the 1929 stock market—and real estate—crash.

Rubloff's survival during the Great Depression might have predicted his fabulous success in later years. Since the time of the Fields and the Palmers, Chicago real estate had been in the hands of immigrants all right, but immigrants from Yankeeland. The developers, the brokers, the owners had names like Warner W. Baird, Farwell, Browne, and Frederick Marsh Bowes. Bowes was one of the men who helped to build what is now Michigan Avenue and the Gold Coast after Potter Palmer and the city wrested the area, in part landfill dumped after the Great Chicago Fire, from old Captain George Wellington Streeter, a single-minded squatter called a "rude, blasphemous, drunken thief" by Palmer.

In any event, Rubloff's name was attached to some of the great real estate developments in modern Chicago history.

As befitting the Windy City, Rubloff took more credit than he deserved, but the buildings went up, the deals were made, many with the fabulous New York investment banking firm Allen & Co., and the money rolled in. As just one example, press reports said Rubloff and his partners picked up a profit of $70 million when they sold Sandburg Village, the huge and initially daring apartment complex that changed the face of the city's Near North Side, to a condominium converter.

Anyone who attended one of Rubloff's dinner parties before his death in 1986 or came to his attention in a service capacity (e.g., worked in the barbershop he patronized) received generous gifts—a money tip, a watch, a cane, a gold-plated shoehorn. Some of the guests at his champagne-and-caviar dinners at his lakeshore apartment were a little taken aback, but Rubloff insisted that gift giving is something he enjoyed.

On a much grander scale, every cause in the city sought his help for years and after his marriage urged Mary Rubloff to join its board. Deliberately, consciously, Rubloff, without a doubt a man of tremendous ego in all his dealings, had meant to do something with his considerable fortune while he lived. The Art Institute gift was only one of the many Rubloff made during his life. He pledged $5 million to the University of Chicago medical center and another $5 million to a law school building at Northwestern University. In 1985 he figured he had already given away a good $30 million, and he did not hesitate to criticize his peers for failing to weigh in in like manner. "Cheap" was a word he often used when he was asked about the generosity of Chicago's aristocracy.

That "cheap" shot may be aimed at old Wasp money, those families where preservation of capital is the cardinal rule and the effort is to live on the interest on the interest. One friend of Rubloff's, an admirer who accepted his "egomania," was always delighted to dine with the Rubloffs at their apartment home at the Carlyle. He swears he never accepts a Lake Forest dinner invitation. For Lake Forest read Wasp. "The meat," he says, "is certain to be the week's supermarket bargain."

John H. Johnson, a Rubloff neighbor in the Carlyle, is listed by *Forbes* among the 400 richest people in America. Malcolm Forbes, publisher and editor-in-chief of *Forbes*, won't talk to his own people about how much money he has but Malcolm has much more than $150 million. Johnson owns *Ebony* magazine and allows his editors to list him among the 100 most influential blacks in America (along with fellow Chicagoans the Reverend Jesse Jackson and John Sengstacke, publisher of the Chicago *Defender*). It is certainly correct that Johnson is among the most influential of blacks. He owns not only *Ebony*, with a circulation of 8 million, but also *Jet*, a pocket-size, less serious magazine that nevertheless, like *Ebony*, emphasizes the positive.

Born in poverty in Arkansas, John Johnson was brought to Chicago by his hard-working, determined mother, who scrubbed floors and made certain Johnson learned what the public schools of Chicago could offer. Working for a black-owned insurance company, Johnson was handed the job of editing a house organ on the strength of the fact that he was bright enough and educated enough to be taking courses at the University of Chicago.

By 1942 Johnson was convinced that there was a need and a place for a black-oriented magazine, and he borrowed $500 on his mother's furniture and launched *Negro Digest*, patterned after *Reader's Digest*. It was something less than a success, and he switched to *Ebony*, patterned after *Life* magazine. Today Johnson owns radio stations in addition to the magazines and has some major real estate holdings, including the eleven-story building he put up on South Michigan Avenue to house the headquarters for his empire. Among the employees are his wife, Eunice, secretary-treasurer of Johnson Publications, and his only child, Linda, a vice-president, bright, striking, hard-working, intent on deserving the right to inherit the publications, and proving it.

Social Chicago, Eppie (Ann Landers) Lederer and Abra
Rockefeller Prentice Anderson, who live across the way, and
the rest of the city, too, apparently approved of Linda's
wedding. It was at least the wedding of 1984, everybody
said. John Johnson was 66, Linda was 26, and the groom, S.
André Rice, a handsome and accomplished stockbroker in
the Chicago offices of Wall Street's prestigious Goldman,
Sachs & Co., was 27. The vows were exchanged in the
Fourth Presbyterian Church, the church of choice in the city
for a large segment of Wasp society. The reception, for 700
including Sammy Davis, Jr., Mayor Harold Washington, and
Cook County state's attorney Richard M. Daley, was held in
the Westin Hotel across Michigan Avenue.

The champagne was Dom Pérignon, the roses were flown
in from South America (Colombia), someone paced off one
of the buffet tables and came up with a measurement of
eighty-four feet, the wedding cake was six feet high, it took
two of the hotel's largest dining rooms to seat the guests for
dinner, Linda's wedding gown was designed by Jean-Louis
Scherrer of Paris, three orchestras played, and everyone had
a very, very good time.

It would seem that two of the country's publishing em-
pires and molders of opinion will be run by women. Both
Linda Johnson, equipped with a journalism degree from the
University of Southern California, and her father made it
clear that Linda would take over someday when she signed
up for Northwestern University courses leading to a master's
degree in business administration.

Over at *Playboy* headquarters, Christie Hefner, also beautiful and bright, already had management experience at age
32 in 1985 as president and chief operating officer. Father
Hugh was spending most of his time on the West Coast and
had no objection when Christie solved a problem for him by
turning the seventy-two-room *Playboy* mansion on the Near
North Side over to the Chicago Art Institute to be used as a
dormitory for students of the institute school.

Most of the city's great institutions, and great wealth, go

back to the industrial and business explosion during and after the Civil War: in the half century after the war the city saw the creation of the Art Institute, the symphony, Hull-House, the Field Museum, the Museum of Science and Industry (Julius Rosenwald, a model for the giving-while-I'm-alive idea), the Newberry and Crerar libraries, the University of Chicago (Rockefeller), the Chicago opera (McCormick and Insull), the Armour Institute (established to train the young poor in basic technology and religion; now the Illinois Institute of Technology).

The Commercial Club of Chicago was founded in 1877, and forty of the original sixty members lived on or about Prairie Avenue. Field, Pullman, and Palmer did not have to go far to put the power structure in gear. It was the Commercial Club that commissioned the Burnham Plan and pushed through his designs (1909) for parks and boulevards and a green lakefront with the dogged help of A. Montgomery Ward, founder of the very first mail-order house. (Ward spent decades and thousands of his dollars in and out of the courts fending off those who thought commercial and industrial development more fitting than beaches and parks for the lakeshore.)

For years it was the Commercial Club, perhaps with some help from the City Club, that sparked major developments in Chicago, supporting or curbing City Hall initiatives. Curiously enough, both clubs withered during the 1960s and 1970s. Curiously enough, both began to show new vigor in the 1980s, with the Commercial Club mounting a major leadership effort to reverse what the club called a long-term erosion of Chicago's economic vitality.

Perhaps the erosion of the business community's leadership in the earlier decades was not so curious. Those were the years when Richard Daley ran Chicago from his office in City Hall. What he wanted got done and what he wanted did not normally demand great effort and more or less got the automatic support of the business community.

Chicago has always been a city with a diverse population.

Richard Daley's home base, the Irish district called Bridgeport, dates back to the Irish laborers who came to the city to build the Illinois and Michigan Canal in the mid-19th century. Bridgeport is located where the Chicago River and the canal meet. French explorers, looking for a passage to India, followed the Indians there and found the portage from Lake Michigan to the Illinois river system and the Mississippi. During the civil rights movement of the 1960s it was pretty generally and at last conceded in Chicago that Jean Baptiste Point Du Sable was "of mixed African and European parentage," as a brochure produced by the Du Sable Museum put it, and in 1779 was the first person other than an Indian to settle permanently in what became Chicago.

In the period around 1900 city notices were often printed in as many as nine languages. Today Spanish-speaking people make up the dominant minority even though the city has elected its first black mayor. Always Chicago boasts of its neighborhoods and ethnic traditions. You name it and someone will tell you that Chicago is the largest or second-largest Polish, Yugoslav, Italian, etc., city in the world, just about every people or culture in the world except Chinese, and that is left out only because China has so many huge cities.

Nathan Cummings's son was the first Jew to sit on the Palm Beach town council. Nate was a self-made man who did not finish grade school. After a couple of false starts in Montreal, where his father owned a shoe company, Cummings bought and sold a candy company, pocketing a half-million profit, and decided to retire. But it wasn't long before he was back in business. He paid something like $200,000 to buy a Baltimore tea and coffee wholesaler. Only a little over 40 at the time, he proceeded to turn the little Maryland company into a multibillion-dollar corporation, Consolidated Foods, now called Sara Lee after its best-known consumer product. Cummings once fired Charles Lubin, the Chicago genius who created Sara Lee and the frozen-dessert industry, because Lubin, angered by a Cummings cross-examination, stalked out of a meeting of the board of directors. Cummings made no comment except to inquire quietly if anyone had a suggestion for a new president for Sara Lee. Much later, when Cummings had retired a second time, this time as chairman of Consolidated, in 1968, he had his successor fired because the man had had the audacity to have Cummings's picture removed from the lobby of the company's headquarters in Chicago. At age 80 Cummings threw a birthday party for himself at the Waldorf with 600 in attendance. Bob Hope was the emcee. Cummings knew where he had bought and how much he had paid for every one of his paintings by Renoir, Picasso, Monet, Matisse, Chagall, Gauguin, Degas, and others, and before his death at age 88 in 1985 he gave the Metropolitan Museum of Art his entire collection of 600 pieces of pre-Columbian art.

Cummings's daughter, Beatrice "Buddy" Mayer, is big in Chicago social and fund-raising activities along with other stars like Sugar Rautbord, the former wife of Clayton Rautbord, an heir to the American Photocopy fortune; Cindy Pritzker, Jay's wife; and Renee Crown, Lester's wife.

Lester Crown, the son of Col. Henry Crown, doesn't need the flak he took in 1985 over the General Dynamics cost overruns on military hardware and his travel expenses. Once when the General Dynamics' board tried to push Col. Crown out—he had sold the family's sand and cement business to Dynamics for a large chunk of GD's preferred stock —Crown turned around and with old friend Nate Cummings bought effective control of Dynamics, the huge defense contractor, now doing an $8 billion annual business. Having donated at least $100 million to good works, the Colonel and his family (Lester has seven children) are worth well over $1 billion, depending on what day the fortune is counted.

That's not a figure of speech. The Crowns own 9.6 million shares of stock in General Dynamics. With the stock jumping around every day, the family can win or lose $10 million or $15 million between breakfast orange juice and after-dinner coffee.

With openhanded people like the Pritzkers, Rubloff, the Crowns, and others, the Jewish community raises spectacular amounts of money for charity and the city's institutions, not counting the millions that have gone into Israeli government bonds over the years and such projects as the Weizmann Institute of Science, the great research center in Rehoboth, Israel.

VIII

McCORMICK

Right up to the last, Cyrus Hall McCormick, the inventor of
the Virginia reaper and the man who did more than Presidents and kings to change the face of the world, was a
fighter. He always knew he was right; in fact, he was pretty
sure that God was often perched on his shoulder, or as he
once put it, his company would not have prospered were it
not for "the fact that Providence has seemed to assist me in
our business." He had a fierce temper, especially when he
felt he had been crossed, and he would fight doggedly to
"put down" his enemies, from legitimate business competitors to casual offenders of the McCormick right.

Once in 1862 the Pennsylvania Railroad offended him
when he was returning to Chicago by way of Philadelphia
from Washington and one of his monumental patent battles.
He was traveling with his wife, two children, a cousin, two
servants, and nine trunks. The Pennsylvania Railroad sought
to assess an excess baggage charge of $8.70 against him.
McCormick protested, refused to pay, ordered his trunks
removed from the train, and retreated to a hotel to plan
battle strategy. He needn't have bothered. As any traveler

might guess, the railroad forgot to remove the McCormick trunks. They went on to Chicago, where a chance bolt of lightning started a fire that destroyed the lot. For once Providence was against him, and the railroad refused to pay what McCormick thought was his due. The courts were always high up on McCormick's list of favorite places and he went to court. He sued and lost. He appealed and lost. He appealed again and lost. Finally, he won. The court awarded him $18,000. But the victory came twenty-three years later and McCormick had been dead for a year.

John Ruff was also a man with a temper. His temper earned him a footnote in history, not as a winner but as a loser. He ordered young Cyrus McCormick to get off his land and stay off.

McCormick was twenty-three years old that midsummer day of 1832 in the Valley of Virginia. He had come to Ruff's farm from the McCormick family's nearby Walnut Grove farm to demonstrate to an assembled crowd of local gentry that he had at last solved a problem that had plagued the world since man evolved from hunter to cultivator. The worst, the backbreaking, part of securing the family's daily bread since before Abraham had been cutting the field of standing grain so that the wheat could be threshed and the separated kernels ground into flour. In every culture, with some few exceptions, the annual harvest had been accomplished by men or women stooping and bending and flailing at the stalks with some form of hand-held knife. Carthage, once the breadbasket of the Mediterranean, apparently made an early stab at a mechanical solution. Crude stone carvings, dated about 150 B.C., show a revolving drum equipped with a circular knife that could only have been used to cut grain. Pliny the Elder reported in 70 A.D. that another cumbersome device was in use in Gaul. It was a wheeled cart armed with teeth and pulled through the grain by oxen to tear off the heads of wheat. Otherwise, the man and his knife. Eventually the knife was curved to catch more grain at a sweep. Until portable electric clippers arrived on the scene, every hardware store in America still carried that same knife, the sickle, the highest state of the art for the homeowner who needed to cut tall grass and weeds. For the grain farmer, a few centuries of man's ingenuity had produced the scythe, simply a longer knife attached to a long curved handle with grips so that the harvester could get two hands on it. It cut wheat faster, if a farmer had the strength to swing it. In McCormick's time, another big advance was the cradle. That was a scythe with long wooden fingers attached to the handle parallel to the knife. In the hands of an expert with big muscles, the cradle was swung so that the cut grain fell on the wooden fingers to be dumped in a neat pile at the end of the swing. This technological breakthrough eased the farmer's labor in gathering the grain for threshing.

Cyrus Hall McCormick was a good sturdy man. But he did not like swinging a scythe or cradle. He invented a cradle that was much lighter than those in standard use. He didn't like that either.

In 1831 he set about trying to find a way to get a horse to do the heavy work. For something close to a century, those clever Scots, among others, had been trying to devise such a horse-drawn machine. In 1780, the English Society of Arts, Manufacturers and Commerce, an official representative of the burgeoning industrial revolution, established a prize for the invention of a mechanical reaper. But little if anything of practical value came of the inventions that did sprout in England then and later in this country.

In the spring of 1831 Cyrus McCormick built his first reaper. In July of that year he demonstrated the machine with success in a field near Steele's Tavern, not far from his home. Now, a year later, on John Ruff's farm, McCormick was going to demonstrate an improved model of his great invention. McCormick's horse-drawn machine did indeed cut wheat, but it was also, as the seventy-five or so spectators and John Ruff could see, flattening and crushing some of Ruff's crop. In short order, Ruff demanded that McCormick get his crazy contraption out of his fields. Fortunately, William Taylor, owner of the adjoining farm, chose to see how much good work McCormick's machine was doing. Taylor lifted down a section of rail fence and invited McCormick to drive on in. And fortunately for McCormick, Mr. Taylor was the owner of some good farmland, level and well cleared. The reaper clipped right along, doing its job, with one of the McCormick slaves, Jo Anderson, walking alongside and raking the cut wheat off the rear platform into manageable piles. McCormick's success was acclaimed locally, and across the Blue Ridge divide in tidewater Virginia, where the rich folks and big farmers lived. Eventually, the story even reached the New York journals.

In a different time and under different circumstances that might have been it for Cyrus McCormick. Overnight fame and fortune.

Properly, McCormick should have been born in, say, the Genesee Valley of New York, where there were large and prosperous wheat farms, where slaves did not take onerous labor from white shoulders, and where a quickening awareness of the industrial revolution might have sparked greater interest in a new labor-saving machine than it did in an isolated Virginia valley.

McCormick's people had come to Virginia by way of Scotland, Northern Ireland (banished there by an English king alarmed over the spread of Presbyterianism in Scotland), and Pennsylvania. Thomas McCormick arrived with his wife in Philadelphia in 1735 and began farming 200 acres in Cumberland County, Pennsylvania. His fifth son, Robert, did well as a farmer, married the daughter of a prosperous neighbor, and for unknown reasons took his wife and five children off to Virginia in 1799. The proceeds from the sale of his Pennsylvania farm were enough to buy 450 acres and a large log house in the Valley of Virginia. Apparently he prospered; by 1800 he owned three slaves and eight horses, little enough by plantation standards but substantial in the mountain country.

A sixth child, also Robert, was born in Virginia. On February 11, 1808, the second Robert married Mary Ann Hall. Mary Ann, whose family lived a couple of miles down the road from the McCormick Walnut Grove farm, brought a dowry of horses and cattle valued at $1,000 to the McCormicks and much more. By all accounts she was not only a handsome woman but also intelligent, witty, sharp-tongued, ambitious, shrewd in money matters, and energetic enough to work in the fields if necessary. Mary Ann was a good match for husband Robert, a quiet, studious man, apparently something more of a dreamer than a doer. Robert loved to tinker. At Walnut Grove he had a blacksmith shop and a carpenter shop and he built a lime kiln, a gristmill to grind his grain, and a distillery. (It was a strict and temperate Presbyterian household with family prayers daily, but Robert wrestled with Calvin and saw no sin in selling the devil's brew to others.) All in all, things went pleasantly for Robert and Mary Ann. They added acres to the original family farm, built an impressive stone-and-brick house (sixty-five feet by fifty feet) in 1822 and by 1830 owned 1,200 acres, nine slaves, and twice that many horses. Along the way they created quite a family.

Cyrus Hall McCormick, the firstborn, came along on February 15, 1809. Then there were William S. (1815), Mary Caroline (1817), Leander J. (1819), John P. (1820, dead at age 29), and Amanda J. (1822).

The young Cyrus was everything that he should have been. He had a strong, handsome face, thick dark brown hair, broad shoulders. Like his father, he was a tinkerer. As a boy he built a revolving world globe, and his first invention very smartly was that grain cradle substantially lighter than those in use in the Virginia fields.

One way or another—through his mother and Presbyterian ministers—Cyrus was better educated than might be expected. Always he was meticulous about grammar and spelling, and as an adult he carried a small dictionary (and, when he traveled, a Bible).

In addition to being a tinkerer and a dreamer, Cyrus was also ambitious, aggressive, and equipped with just that proper dollop of paranoia that makes a fierce and determined competitor. As far back as 1816, his father had dreamed up a reaping machine and had built one. It wouldn't do the job and neither would several successive versions. There was no doubt but that Robert McCormick was handy. He did build his gristmill and he did invent an improved bellows for his blacksmith forge and he did invent a device that automatically stopped his gristmill when the last of the grain reached the grinding stone. In 1834, he was granted a patent on an "Improvement in a Hydraulic Machine for Working Machinery." He also invented a machine to thresh harvested wheat and he actually advertised it for sale.

Then there was the "hemp-breaking" machine invented by Robert. Hemp was a crop recently and ultimately unsuccessfully introduced into Virginia and Kentucky with the idea that its fibers would be sought after as a material for making rope (not its flowers and leaves as a source of hashish). In the fall of 1831, 22-year-old Cyrus charged across the mountains to neighboring Kentucky determined to make his fortune by building and selling the hemp breaker, designed to separate the usable hemp fibers from the stalk. The project was a flop. And rather obviously Cyrus should never have undertaken the venture. He should have been back home, working on the reaper. Or his hillside plow.

Earlier, in 1831, Cyrus had invented a plow that would do a superior job on the hilly farms of Virginia. He had set out to sell it and had been modestly successful, even making a little money at a price of $7 and later $9 per copy.

If he had worked at it, he might have made a real success of the plow. Better yet, he could have devoted his energies to the reaper. He had invented that, too, in the incredibly short time of six weeks. Starting from scratch in the late spring of 1831, Cyrus had produced a reaper that did for a fact cut wheat and did prove its worth in the demonstration on a farm near Steele's Tavern in July 1831. Belatedly, after the excursion into Kentucky, Cyrus went to work trying to improve his reaper, and it was an improved machine that performed so well in farmer Taylor's wheat fields in 1832. Still, McCormick was strangely and uncharacteristically dilatory in pushing ahead with his great invention. Perhaps he didn't quite realize what he had in hand; after the Taylor demonstration, a schoolteacher proclaimed that the reaper was worth $100,000. Cyrus said he would gladly sell it for half that. A good, practical reason may have slowed him up. Virginia suffered a series of crop failures in the 1830s, and Cyrus may have realized that the local farmers were not ready for a revolution, especially one that required a cash outlay. Then there was the fact that Cyrus, as he insisted later, did devote considerable energy to improving the way the reaper was made and the way it worked, particularly in wet fields and on rough terrain.

And, after all, in 1832 Cyrus McCormick was a 23-year-old farmer living in a rustic, isolated section of a nation just beginning to establish itself. He didn't have an engineering degree from MIT or a master's in business administration from the University of Chicago and he didn't have a corporate organization behind him.

But something stirred the McCormick juices in 1833. Cyrus was not the only inventor to take an interest in revolutionizing the production of the world's bread. In England by 1786 the invention of reaping machines was a regular sort of thing. At least one or more patents were filed for reapers almost every year after that. By the early 1800s, Yankees, freed from Britain's attempt to keep all technology in the home country, were regularly inventing reapers too. But few of them materialized, and those that did worked fitfully at best. Then, in 1833, there was Obed Hussey.

It has been argued that Cyrus McCormick was a true inventive genius. Other than profiting from his father's work, it would have been difficult for him to copy the inventions of others, living as he did in his backcountry Virginia valley at a time when communications were something less than instantaneous.

Nevertheless, McCormick certainly did read the April 1834 edition of a publication called *Mechanic's Magazine.* The magazine carried a laudatory announcement of the invention and patenting of a reaper by one Obed Hussey. McCormick, reacting angrily, as he did throughout his life whenever he thought someone was stepping on his toes, fired off a letter to the magazine warning Hussey that he was infringing on McCormick prior invention and rights.

Hussey's machine had been patented in 1833, but weirdly enough, McCormick had made no attempt to patent either his first machine of 1831 or his improved 1832 model. In his letter attacking Hussey, McCormick first made his argument that he had held off his patent application until he could perfect his reaper. Finally, McCormick did obtain his patent on June 21, 1834, paying a fee of $30 to the U.S. Treasury and getting a certificate signed in those uncomplicated days by the President of the United States, Andrew Jackson. His "war," as it was called, with Hussey, a Nantucket whaler and blacksmith who wore a black patch over his sightless left eye and who invented his reaper while unaccountably living on a farm near Cincinnati, continued in the newspapers, in advertisements, in the courts, and in Congress until 1860, when Hussey was killed in a railroad accident. And it went on long after that in regional and national battles waged by firms that obtained Hussey licenses and put improved versions up against the Virginia reaper. (From the early years on, McCormick's real choice of weapons in the war was the field trial, his machine against all comers. He never doubted that he could smash his rivals in head-to-head competition and very often he did. The trials became popular social events in rural America, with the entire community turning out to witness the battle. In some cases later on, the good farmers enjoyed the free beer provided by one or another company in the hope of influencing final judgments.)

The wonder is that schoolchildren today are not reading the story of the one-eyed Nantucket whaler instead of the triumph of the Virginia farm boy. Although McCormick did rush into print to assert vehemently his first rights to a practical reaper and even though he did finally obtain a patent, he left the field pretty much to Hussey and other rivals for the better part of a decade. Once, in later years, McCormick said he did not sell his first reaper until 1839, eight years after his very first model was completed in the family blacksmith shop. The statement is not technically accurate; McCormick probably intended it to indicate the date when he got down to serious business.

If McCormick was diverted from his real mission by a mistaken faith in his father's hemp-breaking machine and if he wasted energy on the real promise of his hillside plow, his iron-ore venture was something that could have ended his career.

The hills around the McCormick Virginia valley were shot full of iron-ore deposits, and the ore had been mined for years, even providing some of the metal for bullets fired in the Revolutionary War. By McCormick's time, the industrial revolution, sparked by Eli Whitney and his cotton gin, was proceeding apace and not only stimulating the invention of machinery but also creating a demand for iron. Other Virginia farmers had prospered mining iron ore, a fact that did not escape the McCormicks, blacksmiths and inventors of machinery.

Enthusiastically, they joined with a monied partner, bought a promising iron-ore site, and set up a smelting furnace. After a long struggle the venture was just beginning to prove itself when the Panic of 1837 swept the country. In Richmond, the price of iron ore dropped from $50 and $55 a ton to $40 and then to $30 and $25. With Scotch determination, the McCormicks hung on until January 1841, when the enterprise collapsed in a welter of debts and bitter feuding between the McCormicks and their partner. The McCormicks escaped debtor's prison a number of times by

raising bail, but in 1842 they were forced to mortgage the
family farm to keep ahead of persistent claimants. (There is
some evidence that it was a "friendly" mortgage, designed
only to tie up title to the farm so that it couldn't be sold out
from under the family.) Despite charges and countercharges
about the partnership's way of keeping books, Cyrus worked
hard to pay his debts. But it took him until 1846 to clear
himself.

The excursion into the iron business may have been a plus
for McCormick. Had it been a roaring success, he might
have spent his life scratching modest wealth from the Virginia hills. And as matters turned out, he gained invaluable
schooling the hard way in business and finance.

In spite of his side excursions, McCormick did not dismiss
the reaper. In fact, during those years he made a major
change and important improvements in the basic design of
the reaper, perfecting a horizontal reciprocating knife that
significantly improved the reaper's cutting ability. Although
Cyrus later claimed that his father's reaper was built on a
principle entirely different from his, the reciprocating knife
may have been adapted from Robert's hemp breaker.

In any event, by 1839 Cyrus was making serious efforts to
manufacture and sell his reaper. It was about time. Cyrus
was already 30 years old. As a farmer, tinkerer, and sometime entrepreneur, he was jumping this way and that in
pursuit of fortune, and he was fighting the iron-ore bankruptcy. He was a very reserved, even aloof man who dressed
meticulously long before he had money to spend on fine
tailors. He was a skilled horseman, he played the fiddle and
liked to sing (hymns), but he made few friends and some
thought him overly conceited. At 30 he was still a bachelor
with no serious entanglements; his younger brother William
often kidded him for not paying enough attention to
women.

Incredibly, McCormick sold only two reapers in 1840,
eight years after his storybook success on the farm of William Taylor. In 1842 he sold seven reapers, all built on the

Walnut Grove farm with its tiny log blacksmith shop. The reaper sold for only $100, and the $700 was enough in those days to be significant in helping Cyrus recover from the iron-ore disaster. By 1843 business was booming; Cyrus sold twenty-seven machines that year and fifty the next. And Walnut Grove was becoming impossible. Cyrus had his father to help oversee construction, and his brothers were also lending a hand. (In 1844, brother William was 29 years old and Leander was 25.) But Cyrus was still handcrafting crucial parts as well as making horseback forays out of the valley for days at a time to drum up sales, collect payments, and arrange shipments (by riverboat and canalboat where possible).

The year 1844 was critical for McCormick. He had the common sense or genius to be impressed by the increasing trickle of orders for the Virginia reaper from faraway places.

In the summer of 1844 McCormick set out on a grueling trip of exploration that took him to Ohio, Michigan, Indiana, Illinois, Wisconsin, Missouri, and back home by way of Cincinnati. At last enthusiastically into the business of selling, he was now convinced that the reaper was what it was in truth: a labor-saving device of vast importance to individual farmers and to a hungry world. Wherever Cyrus went, he was taking orders for the reaper and, dreaming of sales of 400 to 500 reapers in 1845, he was scouting the burgeoning "Western" territories to find men who could manufacture and sell the reaper for him. Long before Ford and General Motors and more than a century before McDonald's, McCormick was franchising. For a fee that might range from $100 to $1,000 depending on the size of the market area, he would grant a monopoly in a county or a region to a likely candidate, extracting an agreement that McCormick also would be paid a hefty $20, approximately one-fifth of the selling price, for every reaper sold.

As matters turned out, most of the local enterprises McCormick chartered proved to be disasters. The machines they produced often failed to perform satisfactorily in the field or simply wouldn't work, especially when the local genius decided to improve on McCormick's design. Worse, perhaps, some of his men, when canceled out by McCormick, signed up with his bitter rival, Hussey, and became competitors, using whatever ideas of both inventors that seemed best to them.

Nevertheless, in 1844, McCormick took the promising fork in the road. He was headed West, where the open land and the flat, broad prairies would make mechanization pay off and where labor, particularly farm labor for hire, was scarce. (A farmer might give up half his crop to anyone who would help with the harvest or see a year's crop rot in the fields.) In a letter to the family in Virginia, McCormick admitted to some awe at the West's great expanses of farmland and said that while the Virginia reaper might be a luxury in its home state, it was a necessity in prairie country.

McCormick could also see fatter profits if he not only sold but also manufactured in the West. "It seems wrong to pay $20 or $25 freight . . . when they [reapers] might be made in the West—considering, too, the greater uncertainty of shipping," he wrote in one of his letters.

Fortunately for McCormick, Obed Hussey chose to concentrate on the East. His two manufacturing plants in the late 1840s were located in Baltimore and New York at a time when the Genesee Valley of New York was the wheat-growing capital of the country and neighboring Pennsylvania was the biggest of the wheat-producing states.

Not that the newly aggressive Cyrus was content to will the Eastern market to the enemy. In time for the 1845 harvest, he signed up a firm, Seymour & Morgan, in Brockport, New York, on the Erie Canal. It turned out that Seymour & Morgan was one of his best local manufacturers —and equally good at scheming against McCormick. In 1847 Cyrus persuaded his younger brother Leander, then 28 years old and newly married, to leave the Virginia valley and move to Cincinnati to oversee operations at his Ohio licensee.

It is not hard to see in the Cincinnati venture a foreshadowing of McCormick's often unhappy relations with his brothers. In return for putting capital into the Cincinnati plant, Leander was to get a salary of $15 a week and share in the profits as a one-third partner. All Leander had to do was to turn out 100 reapers; at that rate he'd get his money out and clear $1,500 too. That was Cyrus's optimistic goal for the factory, optimistic because Cincinnati had never produced for McCormick. Originally, in 1845, Cyrus had hoped Cincinnati would turn out 200 reapers for the Ohio and Western markets. The following year, McCormick and his licensees sold only 328 reapers all told. And more than 100 of those were manufactured by the Brockport shop alone. (Very definitely, the age of the reaper had not arrived; that year, one Chicago manufacturer sold 2,700 cradles, the backbreaking improvement on the age-old scythe that had provided motivation for McCormick years earlier.) In any event, Cyrus closed the Cincinnati operation in a matter of months, and Leander, his pockets empty, went home to Walnut Grove nursing a grudge.

Years later Leander claimed as his own improvements in the reaper of vast importance to McCormick. The most significant of these was the placement of a second seat on the machine, this one for a man who could sit and rake the cut wheat back and off the reaper instead of trotting alongside. Adding a seat to the reaper sounds a simple task. But it wasn't. The entire machine had to be strengthened, balanced, and rearranged to accommodate a platform and the man. Back in Walnut Grove, shortly before his death on the Fourth of July 1846, Cyrus's father, Robert, designed a machine with a raker seat, but it didn't work. In that the father had come up with one solution, it is possible that either of his sons perfected it. Nevertheless, it was Cyrus who succeeded in 1847 in gaining a patent on the much-improved "McCormick's Patent Virginia Reaper." Drawn by two horses instead of one, this was the heavy-duty machine equipped with a seat for the raker that really built McCormick's fortune, revolutionized wheat farming, and made bread cheaper in the cities.

With still later improvements, it was the machine that, in the peculiarly inept phrase of Secretary of War Edwin M. Stanton, was "to the North what slavery" was to the South.

But Chicago may have been of equal importance to McCormick. His decision to plant his flag in Chicago represented a significant turning point in his career. After Chicago, he became a manufacturer rather than a tinkerer and a businessman rather than a floundering amateur. After Chicago, he was ahead of his time. Until then he had been struggling to make a success of an almost impossible concept. If central management of local franchise operations is difficult today, it had to be a herculean challenge in a day when railroading was in its infancy (in 1830 the country boasted all of twenty miles of railroad), water transport was the best means of moving freight, and the horse was the only alternative to foot power in a large part of the nation. Until 1847, McCormick had been trying, quite naturally for the times, to build his business by more or less duplicating the Walnut Grove blacksmithy and carpenter shop. From New York and Virginia to Wisconsin and Missouri, they were linked only by McCormick and his patents.

But in 1847 McCormick made the crucial decision to abandon his patchwork arrangements and concentrate his manufacturing under one roof and under McCormick management. It took more than a little courage and perhaps some genius to choose Chicago as the site.

By 1840 only 4,470 persons claimed permanent residency in Chicago. St. Louis, with 10,000 citizens as early as 1820, and many a town, such as Galena on the Mississippi far to the west of Chicago, had larger populations and boasted far finer amenities. (A wolf hunt took off from downtown Chicago as late as 1841.)

However, Chicago, even though it lacked a good natural harbor, had the Great Lakes to bring in commerce and people from the populous East in addition to its access to the rivers stretching north and south. Its principal rivals were largely limited to the north-south trade that could be developed along the Mississippi.

In 1848, the year after McCormick moved to Chicago, the Illinois and Michigan Canal was completed after twelve years of fitful construction, markedly improving the link between Lake Michigan and the river system. (The Erie Canal had already played an even greater role in the development of Chicago, diverting major commercial traffic and general westward expansion from the Ohio River—and early rival Cincinnati—to the Great Lakes.)

Chicago's gateway position also seems to have attracted to it an extraordinary number of ambitious men seeking profitable investments for Eastern capital or bent on making their own fortune. Naturally enough, they were determined boosters of Chicago's opportunities.

Nevertheless, the city's politicians and businessmen did have something about which to brag and that was growth. McCormick's timing was beautiful. In less than three years, despite the beginnings of the California gold rush, Chicago's population increased by 50 percent, ballooned by waves of Irish and German immigrants. By 1860, the city counted 112,000 citizens and was the country's ninth-largest city. It was the miracle city for businessmen, real estate speculators, politicians, saloonkeepers, gamblers, and prostitutes.

Having realized that his best markets were in the Western territories, where labor was as scarce as the land was broad, McCormick picked Chicago as his capital primarily because he could ship east on the Great Lakes and north, south, and west on the rivers. And 1847 was also the year construction started on Chicago's first railroad, the Galena and Chicago Union. That road, later a part of the Chicago & North Western, was promoted by William B. Ogden, Chicago's first mayor.

Ogden raised $300,000, mainly from believing farmers, to build his railroad to the west of Chicago. The line never did reach Galena on the Mississippi, but in 1848 a wood-burning steam engine, the Pioneer, was hauling trainloads (six cars) of grain and lumber into the city on a track that stretched all of ten miles to what is now the nearby suburb of Oak Park. It was also making carloads of money. Even though a heated debate of the time revolved around the proposition that good plank roads were less expensive and of greater benefit than railroads, Chicago went on a railroad-building spree that once again established the city as the midcontinent crossroads. The rails pushed west, northwest, and south, with Senator Stephen A. Douglas maneuvering through Congress the first of the land grants to encourage railroad building. (The Illinois Central got 2.5 million acres as a carrot to head south toward New Orleans, plus tax benefits, and the right to land that carried the tracks along the lakefront into downtown Chicago as far as the Chicago River. The land, of course, proved to be immensely valuable to the railroad, now the Illinois Central Gulf, especially after modern court rulings established the railroad's authority to build on, or sell, the "air rights" over the downtown tracks. A new city of high rises and plazas continued to blossom in the 1970s and 1980s from the air rights.) Eastern money poured in to finance the rail boom and so did British money. On the Chicago & North Western's dual tracks, the trains still run on the British (left) side of the roadway, baffling and sometimes killing strangers. Boston's rail king, William Weld, who had once laughed Ogden out of his office, and his New York Central colleagues ran the Michigan Central into Chicago in 1852. By the end of the 1850s, the railroads had permanently established Chicago as the crossroads and Queen City of the midcontinent, from the Alleghenies to the Rockies, despite vigorous competition from such cities as Cincinnati and St. Louis. (No doubt St. Louis would have been the capital of the hinterlands if a "think tank" assisted by a computer could have been put in charge in the early 19th century of planning the development of the country.)

McCormick made mistakes during his career but not when he decided to move to Chicago in 1847, just one year ahead of the Illinois and Michigan Canal, the Galena and Chicago Union Railroad, and, not incidentally, the stringing of the last mile of wire that gave Chicago a telegraph connection all the way to New York City.

But McCormick had other reasons for deciding on Chicago. McCormick, who always worried about his health and suffered from a skin disease, was favorably disposed toward Chicago because of its location on Lake Michigan. He thought the lake breezes would keep the summers cool and the air fresh. Not everyone agreed. The newspapers of the times denounced Chicago's mud, pestilential swamplands, and open sewers. One paper called the city a "reeking mass of abominations."

A God-fearing man, raised on the Bible and Virginia Presbyterianism, McCormick was also delighted to discover that Chicago had a strong, Southern-oriented Presbyterian congregation.

Chicago had one other attraction, or so McCormick thought. It was home base for Gray & Warner, a leading firm at the time in the manufacture of harvest cradles. For the 1847 manufacturing season, McCormick had licensed Gray & Warner to make the reaper, and apparently the firm did a reasonable job, good enough at any rate to impel McCormick to seek out Charles M. Gray as his partner for the big move to Chicago.

McCormick did not want to be encumbered with a partner, but he needed one—to provide capital and to help run the business. A dollar had real purchasing power in the 1840s, and the possession of a few thousand in hard cash was enough to set a man off from his fellows. But by 1848, McCormick later testified, only 778 McCormick reapers had been sold. Between the fees he had collected for granting territorial rights to his licensees and the $20 profit he took on each sale, McCormick figured his gross profits over the eight years at $22,643.

On August 30, 1847, McCormick signed a partnership agreement with Gray, establishing the firm of McCormick &

Gray. The same day, the partners completed the purchase of land as the site for the construction of a factory. They bought three lots from William Ogden on the north bank of the Chicago River just east of the present Michigan Avenue bridge and approximately where the Equitable Building now stands. It is a nice touch that International Harvester Co., the successor to McCormick's firm, had its world headquarters in the Equitable for years.

McCormick did not start small. The factory the partners built was a hundred feet long and thirty feet wide, and there were several outbuildings, including one that housed a 30-horsepower steam engine, a small wonder in Chicago at the time. The plant employed thirty-three workers, including ten blacksmiths. Production was scheduled at 500 reapers a year.

This was no handshake partnership. The agreement was lengthy, detailed, and legalistic and characteristic of McCormick. It could also be said that McCormick certainly came off first between equals. Charles Gray was to boss manufacturing and keep the partnership books, subject to McCormick's inspection and advice. Gray was to be paid all of $1,000 a year. McCormick's principal duties were to be selling the reaper and making improvements. He was to collect $30 on each reaper sold as a patent fee. In addition, he would get $2.00 a day as expenses for each day spent on selling trips. Assuming the 500 reapers were sold, McCormick would pocket $15,000 a year plus his compensation for expenses on the road. After all of this and the cost of manufacture, the partners would split any profits that were left 50-50. Each partner agreed to put in $2,000 as start-up capital, and McCormick was to contribute another $2,000 in capital by the end of the year. In 1848, the partners would shoulder any needs for new capital equally. The agreement also spelled out operating methods in detail and contained myriad provisions for penalties in case of non-performance.

The marriage lasted barely long enough for the divorce papers to be filed. McCormick was a tiger when he felt he was being put upon, and that was often. As his grandson once put it, "the fiery zeal of McCormick's nature" could bring him into conflict with almost anyone.

Gray may have had a legitimate complaint. McCormick spent the greater part of the first half of 1848 in Washington waging a patent battle. After the statutory fourteen years, McCormick's original patent of 1834 was running out. McCormick had taken out a patent the previous year on important improvements in the reaper, but he was also determined to get an extension of his first basic patent.

McCormick's New York licensee, Seymour & Morgan, led that fight against McCormick. No doubt the two gentlemen knew what McCormick was up to in Chicago, and they could see a cancellation of their license coming. Beyond that, they would have been delighted to continue manufacturing a reaper without paying McCormick his fee. McCormick's old enemy, Obed Hussey, joined the fight. The Patent Extension Board turned McCormick down. But he was not through. He charged up Capitol Hill and attempted to lobby through a special bill extending his rights. He lost there, too, but he continued his futile campaign in the courts and Congress for eleven years.

The strategy of Seymour & Morgan was remarkably sophisticated for the times. Through agents and advertisements they stirred up farmers against the "monopolist" who was boosting prices of the reaper and milking farmers for his $20 royalty fees. In a way, the patent battle helped McCormick. Of necessity, his opponents were saying that the Virginia reaper was the very best and was needed on every wheat farm. Behind the Patent Extension Board's denial was the argument that McCormick's invention was too valuable to society to be controlled by one man.

By 1850 as many as thirty "inventors" or manufacturers of reapers, all borrowing from or directly copying McCormick, were in the field. But whatever the arguments about McCormick's inventive genius, and they were many and bitter, his real strength was as a manufacturer, businessman, and merchandiser. When the patent war was finally lost, his brother William wrote to say, "Your money has been made not out of your patents but by making and selling the machines."

McCormick did build a machine that worked (Hussey's machine was always more adept at mowing hay than cutting wheat) and stood up to hard use. He backed it with warranties and he sold on easy credit terms. He made use of publicity, staging field competitions against the machines of rival companies at every opportunity, and he conducted extensive advertising campaigns, promising farmers an easier life and new prosperity. He organized a powerful network of sales agents and dealers. He standardized the parts that went into the reaper to make both manufacturing and repair easier, and progressively from the time of the first Chicago factory onward he made use of mass-production methods. He did something else that gave him an advantage. He manufactured for inventory, anticipating sales. "Several hundred [reapers] are now ready for inspection, sale, delivery or shipment to order, at the manufactory in Chicago where a supply will be constantly on hand until all are sold," said an 1850 advertisement. Hussey and later competitors built machines only when orders were in hand, making deliveries uncertain.

In all these things McCormick was an innovator of note. And he had faith—in himself, his machine, and God.

The wonder is that McCormick had the time and energy to accomplish what he did. He devoted weeks and months to the patent controversies and to the various lawsuits that in McCormick's career seemed to follow one upon the other. Even as early as 1846, he was taking long periods off to travel to Avon Springs, New York, for the mineral baths in the belief that the waters would help his skin affliction. And it would seem that he made his early forays to England and the Continent at a time when he could have best left foreign sales to others and concentrated on the vast American market. (His first trip to England came in 1851. The fact that rival Hussey was exhibiting his reaper at London's Exhibition of the Works of Industry of All Nations may have lured McCormick to England. In English field trials, McCormick came off the winner and his machine garnered a Council Medal. The publicity may have made it all worthwhile.)

The suspicion is there that McCormick was fortunate in his associates and partners, even in Charles Gray, obviously a cautious and conservative man. But, while McCormick was doing battle in Washington in early 1848, Gray covered his bets by secretly selling one-half of his one-half interest in McCormick & Gray to William Ogden and another Chicago businessman, William E. Jones. Very shortly Gray and McCormick were in the courts charging each other with breach of contract (one McCormick charge: Gray had failed to supply the required financial statements for his inspection). The important outcome of the falling-out was that Gray sold his remaining interest to Ogden and Jones and McCormick found himself in a new partnership under the banner of McCormick, Ogden & Co. That lasted all of thirteen months. For once, no McCormick lawsuit accompanied the split.

Even more remarkable than the amicable parting of the ways was the settlement. McCormick paid Ogden and Jones $65,000 to get rid of them. This, of course, was pennies compared to what Ogden and Jones could have reaped by sticking to their 50 percent ownership of the firm. But it was a magnificent sum considering the times, the uncertainties of a company only two years old, and the supposed financial status of McCormick.

In fact, McCormick could afford the buy-out price only because of the success of the partnership that year. For the 1849 harvest, the firm had produced and sold 1,500 machines. McCormick's patent fees alone for the Chicago production totaled $30,000.

Finally, Cyrus McCormick had arrived. He was 40 years old, a little late in life, especially considering the fact that he had invented the reaper when he was only 22. He was in sole

command of his company, and the future looked almost
unlimited except for those pesky competitors.

By 1849 Cyrus had help he thought he could depend on.
Late in 1848, Leander had arrived from Walnut Grove with
his wife, Henrietta Hamilton. The three stayed at the old
Sherman House until Leander could have a house built. As
usual, there was an agreement; Leander was to get $750 a
year plus increases based on rising profits. Leander was the
first of the family to join Cyrus in Chicago. In 1849, brother
William S. McCormick, four years older than Leander, followed. Another brother, John P., died in Walnut Grove that
same year at age 29. The eldest of Cyrus's two sisters, Mary
Caroline, had married a minister who insisted upon a mission in the Pennsylvania hills. When he died as poor as a
church mouse, Mary Caroline came to Chicago with her
children. The youngest child, Amanda J., married Hugh Adams, a man making a decent living in Virginia as a grocer.
The couple moved to Chicago in 1857. Cyrus backed him in
a successful wholesale grocery business. Adams also did well
in Chicago real estate with the guidance of William.

After 1850, money was not among Cyrus's problems. The
company sold 1,603 machines that year, and with his off-the-
top fee increased to $30 per reaper, Cyrus had an income of
$48,090 for starters. Sales did drop down to the 1,000 level
in 1851 and 1852 as new competition popped up and as
McCormick wound up the last of his local licensing agreements. (He sued Seymour & Morgan in 1850 for patent
infringements and finally won a court battle, but it took him
seven years.) By 1854 McCormick & Co. had climbed back
to sales of 1,558. That was the year McCormick filed a patent-infringement suit against one of his strongest new competitors, John H. Manny of Waddams Grove, Illinois, who
had some new ideas about reapers along with McCormick's.
McCormick lost, which was not unusual. What was of interest about the trial was that one of the men at the bar for
Manny was a Springfield lawyer named Abraham Lincoln.
Lincoln didn't stay with the case until the end, but he

earned a fee of $1,000. It was Lincoln's first big fee, and the money helped him finance his later campaign against Stephen A. Douglas. Chalk one up for McCormick's windmill tilting.

By the mid-1850s things were really buzzing for McCormick. John Deere was a blacksmith of Grand Detour, Illinois. In spite of its negative name it was one of the Illinois towns on the Mississippi River that thought it would grow up to be the Midwest capital (population today: 400). Deere had had his curved, self-scouring steel plow on the market for nearly twenty years, enabling pioneering Midwesterners to break up the centuries-old sod and the grass (it grew seven and eight feet tall) of the endless prairies. Between Deere's plow (the Deere & Co. farm implement company today) and McCormick's harvester, it was said that cultivation of the prairies was advancing thirty miles a year. Midwestern farmers were not only feeding the Eastern seaboard but also helping, as they still do, to feed the world. Between 1840 and 1850 Illinois wheat production doubled, tripled, and quadrupled. By the 1850s, industrial and wool-growing England was importing one-fifth of its wheat from the United States, the Continent, and Russia. In 1835, McCormick capped a number of European successes—more at exhibitions than on the too small farms—with the sale of his first reaper to Russia. Meanwhile, England had ridden off to the Crimean War (1853–56) and demand for American wheat had zoomed with the war and the closing off of Russian exports. Russia and Poland, with their large farms and estates, were a natural market for the efficient reaper. At one time, before the Russian Revolution, McCormick and Singer were the two largest commercial enterprises in Russia. In the 1920s, after the Revolution, the floundering Bolsheviks asked the McCormicks to come back and run the factory.

The American Civil War multiplied both demand for wheat and the need for labor-saving machinery on the farm. In 1861, McCormick's sales reached 6,000 units. After the war came a remarkable American boom in population, industry, commerce, finance, and agriculture, and McCormick & Co. rode the crest.

Not that Cyrus was marching down a straight road paved with gold. There were turns, bumps, and hills. In 1855 John Manny sold almost 2,000 machines, only about 600 short of McCormick's achievement. But Manny was good enough to die prematurely in 1856 just as McCormick, determined as usual, was taking his patent-infringement suit against Manny to the U.S. Supreme Court. Manny's heirs had no stomach for continuing the court battle, and a deal, or conspiracy as it would be called today, was put together in advance of the Supreme Court ruling. The Manny company and five lesser manufacturers threatened by McCormick's court action agreed that they would pay McCormick his $30-per-machine royalty. In turn, McCormick would drop his suit. The kicker in the scheme in those unfettered, freebooting days was this: McCormick and the other companies would agree to fix the price of the reaper at $160, and they would also set a standard fee to be paid to sales agents. In that the Supreme Court slapped McCormick down on every single point in his petition, the price-fixing plan was never put into operation.

All this left McCormick in an exposed position. The basis of his suit against Manny was his 1847 patent and, win or lose in the courts, that patent was due to run out in 1861. Meanwhile, Obed Hussey, who was to die providentially in a railroad accident in 1860, had sued the master in 1859 for infringement of Hussey's vital cutter-system patent. Hussey not only won but collected damages of $80,000.

But far more important than the patent suits was the Panic of 1857. Having been in business longer and more successfully than his competitors, McCormick suffered least. When sales fell off and hundreds of farmers found themselves unable to pay, many a competitor went bankrupt. McCormick's sales went flat and fell off slightly from 1856 through 1860, but he was still selling about 4,000 machines a year and he was able to carry old customers and finance new ones. The credit he extended to farmers did his reputation—and sales—no harm in later years when the times improved.

Through this period, Cyrus was out of Chicago more than he was in. Rather obviously, William and Leander were running the show even if Cyrus did not see it that way. As he always had with any of his business associates, Cyrus bombarded his brothers with letters. Carrying his Bible and his dictionary and inspired weekly by good Presbyterian sermons from the pulpit, Cyrus gave his brothers detailed instructions for managing the business and uplifting lectures too. For instance, in one letter in 1857, Cyrus ordered William and Leander to get to bed by 9 P.M. if necessary in order to be up at 5 A.M. and at the office by 7 in the morning.

McCormick's grandson Cyrus Hall III may have accounted for Cyrus's seeming inattention to business and his success when he wrote that "perhaps" Cyrus was "one of those rare men . . . afflicted with a disease of superactivity." According to the grandson: "Never has there been a man whose days were more consecrated to the work he had made his own. It was his custom to awake at five, consider his problems in the solitude of early morning, and spend the usual waking hours in consultation with his associates and subordinates. After supper he would sleep for two hours in his chair and then, until midnight, he would again engage in interviews and discussions. In these conferences he sometimes seemed deliberate in making up his mind, but once he reached a decision, his purpose was adamant. . . . He never enjoyed any relaxation except music, never sought the diversion of the theater or society. . . . He found his rest in activity."

However, Cyrus III, not given to finding warts among his grandfather's bold features, does hold that Cyrus could be diverted from business by his love of his children. Once his wife, Nettie, brought an infant son into the room. "Take him away," said Cyrus, "if you want me to have attention for these other matters," the other matters being business, or very possibly religion and politics, two subjects that certainly could grab McCormick's attention at any time.

In all matters, Cyrus had an explosive temper, and the smallest things could ignite the temper. Around the company, everyone knew that they'd best keep telegrams short and terse. An unnecessary word in a telegram could send Cyrus into a rage. One theory has it that to the rich and super-rich a large sum of money is impersonal, a chessman that is moved for a purpose. The emotion the rest of the populace attaches to money can be felt only when the sum is small enough to be held in the hand. Whatever the psychology, McCormick was that way. He once beat upon Potter Palmer until the hotelman lowered meal prices to seventy-five cents even though Palmer complained bitterly that the price did not cover his costs.

In the summer of 1857, Cyrus spent six straight weeks in Chicago, highly unusual for him. Finally, at age 48, a bona fide millionaire, his name known nationally and internationally, Cyrus was taking an active interest in the opposite sex. For years young ladies had been throwing themselves at him, one of the nation's richest bachelors, or had been thrown by their mothers. One thing that stopped Cyrus was a suspicion that the ladies were more interested in his money than in him.

Nancy Maria Fowler, born in Brownsville, New York, on February 8, 1835, was different. The stories vary, but apparently Cyrus first spotted her in comforting surroundings— singing in church. Nancy, or Nettie as she was known in the family, was visiting friends and relatives in Chicago that summer of 1857. It was a fast romance, carried on in part by mail. On September 25, 1857, Cyrus made a formal proposal of marriage in a letter dispatched to Nancy at her mother's home in Clayton, New York. Cyrus also dropped a note to his brother William. "It [the proposal letter] is gone, and I suppose I am in for it," Cyrus said. He was. Nancy accepted promptly, but the wedding was delayed until January 26, 1858. Cyrus was preoccupied with pushing the Manny patent case before the Supreme Court. It was a small wedding followed by a reception for 500 at the home of William and his wife, Mary Ann (Grigsby). Immediately, Cyrus took his 22-year-old bride off on a honeymoon—to Washington, where they stayed through March while Cyrus watched over his ill-fated patent fight.

When Cyrus finally did take a wife he apparently chose wisely. Very quickly Nettie was acting as her husband's confidential secretary, copying out his many personal and business letters and providing him with a sounding board. A pretty woman except perhaps for an overly prominent and sharp nose, Nettie had a charming way with people. In addition to being an excellent corporate wife and bearing Cyrus three sons and two daughters, she had a mellowing effect on Cyrus, often described by friend and enemy as "cold and aloof." Eventually, Nettie became the strong-willed matriarch of the family, and for decades few large or small decisions were made at the company until she had been consulted.

If Cyrus was happy in his marriage and in sons to carry on the name, he was also entering one of the most emotionally frustrating periods of his adult life. He and his brothers were Virginians living in Chicago as the Civil War approached. He had been the owner of slaves (four) until his mother, Mary Ann, died in 1853, and under Virginia law he couldn't set them free; they were still hired out as labor on neighboring farms. Deeply religious, he was committed to the Southern, or Old School, branch of the Presbyterian Church and was dismayed to find his church in Illinois and the West moving steadily over the years toward a pro-Union stance.

Cyrus, like a lot of other people a century later, professed to be a friend of Negroes. He just didn't want to do anything that would upset the status quo. In fact, when called upon, he could cite passages from his Bible that he said proved slavery was no sin against God.

McCormick's response to the unhappy situation was twofold. He fled to London and spent the larger part of the Civil

War in England and on the Continent promoting sales of the
reaper. But before fleeing, he did his best to alter matters
and turn the country from a bloody confrontation. Like
many men who have made a remarkable success in business
or some other career, McCormick obviously thought of himself as endowed with superior knowledge and judgment in
all things, including the great social and political issues of the
time. Having grown up in Virginia and having lived for
years in Chicago, McCormick could easily imagine the horrors of secession and war between the North and the South.
And his horror at the thought of civil war was entwined with
his commitment to fundamental Presbyterianism. To Mc-
Cormick in the 1850s, any right-minded person believed in
the South as part of the Union, Old School Presbyterianism,
and the Democratic Party, then the party of the status quo,
the South, the farmer, and many businessmen.

First, McCormick moved on the religious front. He
brought to Chicago from New Albany, Indiana, a failing
Presbyterian seminary, promising to donate land for buildings and pledging $100,000 to endow four chairs from which
he hoped the gospel according to McCormick would be
spread. Eventually, after a number of vicissitudes, the seminary became the McCormick Theological Seminary and an
influential training ground for the ministry.

McCormick also brought to Chicago a fire-eating St. Louis
pastor and editor, noted for his attacks on abolitionists and
Catholics, among others. For two years Cyrus subsidized the
minister's religious periodical, *The Expositor,* with the hope
that the paper would influence opinion against war with the
South. The paper folded in 1861 as war broke out.

Meanwhile, McCormick was engaged in some warfare of
his own. He had given his support to two Presbyterian
churches in Chicago. When the minister of one shifted increasingly to a pro-North, antislavery stance in his sermons,
McCormick called a loan he had made to the church, withdrew an offer to donate the lot on which the church stood,

and cut off the supply of free coal he had been sending from the McCormick Works.

By 1860 McCormick was ready for bolder steps. To further his views, he was considering running for political office, almost any office, mayor of Chicago, governor, representative, senator, Vice-President. He listened with attention when friends told him he ought to run for President.

In 1860 McCormick bought the Chicago *Herald* and later the same year the Chicago *Daily Times* to further his views, and he did run for the nomination to be the candidate for mayor on the Democratic ticket. He lost. His merged papers were losers too, even though Cyrus, like a relative of his in later days, was very much the militant personal editor. Next to the great cause, his primary interest was in publishing a paper that would not print anything likely to make a maiden blush. He blue-penciled advertising as well as stories.

The Peace Democrats were unwilling to countenance the thought of civil war; thus, McCormick parted company with his old friend and ally Stephen A. Douglas, who did accept war as a last resort to preserve the Union. In April 1861, after Fort Sumter, McCormick published a signed editorial setting the record straight in his fashion.

For past views, McCormick wrote, "I have no regrets to express or apologies to offer. . . . Though a native of the South, I am a citizen of Illinois, and of the United States and as such shall bear true allegiance to the Government. That allegiance I shall never violate or disregard. I am and ever shall be on the side of my country in war—without considering whether my country is right or wrong." By June 1861 McCormick had had enough of newspaper publishing. He sold the *Daily Times* and took off for Europe, where he hoped, among other things, to persuade Napoleon III to intervene in the war as a peace negotiator.

In 1864, back in Chicago after nearly two years, McCormick ran for Congress against Long John Wentworth, a colorful early example of Chicago's long line of machine bosses, and lost by a disastrous three-to-one margin. The Chicago *Tribune* did not help McCormick's cause. The paper ran a series of attacks on McCormick, calling him "poor white trash" from Virginia and more a supporter of slavery than bona fide plantation owners. The *Tribune* even contended that Obed Hussey had really invented the reaper and that McCormick was a pirate who had stolen the invention from Hussey.

Right up to Appomattox, McCormick sincerely believed that there was no way either side could win the war, that the fighting would go on to the point of total exhaustion for both the North and the South, but that the South just might win if the Emancipation Proclamation opened the way for Jefferson Davis to draft blacks into the Confederate Army. He got nowhere with his great scheme to be the savior of the country. He urged the Democratic Party to meet in convention and negotiate, with Lincoln's blessing, a peace treaty with the South. Once he wrote Lincoln and asked permission to travel to Richmond and open peace discussions.

While Cyrus was off to Europe or preoccupied with war and politics, his brothers were doing very well by him. William and Leander were far more conservative fellows than Cyrus, who was always bent on building a grand company of worldwide scope. In the 1850s and through the troubled times of the Civil War, William and Leander kept buying up Chicago real estate with their money and with Cyrus's profits in the company. They also made a pile for Cyrus by buying gold and commodities as the Civil War inflation mounted and as the bank notes, issued almost at will by the country's private banks as the currency of the day, depreciated and many an issuing bank went to the wall. At one time, the McCormick company refused to accept bank notes issued in Pennsylvania, New Jersey, Maryland, and Michigan. In addition, the brothers were most choosy about Ohio and Indiana bank notes.

The brothers lived well in Chicago and prospered, but the basic family situation was one that made for bad blood. Cyrus was the star of the show, the boss, and the man with the real money. Leander particularly resented Cyrus's autocratic rule and less than generous sharing of the wealth. Early on, Leander clashed with Cyrus over European expansion. Leander thought Europe meant more to his brother's ego than it did to sound business development. For years the European operation was a loser even though McCormick reapers won gold medals from London to Hamburg and Cyrus was elected (1879) a member of the French Academy of Sciences "as having done more for agriculture than any other living man." The McCormick machine was too heavy for most European horses to pull easily, it was too expensive, and the competition was rough from other American companies and from national companies that got into the business fairly rapidly. Once Leander outraged Cyrus by demanding that Cyrus pay the company the full retail price for every machine sold in Europe. Another thing that gnawed at Leander was the fact that Cyrus had obtained the 1847 patent in his own name. Leander felt the patent was based on his ideas; the least Cyrus could have done, Leander thought, was to have applied for the patent in the company's name.

Not until 1859, when Cyrus was already in the millionaire class (his royalties alone had been running at $120,000 a year), did McCormick admit his brothers into a real partnership. An agreement in late 1859 gave Leander and William each a one-fourth interest in the firm and the name of the company was changed to Cyrus H. McCormick and Brothers. Leander got a special $5,000 payment in return for granting the company exclusive use of his inventions and allowing Cyrus to patent them.

In 1865, the death of William, who had always been in poor health and who spent his last days under care for what used to be called nervous exhaustion, brought about an open split between Cyrus and his remaining brother. One very sore point: on his return from London, Cyrus had found out about the successful speculations of William and Leander in commodities and gold and he had demanded $25,000 from each of them as his share. William protested in a fifty-page letter to Cyrus, and Cyrus put his lawyers on his brothers. A new partnership agreement in 1864, maintaining the one-fourth interests of the two brothers, handed Cyrus a bonus of $25,000, and that may have cleared up half of the claim. Just before his death, William ordered $12,500 transferred from his company account to Cyrus's, but Leander still held out and finally escaped any further payments when he and Cyrus signed still another partnership agreement nine months after William's death. Leander improved his lot slightly, but Cyrus was still king of the hill; Leander's share in the company was held to one-third with Cyrus taking the two-thirds balance.

The feud between Leander and Cyrus smoldered quietly or flared openly for years in the manner of sisters smiling during family dinners but screeching at each other over a division of their mother's silverware.

The final break came over inheritance, the inheritance of Cyrus's mantle. By 1874, Cyrus was 65 years old and beginning to have some doubts about his immortality. There was his eldest son, Cyrus Hall Jr., in his teens (born 1859), and Leander's eldest, Robert Hall McCormick, the senior of the two and already working for the company. In 1873 Leander had angrily offered, or threatened, to sell his interest to Cyrus, but Cyrus refused to face up to a full break with his brother. A new partnership agreement was signed in 1874. This time Leander gave up something of what he had gained in order to bring his son in on the action. He settled for an interest in the firm of three-sixteenths, with Robert Hall being cut in for one-sixteenth. Leander also agreed that Robert Hall could not cast a vote on company matters in opposition to Cyrus. Cyrus conceded that all new patents and improvements would belong to the firm.

That last turned out to be not much of a concession, except possibly to Leander's pride.

Until the 1860s the machines marketed by McCormick

were as good as, and usually better than, anything offered by the competition. But slowly and surely the firm began to lose out in a developing technological race even though improvements were made in the McCormick machine and even though it was stronger and heavier and worked better. And continued to sell. Because McCormick had the name, the selling force, the advertising muscle, and the production. After the historic Chicago fire of 1871, McCormick was one of the hundreds of Chicagoans who started rebuilding even as the ashes were cooling. He threw up a temporary two-story building on the old site on the north bank of the Chicago River and went to work. The company was lucky in that the fire came in early October; it had a few months' grace to prepare for the spring selling season. At the same time, McCormick made the decision to go ahead with the construction of a grand new factory on a prairie site six miles southwest of the Loop. The first main building was designed as a four-story structure, but Cyrus ordered a fifth story during construction. McCormick's perennial optimism paid off handsomely. The "monster" plant, as it was called at the time, could turn out 10,000 to 15,000 machines a year. In 1874, the company sold 10,114 machines. (The total now included mowing machines for hay fields.) The factory came on stream just as the great Red River valley of the Dakotas was being opened up, and McCormick was in a position to meet the sudden demand from the valley's new wheat farmers. (Wheat farming shifted north and west while Illinois farmers went to corn and other crops.) Originally built at a total cost of $619,000, the McCormick Works lasted nearly ninety years and came to include forty-five buildings. The company eventually abandoned the obsolete and inefficient buildings and sold the site to the Santa Fe Railway for development as an industrial park. The last building was blasted down in 1962.

In 1872 and 1873 Cyrus was spending full-time in Chicago supervising the big construction project and the company's expansion. Between the fire and 1874 he and Nettie did not once visit the Fifth Avenue mansion in New York that had been his real headquarters before 1871. In addition to the factory, Cyrus was also pushing the construction of a number of new Chicago buildings; the fire had cost him $172,000 in annual rents when it burned downtown retail buildings and residences he owned.

In 1873 and 1874 for the first time McCormick was forced to go outside for inventions and technical improvements. After some forty years, the farmer's problem was still what to do with the grain once the reaper's knife cut the stalk. Rakers had to sweep the cut grain off the machine into piles. Then field hands had to bind it for transport to the threshing machine. One improvement was the self-raker. A paddlelike mechanism periodically swept the platform clear. But men on the ground still had to bend and bind the grain into sheaves to be carried off for the threshing. While McCormick watched, dozens of inventors worked on the next step, an attachment that would bind the grain as it was cut. The most successful of a new breed of inventors were Charles W. and William W. Marsh, farmers of Shabona Grove, Illinois. (Mystics might want to make something of Cyrus of Walnut Grove, John Manny of Waddams Grove, and the Marshes of Shabona Grove.) They came up with their own design for a reaper and added variations for binding the grain on the moving machine—they made their first binder in 1858 but didn't get an effective organization going until the 1860s. By 1872, the Marsh company had sold thousands of reaper-binders and were making a real dent in McCormick's market. It was not until 1873 that the McCormicks could bring themselves to pay for a patent and not until the following year that the first McCormick machine incorporating a binder went on the market. From then on, the company bought patents right and left and came out with a succession of machines during the next decade. Patent suits and countersuits proliferated. Cyrus bought a one-fourth interest in the wire-binder patent of one James F. Gordon but never used it, switching to another device. Gordon claimed patent infringement, of course. Ten years later, Cyrus Jr. paid $225,000 privately to end the suit. He paid in cash and small bills, not wishing to have a check extant that might pop up later and be used by rivals to prove that the great McCormick empire had had to seek outside help.

Cyrus and Leander could not make up their minds in a battle of technologies that was of great moment on the farm. The earlier binders used wire because available twines raveled and broke. But the wire binders were dangerous, particularly in that they spewed sharp bits of wire about the fields. The McCormick Works did not offer a twine binder until 1881, and then it was an improvement on a purchased patent right. But with its muscle and the demand for farm machinery the McCormick firm survived the period and prospered. In 1882, the company sold 48,000 reaper and mower models of various designs and uses.

By then Cyrus was 73 years old, tired and in ill health. For most of his life he had had an eczema. For two decades he had suffered increasingly from rheumatism in his right leg and knee. After a severe infection that produced carbuncles and boils during a trip to Paris in 1878, he was considerably weakened (but still strong enough to try his best to knock down the fees of the doctors who may have saved his life), and for the rest of his years he got about with the help of cane, crutch, or wheelchair.

Understandably, Cyrus was determined to bring his eldest son, Cyrus Jr., along as his successor. In 1875, at age 16, Cyrus Jr. was serving as his father's secretary and carrying out various orders. Cyrus, with scant formal education, professed to believe that experience was the best teacher, and he balked at Nettie's plans to give his son a fashionable college education at Princeton. Nevertheless, Cyrus Jr. did complete two Princeton years before his father yanked him home in 1879 to serve as his full-time assistant.

In 1873, in another round of the continuing battles and compromises with Leander, Cyrus had agreed to let Leander's son, Robert Hall, a self-confident, aggressive, and quick-tempered young man, come to work for the company. From Paris, during his 1878 illness, Cyrus wrote to his brother, through a lawyer, proposing that Robert Hall be made a junior partner in the company—if he would agree to stay away from the office. Cyrus backed up his demand with a threat to sell the whole kit and caboodle to the highest bidder.

One response from Leander was an offer to sell out his entire interest to Cyrus for $650,000. That was pennies for Cyrus and a fire-sale price, but for unknown reasons Cyrus refused. Instead he came up with an even more amazing offer: he'd sell to Leander for three times Leander's price. Leander couldn't, or wouldn't, buy. But he came back with a threat of his own: he would set up a rival McCormick factory.

In the next chapter in this script, written either by the Marx Brothers or by one of the Brontë sisters, Cyrus signed a brand-new partnership agreement. Cyrus retained three-fourths of the company while Leander and Robert Hall got the remaining one-fourth interest, with Robert Hall being posted as assistant superintendent of the factory under Leander. The new agreement did not satisfy Leander, who, probably with reason, became more and more convinced that Cyrus was out to get him and his son. Like a child who has been told not to play baseball in the living room, Leander pouted. He stayed away from the office and kept Robert away too.

Meanwhile, Leander had got on his big kick, an attempt to diminish his brother by claiming that the original reaper actually had been invented by their father and that Leander was responsible for the important improvements. Cyrus found it necessary to come back at Leander, face to face and in writing. His standard defense was to challenge Leander to show that any important part on his first reaper was the same as a part on his father's design. This was a telling challenge, but possibly a little difficult to take up a half century after the fact.

By 1880, Cyrus, even more crusty in his old age and illness, was ready for full-scale battle. The last partnership agreement had a five-year term and by the end of 1879 it had run out. Cyrus had the board of directors adopt a motion of censure against Leander, charging breach of contract and disloyalty, and both Leander and his son were ordered to relinquish their jobs with the company. Finally, Cyrus, through his son and his loyal general manager, had full and complete control of his empire. But it is probable that by then his wife, Nettie, was the real power, if not on the throne, then behind it. Her grandson wrote much later that in another age she would no doubt have been chairman of the board, and effective. There was precedent in the family; her father had been killed by a kicking horse when she was still an infant and her mother had taken over the running of his small rural store in New York.

By this time Nettie occupied the last of the cluster of McCormick mansions around the 600 and 700 blocks of North Rush Street. At 675 Rush, the mansion, with its straight lines and lack of gingerbread, uncharacteristic of the times, had been completed in 1879 after three years of construction and the expenditure of $175,000. The dining-room ceiling was painted with representations of the reaper and Cyrus's medal of the French Legion of Honor. The house was opened with a grand party in early 1880 in honor of the 21st birthday of Cyrus Jr.

Cyrus the first died in the house four years later on May 13. He was three months past his 75th birthday. No specific illness killed him, just a combination with age. On April 30 he had fired off his last known set of orders. And he was still tilting at windmills. He sent a telegram to Cyrus Jr. in New York City ordering him to see Samuel J. Tilden, the Democratic candidate for President in 1876, and persuade Tilden to reconsider his decision not to run for the nomination again. That same night Cyrus weakened visibly. On May 7 the family gathered in his bedroom for hymns and prayers. "It's all right," Cyrus said. "It's all right. I only want

Heaven." Six days later, he was dead. His last known words were appropriate. "Life is a battle," he said.

Cyrus died the richest man in Illinois. (Not counting the factory site, he was the largest landlord in the city by 1868.) The estimate was that his estate was worth $10 million. That had to be very conservative; in 1878 alone the company turned a profit of $600,000. But there was another and surprising side to Cyrus, normally the hardheaded businessman. On the side, he was a plunger. He went into speculative stock market deals, sometimes, as in the fashion of the day, into stock deals that supposedly were rigged on the basis of insider control and information. The big one was the Crédit Mobilier or, as it is usually written, the Crédit Mobilier Scandal. The company, with a blue-chip list of stockholders, had a fat contract to build the Union Pacific Railroad west of the 100th meridian (mid-Nebraska). There was a little kicker in the deal. As the company in charge of construction, Crédit Mobilier would always know exactly where the rail line would run. Well in advance, it would buy up land where new towns might mushroom and make huge profits reselling the land and houses and buildings that the company would construct. Among other things, the company made sure that a number of congressmen had stock. The idea was to head off unseemly questions about the construction contract, the land deals, and the federal subsidies Congress might grant the road. Fortunately for McCormick, he was in Europe for long periods of time in 1867 and 1868 and he was dropped from the Crédit Mobilier board of directors, so that when the stock collapsed and scandal broke he was not among those publicly blamed. The Union Pacific screamed at the firm's bills and withheld payment of millions. Congress, despite the bribes, took its usual good time in approving the subsidies. The stock manipulators in charge of Crédit Mobilier never got around to the big land deals; only eighty acres of Nebraska land was bought and only a handful of houses built. McCormick nevertheless may have made money on this one. Suspecting something funny, he violated the stock pool agreement and secretly dumped stock. "There is little doubt, I suppose, that there has been enormous stealing in some way in connection with the building of the Road," he wrote.

Otherwise, McCormick put large sums into a railroad that never ran anywhere; it was supposed to go from Virginia to New Orleans. He lost money on an early scheme to build the Panama Canal and lay an Atlantic telegraph cable. Having ignored the California gold rush, except to use the flight of the local populace as a selling point for his labor-saving reaper to the farmers who remained behind, McCormick sank $120,000 in a largely worthless South Carolina gold mine. For years he bought gold- and silver-mining claims in the West and lost on most of them. Once he came out merely a $90,000 loser, by his count, only because he successfully sued an old friend and fellow churchman, John V. Farwell, an organizer of the venture, a prominent retailer and real estate man and progenitor of one of Chicago's finer families. The promoters of the South Carolina gold mine convinced him that another large infusion of McCormick money would allow the mine to profitably produce not gold but manganese. At the same time (the late 1870s), Cyrus bought up 1,200 acres of land near the mine with the idea that when a Georgia–South Carolina railroad went through he'd make a small fortune on timber and on the sale of lots for a town. He called his proposed town McCormick and laid out streets named after members of the family. The railroad was three miles short of the town when it ran out of steam, but McCormick was still incorporated in 1882. The following year Mrs. McCormick ordered the mine shut down, not wishing to throw more good money after bad. Whether in honor of her husband or not, Nettie proceeded with plans for the town, but as a social experiment rather than a profit-making venture. She donated town lots for churches and a cemetery and built store buildings, a "temperance" hotel, and later an orphanage. In 1906 a local group bought the old mine from Nettie for $27,183, about a tenth of what Cyrus had put into it. In the 1980s the town of McCormick was listed as having a population of 1,725.

Another Cyrus speculation says at least a small volume about the temper of the times in the expansion years after the Civil War. McCormick bought up land in Santo Domingo on the theory that the United States would soon annex the Dominican Republic.

At age 25, with Nettie and an able general manager behind him, Cyrus Jr. took over as president of the McCormick Harvesting Machine Company, as it was then known. Junior did not have the fiery temperament of his father, a lack that was probably all to the good. The big battles were over, and the company was firmly entrenched as the leader in its field both at home and abroad. (More than 54,000 machines were sold by the company in the year of Cyrus's death.) The times seemed to demand conservative, sound business management to consolidate and improve on what already existed. Cyrus Jr., a hard-working executive, did just that. His forte was efficiency and cost savings in the operation of both factory and office.

But he did have a certain flair. He had been president of the company less than a year when he made a dramatic, and foolish, attempt to end a strike at the McCormick Works by riding alone in a buggy through a crowd of angry strikers to the plant gate and then inviting anyone who wanted to work to come on in. This at a time when Chicago, newly inundated by waves of German and Middle European immigrants, was seething with labor unrest. The ten-hour day and the six-day week had been the rule, and employers, presented with an unending supply of labor, had been happily lowering wages. At the time real anarchists were appearing in Chicago to convince employers that their fears had been correct all along, and the city was building toward the tragedy of the Haymarket Riot of 1886. (Score: Seven policemen killed by an anarchist's bomb and more than half a hundred wounded. Some 200 in the crowd wounded, mostly by police gunfire, and an unknown number killed. Four sent to the gallows—a fifth, sentenced to death, committed suicide —including the editor and assistant editor of the *Arbeiter Zeitung,* a militant socialist newspaper, on the nightmarish charge that they had incited the unknown bomb thrower.)

Nettie McCormick, who supported schools, colleges, missionary schools, and the Y, had a different view of the world. She influenced Cyrus Jr. to raise wages after the prolonged and bitter strike of 1886 at the McCormick Works. And she also got Cyrus to fire the hard-nosed general manager she blamed for precipitating the strike. In a day when most businessmen firmly believed that they were fulfilling a great social purpose simply by providing jobs and that labor unrest was created only by a handful of agitators who misled honest workingmen, Nettie wrote this: "Concessions on both sides, I think, is the right way. . . . It is evident that as a class, those who win strikes are not much better satisfied than those who lose." At the turn of the century, she was responsible for a pioneering profit-sharing plan that encompassed some 3,500 McCormick employees and for early pension and workmen's compensation programs. Still later she stopped the McCormick general manager when he had decided on an iron-fisted plan to beat a strike at one of the company's smaller plants in New York by moving the plant elsewhere. She may have given the general manager of that day a hint when she wrote that she feared a repeat of "the awful episode in 1886 . . . all arising from the unwisdom" of the general manager.

Nettie also did what she could, and that wasn't too much, to heal the breach between her branch of the family and Leander's. Cyrus had become an obsession with Leander. He spent the best part of seven years collecting "evidence" against Cyrus, going so far as to interview relatives and everyone he could find in the Virginia valley who might have known about his father's and Cyrus's work in the Walnut Grove days. (In 1882, Cyrus took title to the old farm and had the house and buildings fixed up. It had been inherited by William's sons. They released it to Cyrus in return for wiping out most of a debt of $17,064 they owed Cyrus. The farm remains a point of interest for tourists today.)

Shortly after the death of Cyrus, Cyrus Jr., perhaps anticipating Leander, published a memorial volume lauding his father. Leander followed in 1885 with *The Memorial of Robert McCormick.* It was an all-out attack on Cyrus. The first sixteen pages consisted of statements from Leander and his wife, from Cyrus's sister Mary Caroline Shields, and from Virginia cousins and others, all supporting Leander's thesis that the father, Robert, was the great inventor.

Leander's story was that Cyrus, the eldest son, had always been the favorite child of their mother, that Cyrus had persuaded his mother to persuade his father to credit Cyrus with the reaper invention, actually the sole work of his father. Robert McCormick, Leander said, had agreed but only on condition that Cyrus split any profits from the reaper equally among all the children. Furthermore, Leander was the real mechanical genius in the family and it was Leander who was responsible for the improvements in the reaper over the years and even for some of the work on the original. Particularly, Leander had figured out the way to make it possible for a raker to ride on the machine, an improvement critical to the reaper's success. Said Leander: "I made the Raker stand improvement at my father's farm in Va[.] in the summer of 1845[.] Cyrus patented it without my permition [sic] in 1847 when he had nothing whatever to do with it[.] This is true as their [sic] is a God in heaven."

Having claimed the reaper for his father and for himself, Leander then went overboard. The McCormick reaper had really been derived from the invention of Obed Hussey and others, he wrote.

One way or another, Leander was going to put his brother down.

In 1900, nine years after Leander's death, his son, Robert Hall, and a nephew, James Hall Shields, republished the polemic volume in expanded form.

In making his case totally one-sided, Leander defeated

himself. He came off as the younger brother consumed with jealousy. But there are points on his side. It seems improbable that the reaper sprang full-blown from young Cyrus's brain in six weeks with no contribution from the long years of his father's work. To have invented the raker-seat arrangement and patented it in 1847, Cyrus would have had to be very fast on his feet; in that period he was traveling almost constantly and also getting ready for his big move to Chicago.

But apart from the question of who did contribute to the birth of the reaper and to its growth, Leander refused to give Cyrus credit for what he undoubtedly did do. While Leander and William were still back on the farm, Cyrus was beating his way about the country selling the machine and establishing sales agents and local manufacturers. He made the decision and the arrangements for the big factory in Chicago and got a viable organization going. He was the man at the helm in the years when the reaper revolutionized farm labor and made cheap bread a staple. And even though Leander was on the spot in charge of reaper production while William kept an eye on the mushrooming sales organization and the company finances, Cyrus was the one giving the final orders and pushing. Henry Ford did not have to "invent" the automobile to secure his place in history.

In the blood feud between Cyrus and Leander, the only objective evidence for either side may be the will of their father, Robert McCormick. The will directed Robert's executor to pay Cyrus $15 for each reaper made at Walnut Grove in the year of his death, 1846. Significantly, he did not say that what was obviously a patent or royalty fee should be paid into his estate or divided among the children.

Despite Leander's public attack, Nettie and Cyrus Jr. negotiated one peace treaty with him in 1886. For $60,000 they settled Leander's long-standing laments about the accounting for royalty payments on foreign sales. They adjusted Leander's salary claims against the company, and they had the 1880 censure expunged from the corporate record on the grounds that it dealt with a personal rather than a business matter.

In 1890, the year before Leander died, Mrs. McCormick and Cyrus Jr. negotiated another and final settlement with him. They bought him out for $3,250,000. Part of that money went to a foundation that still supports a small Chicago museum dedicated to Robert and Leander.

That was also the year of the Sherman Antitrust Act. If young Cyrus took over the family company at a time when the need was to polish an existing organization, he also stepped in just as American business was moving into its first turbulent era of giantism. Having arrived, the country's young companies began to look to ways and means of keeping what they had. A preliminary step was price-fixing and market-share agreements that would assure the operating companies a profit and keep newcomers down. The final goal was consolidation, a trust big enough to control prices, crush competition, and efficiently serve a national economy of vast new size.

Between 1880 and 1884, the McCormick company tripled its sales and tripled them again by 1892 with an expanded product line and increasing sales overseas. But growth on that order couldn't continue indefinitely. Increasingly, as the decade of the 1890s wore on, the Panic of 1893 aside, the farm equipment companies found themselves pushing machinery on reluctant buyers. Alarmingly, they began to wind up a year's sales effort with unsold machines on their hands.

In 1890 the industry had almost backed into an amazing consolidation, one big monopoly. The impetus came from a small parts manufacturer who wanted to guarantee the future of his business. He badgered all of his corporate customers into agreeing to a price at which they would sell out to a combine of all harvesting companies and presented his findings to McCormick and William Deering, McCormick's major competitor. In December 1890 the American Harvester Company came into being—on paper. Cyrus Jr. was elected president and Deering chairman of the board. One month later the scheme was dead. The bankers were not about to provide the big financing necessary for the hastily contrived amalgamation even though McCormick and Deering went to New York together to look for money.

By that time, William Deering was a man of real substance on his own. Born in 1826 in South Paris, Maine, he was the son of the president of the local woolen mill and the grandson of a master shipbuilder. He wanted to become a doctor, but his father, in ill health, pulled him out of college to help run the mill. Deering took to business and eventually founded a woolen-goods commission house in Portland, Maine, with Seth Milliken. Deering, Milliken & Co. was quite successful, with offices in Boston, New York, and Chicago. The Chicago office sparked Deering's interest in Chicago and Midwest real estate.

Health, or rather ill health, played a remarkable role in Deering's career. He fell ill in 1870 and retired from his commission business. That year he arrived in Chicago with $40,000, which he intended to put safely into Chicago real estate. Fortunately for him, he ran into a man he had known in Maine, E. H. Gammon, a Methodist minister who had resigned the pulpit to seek his fortune in the West. Gammon had done well selling reapers for the Marsh brothers, and he had moved into control of their company at Plano, Illinois. Deering was foolish enough or smart enough to put his $40,000 into the company. Whatever, he may have escaped an unknown disaster in the Chicago fire of 1871 by choosing Plano instead of Chicago real estate. In the summer of 1873 Gammon became ill and he urged Deering to manage the firm for a few months. Deering did and stayed on to take over when Gammon's health forced him to retire in 1879.

What Gammon and Deering had was the factory and the designs of the Marsh brothers for a reaper that offered a first solution to the problem of binding the cut grain.

Deering, a man of unusual perception and judgment and possessed of a fine gambling instinct, was always an innovator. Historians of the industry give Deering special marks for his accomplishments because he was an outsider, a New England wool merchant, not exactly an expert on either wheat farming or manufacturing. That may have been an advantage; he came to the business without preconceived notions. Deering first worked with the inventor of a wire binder and then put his money on the twine binder of a Wisconsin inventor, John F. Appleby. (McCormick earlier turned down Appleby's wire binder at a time when Appleby would have thrown in his experiments with twine for free.) In fact, Deering had his company and his fortune riding on the Appleby mechanism. In 1879 Deering built a large plant in Chicago (Fullerton Avenue and Clybourn on the Near Northwest Side), abandoning the old Plano factory, and started manufacturing the Appleby-equipped reaper. Meanwhile, Deering had solved the number one problem with twine binding. Deering spent a small fortune experimenting with twines made of grass, twine, paper, straw, and flax before he went to the country's top rope maker, E. H. Fitler, and backed him in what became a successful effort to make a strong, single-ply twine. Fitler made what was for him a million-dollar deal with Deering on the basis of a two-minute conversation and a handshake. McCormick later lost a million on a flax experiment and a St. Paul factory; the problem with flax twine was that grasshoppers loved it.

In 1880, Deering's Chicago plant turned out and sold 3,000 twine-binder machines. That success sent the industry scrambling; McCormick and other manufacturers paid to get rights to the Appleby binder, and McCormick was able to get his machine on the market in 1881. But the McCormicks had let Deering in the door. By 1883 some twenty-five firms were making twine-binder machines and an estimated 77,000 were sold, but Deering, virtually matching McCormick production, was the only one the McCormicks feared.

The worry at McCormick headquarters only increased as the years went by. Everybody in the business was building a similar machine—the Appleby binder on a Marsh harvester based on the McCormick frame and cutting mechanism. But Deering spent money on research to improve materials and machines, and he apparently developed more than a little genius at manufacturing. His plant was noted for low-cost production and new techniques. He may have had a happier labor force than the McCormicks. When the wage rate in Chicago fell to a dollar a day in the aftermath of the Panic of 1893, Deering declared that no man could support a family on that wage; he paid his men $1.35 a day. Deering stole a march on the McCormick company by manufacturing peripheral equipment such as hay rakes in his own plants and by making a number of his own parts. He was not only ahead of McCormick but of his times in moving toward vertical integration of the company. He bought coal mines in Kentucky, iron-ore leases on the Mesabi Range in Minnesota, timberlands in Missouri and Mississippi. He acquired control of a Chicago blast furnace and bought land for the construction of a steel mill near his plant and for a plant in Canada.

By 1900 it was evident to Cyrus Jr., his mother, and two brothers, Harold and Stanley, that, efforts to bring about a consolidation having failed, something else had to be done. The what else was modernizing the McCormick plants, broadening the product line, following Deering into iron, steel, and lumber, and pushing the company's sales overseas, where McCormick was far ahead of Deering and where farms were still underequipped.

The plans Cyrus had in mind required new capital, lots of it. The McCormick family was not about to risk that much of its own money. After all, several times in the 1890s the annual profits of the company had fallen below $1,500,000.

In June 1902, Cyrus went where the money was. He got on a train for New York and paid a visit to the House of Morgan. Cyrus felt it necessary to carry a letter of introduction with him. For that, he gained an audience with George W. Perkins, then the youngest Morgan partner but later J.P.'s right hand. During the course of a conversation that

lasted for hours, Perkins assured McCormick, then a sea-
soned veteran of manufacturing at age 43 but no expert in
high finance, that raising a bundle of almost any number of
millions was easy. But, no fool when it came to the ways a
banking house can make money, Perkins dropped several
remarks about the advantages of creating a brand-new company out of a series of mergers. A week later at a second
meeting, having found Cyrus receptive to the one-big-com-
pany idea, Perkins indicated that the House of Morgan
might be interested in putting in capital in return for a piece
of the action. That apparently went over well. Now the
House of Morgan had the ball. Perkins rounded up McCormick, Deering, and several of the smaller competitors for a
series of New York conferences that lasted through three
weeks of a non-air-conditioned New York summer. Appropriately, the final handshake came on board J. P. Morgan's
yacht. The time was late in the afternoon of August 12, 1902.
Aboard the yacht were Perkins (Morgan was in Europe,
being kept informed by cable); Cyrus and his brother Harold; Charles Deering, William Deering's older son (by this
time Deering was 76, ailing and spending long periods of
time at his winter home at Coconut Grove, Florida); and
representatives of three smaller companies: Warder, Bushnell & Glessner Co. of Springfield, Ohio; Milwaukee Harvester Co.; and Plano Co. (Deering's abandoned Plano factory had been taken over by another group of investors).

In any merger, ego, prestige, emotion can be as powerful
as cold calculations of profit. In less than thirty years William
Deering had built a company that rivaled the McCormick
empire of more than twice that age. He was not about to
admit that he was second to the McCormicks. But finally he
swallowed his pride; in the new, giant company, capitalized
at $120 million, the Deerings received 37 percent of the
stock while the McCormicks got 43 percent. The Milwaukee
company was owned by heirs no longer interested in the
business and they sold out for cash. That left a 20 percent
interest to be divided among the Plano people, the Cham-

pion owners (Warder, Bushnell & Glessner)—and the House of Morgan. The Morgan firm put $10 million into the combine in exchange for stock, and it was a very profitable investment.

Another emotion, fear, almost busted the grand scheme. Harold McCormick, the second son of Cyrus, had married Edith Rockefeller, John D.'s daughter. The Deerings feared that the Rockefellers would buy into the new company through Morgan and then in combination with the McCormicks loot the Deerings of their rightful interest. George Perkins came up with a device that allayed this fear and other fears on both sides of the table—this was a marriage of old and bitter enemies, not of friends. A clause in the agreement of merger read this way:

"To prevent either of the two principal interests from securing control as against the other, and also to insure that neither will sell down his holdings, the McCormicks and the Deerings shall deposit with a board of trustees, consisting of J. P. Morgan, one Deering and one McCormick, sufficient amounts of stock in the company, pro rata, to prevent control passing to either of the two parties, McCormick or Deering, while the other retains the amount of stock originally received by that party." The trustees would hold and vote the stock for ten years.

Despite all the infighting and jockeying for position, the McCormicks came out on top and in control of the operating company. William Deering, succeeded by Charles Deering, was designated chairman of the board. But the chairman was not made an officer of the company; he presided at meetings of the board and had his vote, but operations were in the hands of the president. The president was Cyrus Jr.

The name chosen for the trust was International Harvester Co. Some accounts say J. P. Morgan suggested the name. Others say he objected; supposedly, Morgan thought Europeans would resent the raw Americans crowning themselves international. In any event, Nettie McCormick held up the final agreement for four days. She could not stomach the disappearance of Cyrus's name.

By 1902 the reaper, or harvester, was no longer enough. As far back as the 1850s the McCormick firm had made hay-mowing machines a permanent part of the line, and other implements had been added as time went by. The Deering firm had moved more aggressively in diversifying its product line. Still, there were many companies, particularly specialists, supplying one or another of the implements needed to operate a farm in the slowly maturing age of mechanization that McCormick had created. The new International Harvester Co. would have the muscle to move strongly across the board.

That was one of the business reasons for the merger. In a 1976 University of Virginia doctoral thesis on the American Multinational Corporation in Imperial Russia, Frederick Vernon Carstensen summed up: "It was tough competition at home, surplus capacity in the factories, the desire to offer a full line of implements, and promising but largely untapped markets abroad that led in 1902 to the creation of International Harvester under the tutelage of George W. Perkins. . . . Indeed, one of Harvester's principal defenses against government antitrust charges ten years later would be that it was created precisely to permit efficient development of these foreign markets, not to restrain trade in America."

In the years immediately following the big merger, once the shakedown cruise was over and bitter enemies became colleagues, superior or subordinate, International Harvester gobbled up a number of specialty companies, giving the Justice Department new antitrust ammunition. Very quickly the company was producing such equipment as harrows, manure spreaders, cultivators, and, for dairy farmers, cream separators. Cyrus Jr., Harold, and Stanley were gung ho for developing foreign sales, and that end of the business increased rapidly, although Stanley may have been faking his interest. His first love was not the McCormick empire, but art, and any excuse to get to Paris was probably a good one.

At the same time, Cyrus Jr., with new capital behind him, was busy making good on the forward-looking moves initiated by the old Deering company: construction got underway on a full-fledged steel mill and on a Canadian plant. Development of the Kentucky coal fields and the Mesabi Range iron-ore deposits began.

Meanwhile, the age of the internal-combustion engine was descending upon the country and International Harvester. Strangely enough, little had been done over the decades of the 19th century to apply steam power to agriculture. By the turn of the century, the steam power that was in use on the farm was largely in the form of a stationary engine used with a belt drive to run threshing machines.

Too late, steam engineers and inventors went to work earnestly trying to adapt the bulky, heavyweight engine of the railroad locomotive for use in the field to replace the horse. The major impetus came from Canada, where the vast western territories were being opened up to wheat farming and where farms were measured in miles rather than acres.

In his book *The Century of the Reaper*, Cyrus III gives his version of what happened: "When specially designed steam apparatus was produced, it was not successful. The field locomotive was too cumbersome and too costly for individual farm use.

"The solution of the problem of the tractor lay in the Otto internal combustion engine of 1876. [Nikolaus August Otto, German inventor, 1832–91.] When the Otto patents ran out in 1890, so many companies in different parts of the world leaped into engine activity that by 1899 there were more than a hundred kinds of four-cycle engines on the market. Today they are all nameless, for, with the exception of Otto, who pioneered the original process and its theoretical background, no single inventor can be credited with the discovery of the gasoline engine. Otto's name may, if you will, be added to those of Whitney and McCormick to make up the trio whose practical researches have for all time been of the greatest benefit to farmers; but Otto was interested in power and in the functioning of his device as a prime mover for all purposes, not in agricultural power as such. The tractor of today derives its heritage more directly from the possibly many unnamed individuals who, for and by themselves, mounted stationary gasoline engines on movable frames."

In 1908 a great tractor plowing contest was staged at Winnipeg. Five steam-powered tractors went up against five gasoline-powered machines. The gasoline tractors carried the day, placing first and second, with the Harvester entry second. For practical purposes, the brief run of steam power on the farm was over.

As usual, William Deering had been ahead of the McCormicks. As early as 1889 Deering signed on a young inventor and supported his research on a practical internal-combustion engine. By 1891 Deering had a small gasoline engine that was geared to propel a lightweight mowing machine. (The French Legion of Honor later recognized Deering as the manufacturer of the first motor-powered mowing machine.) In 1892, Deering's inventor, George Ellis, completed his first horseless buggy, and for a time Deering toyed with the idea of going into automobile manufacture after he was driven at thirty miles an hour across Daytona Beach in an improved model. Deering's decision was to stick to farm equipment; the Ellis automobile, he said, frightened horses.

Meanwhile, McCormick had found his own young inventor, and by 1900 he, too, marketed a gasoline-powered mower, not much bigger than the "garden"-type tractor mowers sold today to cut large lawns. Gasoline power did not immediately revolutionize farming. With its muscle and sales organization, International Harvester was the leading manufacturer of tractors by 1910, selling a third of the tractors produced in the country, but in 1912 it was turning out only slightly more than 3,000. Manufacturers mistakenly concentrated on competing with each other to build larger and heavier tractors, needed in western Canada for plowing, and neglected the need of the average American farmer for an all-purpose tractor that would, among other things, pull a plow or a reaper. And farmers were, of course, reluctant to give up their all-purpose horses and mules. In fact, between 1890 and 1919, the work-animal population on U.S. farms increased remarkably from 17 million to more than 26 million. It was not until 1924 that International Harvester finally got into quantity tractor production, doing away with any real need for horses, and completing the farm revolution.

In 1931, one hundred years after Cyrus the first built his first reaper at Walnut Grove, International Harvester noted with some pride: "With the sickle, which was the harvesting tool for many centuries, a man could cut one-half acre of grain a day. With the cradle, he might cut two acres a day. The very first reaper that McCormick put in the field had a capacity of 10 acres a day, replacing 5 cradlers or 20 men with sickles. Today one man with a 10-foot tractor binder can cut and bind 35 acres a day."

Traditionally—tradition in Chicago being measured in decades and maybe in years—wealthy Chicagoans have maintained a home in the city and a summer home along the Lake Michigan shore in one of the suburbs to the north of the city, preferably Lake Forest. (The super-rich, once the money has been made in Chicago, have also often kept mansions in Manhattan, summer estates on Long Island, and occasional houses in other attractive spots, from Maine to Florida to the West Coast.) In 1916, the McCormick family moved Nettie, now 81, away from the noise and dirt of "McCormicksville," the cluster of McCormick mansions on Rush Street a half dozen blocks north of Chicago's Loop, and installed her in Lake Forest near the estate of Cyrus Jr. In the winter of 1923 the doctors ordered her to California for her health, but back in Chicago in June a cold developed into pneumonia and the matriarch of the family died on July 5, 1923.

The original Cyrus had fathered four sons, Cyrus Hall Jr., Harold Fowler, and the youngest child, Stanley. (Robert, born in England during the Civil War sojourn, died at the age of three.) Just older than Harold was a daughter, Anita, who married Emmons Blaine, the son of James G. Blaine, the unsuccessful Republican candidate for the presidency. Nettie succeeded briefly in luring the art-oriented Stanley back to the family home and back to the McCormick Works (he served as superintendent in 1901). In the fall of 1903, Stanley married a remarkable young lady, Katherine Dexter, the daughter of a wealthy Chicago lawyer, then in her final year of study at the Massachusetts Institute of Technology. The marriage took place in France, with Nettie and the entire tribe in attendance, and Stanley disappeared from the center of McCormick power. Unhappily, he was doomed to spend the greater part of his life in mental institutions.

Harold, it turned out, evolved into the spectacular member of the trio of brothers. His career with the family business was correct; he served under brother Cyrus until Cyrus moved up from president of International Harvester in 1918 to board chairman. Then Harold became president, and through the 1920s and 1930s he served either as chairman or as chairman of the executive committee. But it was his personal life that was of greater interest, especially to the gossips of the day. Barely out of Princeton, which he attended with Stanley, Harold married Edith Rockefeller, daughter of John D. Prophetic perhaps of later troubles, Harold became ill on his wedding day and could not attend the lavish Rockefeller reception. Nettie turned over her New York hotel apartment to the couple so, she said, the young people could set up housekeeping on their own. In Chicago, Harold bought a castlelike mansion at 1000 Lake Shore Drive (now the site of a luxury condominium), and the couple lived in royal style (menus for family meals were printed in French, and the house was furnished and decorated with what money could buy from the effects of European royalty, from Napoleon to the Czars). The death of the eldest child, John Rockefeller McCormick, in 1901, may have been too much for Edith McCormick. In any event, in 1913 she gave up her position as queen of Chicago society and chief sponsor with Harold of Chicago opera and took off for Europe with Harold and their three children. Edith stayed on for eight years. The greater part of that time she spent in Switzerland at the feet of Carl Jung, the apostate, sometime disciple of Sigmund Freud.

For a long time, starting with Alexander Legge, a man of fire and force who became general manager in 1922, the fortunes of International Harvester were really in the hands of what are known these days as professional managers. Along the way, Harvester lost its position as the leading manufacturer of farm equipment to the successors of John Deere, the inventor of the prairie plow. Deere & Co. evolved into a manufacturer of quality farm machinery of all kinds while Harvester took another fork in the road. The turning traces back to the company's development of gasoline engines.

In 1907 Harvester introduced its Auto Buggy, a horseless carriage designed with high wheels for travel on rutted and muddy rural roads. This was followed in 1909 by the Auto Wagon, an improved vehicle with an open wagon bed behind the driver's seat, but produced in variations as a two- and three-seat automobile. The company's interest in passenger cars lasted only a couple of years. Management rightly sensed that Henry Ford and the dozens of other automobile companies of the time presented too much competition. However, it was natural for Harvester to move on from the Auto Wagon to farm trucks and then to commercial trucks. Starting in World War I, with the government urging greater farm production, Henry Ford set out to do for farm tractors what he had done for automobiles; he started producing a Tin Lizzie farm tractor at a price hundreds of dollars below Harvester's bottom price and hoped that mass production and mass sales would bring a respectable profit. Inside of just two years Ford was producing three-fourths of all the tractors sold in the country. Harvester fought back desperately. Sticking to its heavier, quality tractor, Harvester counterattacked by reverting to Cyrus McCormick's original sales technique, the field trial. Naturally enough, Harvester's heavy-duty model triumphed against the Fordson. By 1927 Harvester had overhauled Ford and was once again number one in tractor sales. The next year Ford gave up. He had lost a pile; General Motors had briefly entered the contest and had quit, writing off a $33 million loss in 1922. In the modern era, Harvester has often been more a truck-manufacturing concern than a farm-equipment company. In 1972, trucks accounted for more than 52 percent of combined sales and agricultural equipment only 30 percent. Other years, when farm demand was high, farm equipment and truck sales ran just about neck and neck. Of course, many Harvester trucks are used on the farm. But the one area where the onetime farm king could brag was that it was number one in the production of heavy-duty highway trucks.

Of the second Cyrus's two sons, one entered the business. Appropriately, this was another Cyrus. He did not have a middle name. His father was born Cyrus Rice McCormick, but his name was changed to Cyrus Hall. In the company and the family he was known as Cyrus H. The descending order may be appropriate: Cyrus Hall McCormick, Cyrus H. McCormick, Cyrus McCormick. Born in 1890, Cyrus followed his predecessors to Princeton and then jumped to England to study at Oxford. But he returned to the company, eventually becoming vice-president for manufacturing and the heir apparent. Alexander Legge, a cowpuncher who had started with Harvester collecting company money from Nebraska farmers and had bulled his way to the top, convinced the Harvester board and the family that the third generation did not have the stuff, and Cyrus number three retired to New Mexico to write. He did not have children of his own despite two marriages.

Latter-day McCormicks have had a tough time with the professionals who nominally worked for them. Harold Fowler McCormick's son, also Harold Fowler and known as Fowler, became president of Harvester in 1941 and chairman and chief executive officer in 1946. In a showdown with John L. McCaffrey, who then was president but not chief executive officer, Fowler lost. The board of directors, rather than fire McCaffrey, designated McCaffrey chief executive officer, or as the early McCormick corporate notes quaintly put it for years, the man "in charge of the business." Declining to assume the role of figurehead chairman, Fowler resigned at age 53. A brilliant man, and a lifelong follower of Jung, he sported a small mustache and looked like a more rugged David Niven. Fowler once had been endorsed by Alexander Legge. "Fowler McCormick," Legge said, "is a man you could toss out of an aeroplane with a parachute and wherever he landed he could go to work." But even talent and name and the McCormick stock, widely dispersed among family heirs, apparently was not enough at Harvester. (If ever a man had name and family, it was Fowler; he was the grandson of both Cyrus and John D. Rockefeller.)

Brooks McCormick, the man very definitely in charge of the business these past years, worked for the company eighteen years before being elected to the board of directors. After graduation from Yale in 1940, he immediately joined Harvester as a sales and management trainee. A dozen years later he was running Harvester's British subsidiary. Returning home in 1954, he was made director of manufacturing. From there he moved to executive vice-president (1957), president and chief operating officer (1968) and president and chief executive officer (1971).

Brooks McCormick is a descendant of another and noteworthy branch of the family. His great-grandfather was William Sanderson McCormick, the peacemaker brother of Cyrus who wasted away and died early. (Another of William's descendants turned out to be Colonel Robert McCormick, of the Chicago *Tribune.*) Brooks's father was Chauncey Brooks McCormick, a longtime director of Harvester who did a very good dynastic thing. He married Marion Deering, one of the principal heirs to the Deering fortune. Brooks is the second of three sons. The youngest, Rogers, was an inexplicable suicide. The elder brother, Charles Deering, moved to old Deering haunts, Miami, to run several prospering businesses.

Born in 1917, Brooks was 54 years old when he took full charge of Harvester. He walked into a pile of trouble. It would have been easy enough for Brooks simply to enjoy his position—by some standards, he had everything, including a beautiful, energetic wife, Hope. In Chicago a major title on an important door is almost everything. Only next to business prominence is old money. Brooks had hundred-year-old money.

Even before he became executive vice-president, Brooks had been pushing hard to pump new life into the aging company. Once in full command, he went to work with a will. The problems were basic: obsolete and high-cost manufacturing plants, a stale product line, an organization content to rest on its oars against hard-hitting competition. Deere & Co., with headquarters in Moline, Illinois, a billion-dollar company in 1967, was the world's largest producer of farm equipment and the leader in sales of combines, the ultimate refinement of Cyrus's Virginia reaper, and of tractors. Deere, Harvester, and others had progressively added construction machinery to their tractor and farm-machinery lines, but here Caterpillar, with world headquarters in Peoria, was the clear leader. In its important truck business, Harvester was up against full-line competition from General Motors and Ford and had to fight for shares of specific markets with such as White, Mack, and Diamond T.

A single decision in 1971 dramatized a new era for Harvester. As one of his first acts as chief executive officer, McCormick persuaded the board of directors to cut the dividend. In the conservative corporate and stockholder world, that's akin to leaving the Church. But rather obviously something had to be done. The company had paid out $1.80 a share in dividends the previous year even though it had earned only $1.92 a share.

McCormick closed plants, dropped losing products, and instituted a reorganization that was aimed as much as anything at placing profit responsibility down the line where it belonged. The curious thing was that Harvester's sales had been increasing steadily in the late 1960s, moving from $2.5 billion in 1966 to just over $3 billion in 1971. But profits had been dropping even more rapidly. The year 1966 had been a record profit year to that time, with the corporation netting over $100 million. By 1971 the take had dropped disastrously to $45 million. Quite literally, McCormick said later, the question was what the company could do to "survive."

In the 1980s Brooks McCormick was a wealthy man by most standards even if he was not in the megabuck class. Descended from William McCormick, a brother of Cyrus the first, McCormick also had Deering family money. And for years he had earned the kind of salary from Harvester that permits substantial savings and investment.

Tall, trim, handsome except for an odd, bashed-in look about the mouth, he was a gentleman through and through.

One foundation for his wealth was the ownership of 46,616 shares of Harvester stock. In 1978, the year he decided to resign as chief executive officer, the Harvester stock represented a sizable nest egg. At its high for the year its stock market value exceeded $2 million, but a half dozen years later the same shares would fetch less than $400,000 on the open market. Another 37,000 shares held in trust or beneficially owned by his wife, Hope McCormick, or his four children, hardly placed the family among the super-rich.

By 1980 the heirs of Cyrus, William, Leander, and the rest owned less than 3 percent of Harvester's 30 million shares, and the stock was headed down to $8 a share on the New

York Stock Exchange, with the company piling up a series of disastrous deficits that equaled $20 a share in 1981.

In the late 1970s Brooks was being paid a salary and bonuses that totaled more than $400,000. He was also a beneficiary of a little-known company called the Miami Corp. It was established as a holding company, a profit-making corporation, for the Deering family. As a Deering heir, Brooks was the top family representative on the board of the corporation, but it was run day-to-day by professionals.

Early on called the Deering-Harvester Corp., the holding company began with the greater part of the personal wealth of William Deering, and he had far more than Cyrus the first. The name was changed to the Miami Corp. in 1919 simply because it was in Miami that the Deerings had homes, including the fabulous Viscaya estate with its formal gardens, its indoor-outdoor swimming pool, and its Roman galley of stone sitting in the harbor in front of the mansion. (Viscaya, ceded to Dade County, is now a public park.)

Among the holdings of the Miami Corp. is the Boulevard Bank, a prospering, $550 million (assets) bank located in the Wrigley Building on Michigan Avenue. What is even more important to the Miami Corp. is a large chunk of stock in Socony Mobil, now the Mobil Corp. The stock was purchased with great foresight in 1907, and the annual dividends now exceed the original cost.

Another pleasant holding is 300,000 acres of Louisiana land. It is swampland, and the Deerings had the idea that it could easily be turned to rice farming. That didn't work out, and for years the acreage provided nothing but tax bills and good hunting grounds for family and friends.

Today the area is rated the largest single oil- and natural-gas-producing area of Louisiana, and Amoco Oil pays the Miami Corp. handsome royalties on the oil and gas it pumps out of the ground. Beyond that gem the corporation owns 15,000 acres of timberland in Oregon and another 60,000 acres northeast of Orlando in the booming Disney World sector of Florida. Counting a couple of hundred million dollars in stocks and bonds, the total value of the private corporation is someplace between $500 million and $1 billion, depending on the day's value of oil and someone's guess as to the value of timberlands.

But then Brooks is only one of some 150 heirs who collect dividends from the company.

Brooks is no doubt the last of the McCormicks in the old business. He did not play the heavy father with his two sons, and he made no effort to push them into the company, although Mark, the holder of a master's degree in business administration and a Wall Street investment banker, might have been very well qualified.

Outside of Chicago, Brooks was not given high marks as a manager, but the truth is that he spent his years in top management trying to repair the mistakes of omission and commission of more than one professional manager. In general, they failed in the efforts they did make to tap new technology and they allowed corporate debt to pile up. In addition, they kept putting money into Wisconsin Steel, the company the Deerings started to assure Harvester of adequate supplies of supposedly low-cost steel. The millions they put into the steel company was a drain but also on the order of a starvation diet—enough to keep the company going but not really enough to keep it modern and efficient.

Finally Brooks made the tough management decision. To get rid of an albatross, he sold Wisconsin Steel under a costly arrangement that in effect subsidized the buyer. (The buyer was later forced into a bankruptcy filing and the mill was closed.)

McCormick was bedeviled by something he could not control. By happenstance, his timing was terrible. His efforts to turn the huge corporation around ran right into the ruinous inflation and interest rates of the late 1970s, the world price and supply squeeze engineered by the Organization of Petroleum Exporting Countries, and a developing farm depression. It was something less than the best of times for a maker of trucks and farm machinery.

In the face of such adversities, McCormick made one disastrous mistake. With the board's approval he instituted a search and found the very model of a modern manager to come in and complete his reorganization and the cost-cutting shakeup necessary to shape Harvester for new growth.

To lure Archie R. McCardell away from Xerox where his labor since 1966 had won him the presidency, McCormick and the board approved an outsized package of benefits: a base salary of $460,000, a signing bonus of $1.5 million to make up for lost Xerox perks, a deferred compensation plan worth $1.7 million, and a sweetheart loan that would allow McCardell to buy about $1.8 million in Harvester stock.

McCardell did know something of the truck business, having worked for 17 years as a young man for the Ford Motor Co. But in 1978 he was an executive whose primary concerns were with keeping up with technology and with demand for Xerox machines. His primary contribution to Harvester was to take on the United Automobile Workers at a time when the unions still had not recognized a new era. The stubborn strike was a disaster for the UAW, for McCardell, and for International Harvester.

The banks, owed hundreds of millions, and the Chicago business establishment moved in, restructured the debt, reorganized the company, and finally sold off Cyrus McCormick's Virginia Reaper and its descendants.

In the 1970s the company had grown under McCormick's direction from $3 billion in sales to $5.4 billion while profits climbed from $45 million to $174 million.

But it was not enough to provide the kind of cash injection Harvester needed to rebuild. By comparison, Xerox was only slightly larger in sales but it was earning nearly $500 million.

There was a time when it looked as if McCardell had picked the right moment to take a strike. A strike of reasonable duration might produce concessions from the UAW on some of the union's costly and archaic work rules, and at a point when farm equipment sales were soft he could let

Harvester dealers clear out their inventories. But the strike dragged on for months against a background of worsening economic conditions.

The banks put trusted Chicago businessmen in charge to restructure and reorganize the company. To raise cash and stem losses, Cyrus McCormick's legacy, the farm-equipment business, was sold to another struggling agricultural-machinery company, J. I. Case. Harvester was now a truck company.

In addition to the business, J. I. Case also got the venerable Harvester name. A consulting firm, after thousands of dollars and months of brainstorming, came up in 1986 with a new name for the truck company, one for the future. It was Navistar International Corp.

The new corporation could thus keep the name International on its trucks, while Navistar would be suitable if the old company of Cyrus McCormick and the Virginia reaper might somehow, someday create a new enterprise that would once again revolutionize the workaday world.

As the last decade of the century drew near, it did not seem probable that a major new industry would emerge from the truck company. Intelligent people in the 19th century managed to believe that everything needed or useful had been invented. With far more justification it could be said in the late 1980s that a truck is a truck. No doubt truck efficiency and comfort could be improved, but it was not likely that anyone would invent a revolutionary replacement or that Navistar engineers would perfect a brand-new technology.

Very few of the world's inventions were ever in the "Eureka, I've got it!" class. That McCormick put together a working machine in the isolation of the Virginia hills is remarkable. Equally remarkable is the fact that others here and abroad were more or less simultaneously "inventing" the reaper.

Leander McCormick, even after he was paid off to the tune of $3,250,000, claimed that the reaper was his and his father's as much as it was Cyrus's. The vehemently voiced assertions of Leander no doubt had more than a kernel of truth behind them. However, what's more important, Mc-Cormick built a company that made increasingly improved farm machinery available in the Midwest and as far away as Russia at a reasonable price.

It is something Chicago has done well over the decades and something it continues to do.

In the late 1920s, when radios were just out of the novelty category, Paul Galvin decided that all those people who were buying automobiles might like to take a radio along on the newly popular Sunday-afternoon drive. He had to do something anyway. The battery company that employed him went bad and he needed a job. It turned out that Galvin was spectacularly correct about a marriage of the car and the radio. In his first full year his new company sold thousands of car radios even though the units were cumbersome and the reception uncertain.

Today the company, Motorola, Inc., racks up sales of about $4 billion. It still makes car radios and particularly two-way communication equipment for police and emergency vehicles. Other products include CB radios and mobile telephones. Huge semiconductor and electronics divisions turn out a variety of sophisticated equipment and components (MOS chips, microprocessors) for industry, the military, and the space program. Son Robert Galvin became a director of the company in 1945 when he was 23 years old. With his father's death in 1959 he assumed full charge of the company. A recent estimate put his personal fortune at $300 million, a sum that is not unreasonable in view of his stock holdings and his compensation in recent years of a half million dollars.

Over the years Motorola's engineers developed the walkie-talkie of World War II, the alternator, and many an advance in semiconductors. Still, it is a company known more for improvements and advances in the state of the art rather than significant invention.

A handsome, very low-key executive, Galvin has often quoted a piece of advice from his father. To get something done, to succeed, the elder Galvin said, try to keep "purposefully in motion."

The phrase has a Chicago sound to it. Have a purpose, keep moving, stir the pot, good things will happen.

INDEX